WOMEN DON'T ASK

The High Cost of Avoiding Negotiation— and Positive Strategies for Change

LINDA BABCOCK

and

SARA LASCHEVER

BANTAM BOOKS
New York Toronto London Sydney Auckland

WOMEN DON'T ASK
A Bantam Book

PUBLISHING HISTORY
Princeton University Press hardcover edition published September 2003
Bantam trade paperback edition / March 2007

Published by Bantam Dell
A Division of Random House, Inc.
New York, New York

Book design by Helene Berinsky

Library of Congress Catalog Card Number: 2003049842

Bantam Books and the rooster colophon are
registered trademarks of Random House, Inc.

ISBN 978-0-553-38387-4

Printed in the United States of America
Published simultaneously in Canada

www.bantamdell.com

BVG   10

For our children, Alexandra, Moses, and Adam,
in the hope that they will grow up in a world
more accepting of women who ask

CONTENTS

PREFACE

Why Negotiation, and Why Now?

Women don't ask. They don't ask for raises and promotions and better job opportunities. They don't ask for recognition for the good work they do. They don't ask for more help at home. In other words, women are much less likely than men to use negotiation to get what they want. Why does this matter? Although negotiation has always been an important workplace skill, it has long been thought to be the province of men: a competitive realm in which men excelled and women felt less capable. But ideas about what make a successful negotiation have changed in recent years. Rather than a battle between adversaries, negotiation has increasingly been seen as, ideally, a collaborative process aimed at finding the best solutions for everyone involved. This not only makes the process of negotiating less combative, it has been shown to produce superior agreements: Everyone walks away with more of what he or she wants.

This change in attitudes makes negotiation more attractive to women, because many women have disliked the competitive nature of much negotiation. In addition, people often react negatively to women behaving in competitive ways, making negotiation a less effective strategy for women to get what they want. The new understanding of negotiation as a collaborative process has eased this problem.

But why do women need to negotiate more now than before—and

why is it good news that women can begin to discover their strength as negotiators? Recent changes in workplace culture are making it essential for
women to exercise far more control over their careers than in the past. The
rise of Internet-based commerce, especially the boom in online auction
and trading sites, has created a whole new realm for buying, selling, and
doing business—further changing the landscape in which women live and
work. At the same time, ongoing changes in the roles women play at home
force them to manage a clamor of conflicting commitments in their lives.
In the midst of so much rapid-fire professional and personal change, negotiation is no longer optional. It's become a basic survival skill.

A Brave New World of Work

In many industries, and in offices of every size, businesses have become
less bureaucratic, levels of hierarchy have become fewer and flatter, and job
responsibilities and lines of report have become less formalized.[1] Management styles have become less "top-down," less "command-and-control."
Traditional job ladders have given way to more diffuse organizational
structures and new business models seem to emerge daily. Employees, as a
result, often find themselves with few hard-and-fast rules to follow about
how things are run.

Many organizations are also making increasing use of "idiosyncratic
deals" (called I-deals). I-deals are customized employment contracts designed to meet the individual needs of employees. They can allow varying
degrees of flexibility in travel requirements, hours worked, or rates of skill
development for different people doing the same job. They make more elements of an employee's work life negotiable.[2]

Although the number of mergers and acquisitions has declined from
its height in the past decade, companies are still being bought, sold, and
combined at a brisk pace, with a direct impact on thousands of workers
each year. In most cases, workers whose companies are acquired by other
firms must renegotiate every aspect of their working lives, from compensation, hours, and benefits to titles, job responsibilities, and even office
space. In addition, when two firms merge, a vast array of large and small

issues must be resolved in order to integrate two different cultures and ways of doing business.

Most workers' career experiences have also changed radically. Up until the middle of the twentieth century, many workers spent their entire careers at one organization. In today's economy, this is extremely rare. In the year 2000, about 25 percent of all workers in the United States had been with their employers for 12 months or less. The average amount of time all workers had been with their employers that same year was a meager 3.5 years.[3] Between May 2001 and May 2002, 52.9 million workers in the United States were laid off, fired, or quit—meaning that 39 percent of the American work force changed jobs during that one 12-month period.[4] Every time a worker changes jobs, he or she must be on the alert for new opportunities—and must negotiate a new employment contract.

The percentage of workers in the United States who are union members has also dropped precipitously. Whereas 20.1 percent of U.S. workers were unionized in 1983, this figure had fallen to 13.5 percent by 2001—a drop of 33 percent.[5] Since unionized workers do not need to negotiate most aspects of their employment, such as wages, benefits, job assignments, and vacation time, the implications of this reduction in union membership are staggering. Thousands, perhaps millions, of people, many of them women, who have not been accustomed to negotiating on their own behalf must now do so.

More women are also participating in the work force than at any time in recent memory. In the year 2000 in the United States, 76.8 percent of women aged 25 to 54 worked outside the home compared to 64 percent of women in that age group in 1980, a 20 percent increase in 20 years.[6] Women's share of self-employment also increased from 22 percent in 1976 to 38 percent in 2000, with a total of 3.8 million women in the United States self-employed in the year 2000.[7] Women who run their own businesses must negotiate everything from consulting fees, real estate contracts, and rates for subcontractors to their own benefit arrangements from insurance companies.

Multiple Roles and Conflicting Commitments

As more and more women work outside the home, millions of them must play more roles in their lives than ever before (boss, coworker, employee, daughter, wife, mother, friend). On top of the demands of working and raising their own children, many adults—especially women—bear increasing responsibility for the care of their elderly parents. This frequently requires negotiating with doctors' offices, nursing homes, supplemental caregivers, insurance companies, government programs, their own employers, and their parents themselves.

Between 40 and 50 percent of marriages now end in divorce as well, making women more likely than in the past to find themselves self-supporting or supporting a family by themselves.[8] In the United States alone, almost 20 million people have been divorced.[9] Half of them are women, and for most of them, in addition to the other dislocations and adjustments they must endure, divorce means a sudden drop in their standard of living.[10] In *The Divorce Revolution: The Unexpected Social and Economic Consequences for Women and Children in America*, Lenore J. Weitzman estimates that women's standard of living falls by 73 percent on average after a divorce while men's rises by 42 percent on average. Census data also show that about 85 percent of all divorced women receive no alimony. The percentage of births to single mothers (out of all mothers) has risen steeply as well, from 10 percent in 1970 to 33 percent today.[11] For both divorced women and single mothers who have never been married, shouldering the burden of child rearing without a partner to share the work and decision making means finding other forms of support and assistance—sometimes from friends and relatives, often from local, state, or federal government programs. Whatever the source, women must be prepared to actively pursue what they need to care for themselves and their children.

Miles to Go

Over the past 35 years, affirmative action, changes in social norms, reduced gender discrimination, a decline in occupational segregation, and an increase in access to higher education for women all contributed to a dramatic improvement in women's economic status. But our assumptions about women's progress often far outstrip reality. Much of that progress slowed almost to a standstill in the 1990s. For full-time workers, the ratio of women's to men's annual earnings increased from 60.2 percent in 1980 to 71.6 percent in 1990, but between 1990 and 2000 that ratio increased only 1.6 percentage points, from 71.6 percent to 73.2.[12]

Women's progress into positions of leadership in professions that were previously closed to them has also been far from complete. In Linda's field,* economics, the percentage of female full professors doubled between 1981 and 1991 (from 3 percent to 6 percent) but still remains shockingly low and has remained flat ever since. (In 2001, women still made up only 6 percent of all full professors in economics.) This is true even though 25 percent of all Ph.D.s in economics for the past two decades were awarded to women, meaning that there have been plenty of women in the "pipeline" who were not allowed to advance.[13] The number of women hired as college presidents has also slowed. From the mid-1980s to the mid-1990s, the percentage of college presidents who were women more than doubled, from 9.5 percent to 21.1 percent. But between 1998 and 2001, this percentage increased by only 1.8 percentage points.[14]

These stagnating figures suggest that we may have gotten as much mileage as possible out of the changes we've already made—and that new solutions need to be found if women's progress is to continue. One of these solutions must be a change in society's attitudes toward women who assert themselves. Another, we're convinced, will come from encouraging women to speak up for what they deserve—to recognize more opportunities in their circumstances, appreciate the value of their work, and ask for what they want.

* Because we wrote this book together, when we describe incidents from our own lives we refer to ourselves by our first names, as Linda and Sara.

WOMEN DON'T ASK

INTRODUCTION

Women Don't Ask

A FEW YEARS AGO, when Linda was serving as the director of the Ph.D. program at her school, a delegation of women graduate students came to her office. Many of the male graduate students were teaching courses of their own, the women explained, while most of the female graduate students had been assigned to work as teaching assistants to regular faculty. Linda agreed that this didn't sound fair, and that afternoon she asked the associate dean who handled teaching assignments about the women's complaint. She received a simple answer: "I try to find teaching opportunities for any student who approaches me with a good idea for a course, the ability to teach, and a reasonable offer about what it will cost," he explained. "More men ask. The women just don't ask."

The women just don't ask. This incident and the associate dean's explanation suggested to Linda the existence of a more pervasive problem. Could it be that women don't get more of the things they want in life in part because they don't think to ask for them? Are there external pressures that discourage women from asking as much as men do—and even keep them from realizing that they can ask? Are women really less likely than men to ask for what they want?

To explore this question, Linda conducted a study that looked at the starting salaries of students graduating from Carnegie Mellon University

1

with their master's degrees.[1] When Linda looked exclusively at gender, the difference was fairly large: The starting salaries of the men were 7.6 percent or almost $4,000 higher on average than those of the women. Trying to explain this difference, Linda looked next at who had negotiated his or her salary (who had asked for more money) and who had simply accepted the initial offer he or she had received. It turned out that only 7 percent of the female students had negotiated but 57 percent (eight times as many) of the men had asked for more money. Linda was particularly surprised to find such a dramatic difference between men and women at Carnegie Mellon because graduating students are strongly advised by the school's Career Services department to negotiate their job offers. Nonetheless, hardly any of the women had done so. The most striking finding, however, was that the students who had negotiated (most of them men) were able to increase their starting salaries by 7.4 percent on average, or $4,053— almost exactly the difference between men's and women's average starting pay. This suggests that the salary differences between the men and the women might have been eliminated if the women had negotiated their offers.

Spurred on by this finding, Linda and two colleagues, Deborah Small and Michele Gelfand, designed another study to look at the propensity of men and women to ask for more than they are offered.[2] They recruited students at Carnegie Mellon for an experiment and told them that they would be paid between three and ten dollars for playing *Boggle*™, a game by Milton Bradley. In *Boggle*, players shake a cube of tile letters until all the letters fall into a grid at the bottom of the cube. They must then identify words that can be formed from the letters vertically, horizontally, or diagonally. Each research subject was asked to play four rounds of the game, and then an experimenter handed him or her three dollars and said, "Here's three dollars. Is three dollars okay?" If a subject asked for more money, the experimenters would pay that participant ten dollars, but they would not give anyone more money if he or she just complained about the compensation (an indirect method of asking). The results were striking—almost *nine times* as many male as female subjects asked for more money.[3] Both male and female subjects rated how well they'd played the game about equally, meaning that women didn't feel they should be paid less or should accept less because they'd played poorly. There were also no gender differences in how much men and women complained about the compensation (there was plenty of complaining all around). The significant factor seemed to be that for men, unhappiness with what they were offered was more likely to make them try to fix their unhappiness—by asking for more.

In a much larger study, Linda, Michele Gelfand, Deborah Small, and another colleague, Heidi Stayn, conducted a survey of several hundred people with access to the Internet (subjects were paid ten dollars to log on to a website and answer a series of questions).[4] The survey asked respondents about the most recent negotiations they'd attempted or initiated (as opposed to negotiations they'd participated in that had been prompted or initiated by others). For the men, the most recent negotiation they'd initiated themselves had occurred two weeks earlier on average, while for the women the most recent negotiation they'd initiated had occurred a full month before. Averages for the second-most-recent negotiations attempted or initiated were about seven weeks earlier for men and twenty-four weeks earlier for women.

These results suggest that men are asking for things they want and initiating negotiations much more often than women—two to three times as often.[5] Linda and her colleagues wanted to be sure that this discrepancy was not produced simply by memory lapses, however, so the survey also asked people about the *next* negotiation they planned to initiate. In keeping with the earlier findings, the negotiations planned by the women were much further in the future than those being planned by the men—one month ahead for the women but only one week ahead for the men. This means that men may be initiating *four* times as many negotiations as women. The sheer magnitude of this difference is dramatic, especially since respondents to the survey included people of all ages, from a wide range of professions, and with varied levels of education. It confirms that men really do take a more active approach than women to getting what they want by asking for it.

The more than 100 interviews we conducted in the process of writing this book—with men and women from a range of professions (including full-time mothers) and from Britain and Europe as well as the United States—supported these findings.[6] When asked to identify the last negotiation in which they had participated, the majority of the women we talked to named an event several months in the past and described a recognized type of structured negotiation, such as buying a car. (The exceptions were women with small children, who uniformly said, "I negotiate with my kids all the time.") The majority of the men described an event that had occurred within the preceding week, and frequently identified more informal transactions, such as negotiating with a spouse over who would take the kids to soccer practice, with a boss to pay for a larger-size rental car because of a strained back, or with a colleague about which parts of a joint project each team member would undertake. Men were also more likely to mention more ambiguous situations—situations that could be construed as negotiations but might not be by many people. For the most part, the men we talked to saw negotiation as a bigger part of their lives and a more common event than the women did.

One particularly striking aspect of our findings was how they broke down by age. The changes brought about by the women's movement over the last 40 years had led us to expect greater differences between older men and women than between their younger counterparts. And indeed when we discussed the ideas in the book with younger women they often suggested that the problems we were studying were "boomer" problems, afflicting older women but not themselves. To our surprise, however, when we looked exclusively at respondents to the web survey who were in their twenties and early thirties, the gender differences in how often they initiated negotiations were similar to or slightly *larger* than the differences in older cohorts (with men attempting many more negotiations than women).[7] In addition, both the starting salary study and the *Boggle* study used subjects who were in their twenties. This persuaded us that the tendency among women to accept what they're offered and not ask for more is far from just a "boomer" problem.

The Asking Advantage

But just because women don't ask for things as often as men do, is that necessarily a problem? Perhaps directly negotiating for advantage—asking for what you want—is a male strategy and women simply employ other equally effective strategies to get what they want. This is an important point, but only partly accurate. Women often worry more than men about the impact their actions will have on their relationships. This can prompt them to change their behavior to protect personal connections, sometimes by asking for things indirectly, sometimes by asking for less than they really want, and sometimes simply by trying to be more deserving of what they want (say, by working harder) so they'll be given what they want without asking. Women also frequently take a more collaborative approach to problem-solving than men take, trying to find solutions that benefit both parties or trying to align their own requests with shared goals. In many situations, women's methods can be superior to those typically employed by men (we explore the advantages of women's different approaches and styles in the last chapter of the book). Unfortunately, however, in our largely male-defined work culture, women's strategies can often be misinterpreted and can leave them operating from a position of weakness. And in many cases, the only way to get something is to ask for it directly.

So let's look at the importance of asking.

First, consider the situation of the graduating students at Carnegie Mellon, in which eight times as many men as women negotiated their starting salaries. The women who did not negotiate started out not just behind their male peers, but behind where they could and should have been. With every future raise predicated on this starting point, they could be paying for this error for a long time—perhaps for the rest of their careers.

Liliane, now 46, is an electrical engineer and a successful software designer in New England's competitive high-tech industry. Although she earned excellent grades in college, she was so insecure when she started out in her field that she felt she didn't even deserve to be interviewed for an engineering job—she was only "faking it." Despite her doubts, she quickly received an offer from a highly regarded company. When the company's personnel manager asked her what kind of salary she was looking for, she said, "I don't care what you pay me as long as you give me a job." A big smile spread across the personnel manager's face, she remembers. She later learned that he gave her the absolute bottom of the range for her position, which was 10 to 20 percent less than her peers were earning. It took her ten years to fix this inequity, and she only did so, finally, by changing jobs.

Quantifying—in terms of dollars and cents—the loss to Liliane and women like her from not negotiating their salaries produces sobering results. Take the following example. Suppose that at age 22 an equally qualified man and woman receive job offers for $25,000 a year. The man negotiates and gets his offer raised to $$30,000. The woman does not negotiate and accepts the job for $25,000. Even if each of them receives identical 3 percent raises every year throughout their careers (which is unlikely, given their different propensity to negotiate and other research showing that women's achievements tend to be undervalued), by the time they reach age 60 the gap between their salaries will have widened to more than $15,000 a year, with the man earning $92,243 and the woman only $76,870. While that may not seem like an enormous spread, remember that the man will have been making more all along, with his extra earnings over the 38 years totaling $361,171. If the man had simply banked the difference every year in a savings account earning 3 percent interest, by age 60 he would have $568,834 more than the woman—enough to underwrite a comfortable retirement nest egg, purchase a second home, or pay for the college education of a few children. This is an enormous "return on investment" for a *one-time* negotiation. It can mean a higher standard of living throughout one's working years, financial security in old age, or a top-flight education for one's kids.

The impact of neglecting to negotiate in this one instance—when starting a new job—is so substantial and difficult to overcome that some researchers who study the persistence of the wage gap between men and women speculate that much of the disparity can be traced to differences in entering salaries rather than differences in raises.[8]

Another estimate of a woman's potential lost earnings from not negotiating appears in the book *Get Paid What You're Worth* by two professors

of management, Robin L. Pinkley and Gregory B. Northcraft. They estimate that a woman who routinely negotiates her salary increases will earn
over one million dollars more by the time she retires than a woman who
accepts what she's offered every time without asking for more. And that
figure doesn't include the interest on the extra amount earned.[9] Even in
such a small matter as the *Boggle* experiment, the gains to asking were
great. Everyone who asked for more money received ten dollars, more
than three times as much as those who didn't ask and received only three
dollars.

We all know that few employers will pay us any more than they need
to. They're prepared to spend extra to get an applicant they want, but
happy to pay less if they can. Assuming applicants will negotiate, they routinely offer less than they're able to pay.[10] But if we fail to ask for more, it's
a rare employer who will insist that we're not being paid enough. A recent
study shows that this is true even at institutions with a committed policy
against discriminating between men and women. This study describes a
man and a woman with equivalent credentials who were offered assistant
professorships by the same large university. Shortly after the two were
hired, a male administrator noticed that the man's salary was significantly
higher than the woman's. Looking into it, he learned that both were offered the same starting salary. The man negotiated for more, but the
woman accepted what she was offered. Satisfied, the administrator let the
matter drop. He didn't try to adjust the discrepancy or alert the female
professor to her mistake. The university was saving money and enjoying
the benefits of a talented woman's hard work and expertise. He didn't see
the long-term damage to his institution and to society from not correcting
such inequities (which we explore later in the book), and she didn't know
how much she had sacrificed by not negotiating the offer she'd received.[11]

Other new research emphasizes how important asking can be. Deepak
Malhotra, who is now a professor at the Harvard Business School, assigned every student in a negotiation class he was teaching at the Kellogg
School of Management to "go negotiate something in the real world." The
students were then asked to write a report about what had happened. All
of the students were part-timers who worked during the day and took
classes at night. Of the 45 students in the class, 35 negotiated something

for themselves (the purchase of an antique, the rental fee for an apartment, the salary for a job) and ten negotiated something on behalf of an employer (a contract with a consultant or supplier, a work agreement with a client). The median amount of money saved by the students who negotiated something for themselves was $2,200. The median amount saved by those who negotiated something for their employers was $390,000 (and these are just the medians; some people saved much more). More significant than the amounts saved, however, was the answer the students gave when asked to name the most important tactic that enabled them to achieve such extraordinary results: "Choosing to negotiate at all." They reported that the biggest benefit of completing the exercise was learning that they could negotiate for things (such as rental fees) that they never knew were negotiable.[12]

Because Molehills Become Mountains

We've demonstrated how negotiating your starting salary for your first job can produce a gain of more than a half-million dollars by the end of your career. This one example illustrates a truth that has become better understood in recent years—that even small initial differences can quickly turn into big discrepancies over time. As a result, the cumulative effects of the gender gap in asking can be enormous. In the realm of social equity, small inequalities between men and women, between racial groups, or between heterosexuals and homosexuals have been shown to accumulate rapidly and dramatically to one group's advantage and the other's disadvantage.

To illustrate this phenomenon, three psychologists, Richard Martell, David Lane, and Cynthia Emrich, looked at what would happen if men in an organization consistently received slightly higher performance evaluations than women.[13] (In chapter 4 we explore the dynamics of how this can occur even when there are no real differences in performance or productivity.) The researchers constructed a hypothetical "pyramid structure" organization, in which many people labor at the bottom levels of the organization and successively fewer people are promoted upward to the organization's top levels. In this type of organization, people with the highest performance evaluations tend to be promoted more quickly from lower levels to higher ones. They also tend to go further—to get promoted higher up the ladders of responsibility and power than people with lower evaluations. The researchers noted that even when differences in the performance evaluations awarded to men and women were miniscule (as low as 1 percent), and men and women started out in identical positions in the organization, it didn't take long before the overwhelming majority of people at the highest levels were men.

This is what sociologists call "accumulation of disadvantage." As the psychologist Virginia Valian writes in her book *Why So Slow: The Advancement of Women*: "It is unfair to neglect even minor instances of group-based bias, because they add up to major inequalities."[14] The bottom line is that even if women were asking for comparable things and were equally successful at getting what they ask for when they *do* ask, this simple difference in the "asking propensity" of men and women would inevitably lead to men having more opportunities and accumulating more resources. But women don't ask for comparable things—they ask for less when they do ask, and they usually get less, too. The net result is a huge imbalance in the distribution of resources and opportunities between men and women. Because women ask for what they want less often than men do, and therefore get what they want much less of the time, the inequities in our society, and all the problems they create, continue to pile up. Or, as Virginia Valian has written, "molehills become mountains."[15]

More than Money

The penalties for not negotiating extend far beyond the merely monetary, too. As Pinkley and Northcraft demonstrate,

> Applicants with identical experience and performance records but different salary histories are rated differently by employers. If your compensation record is better than others, employers will assume that your performance is better too.... Accepting less will imply that you have less value than other new hires.[16]

In many cases, employers actually respect candidates more for pushing to get paid what they're worth. This means that women don't merely sacrifice additional income when they don't push to be paid more, they may sacrifice some of their employers' regard too. The experience of Hope, a business school professor, tells this story clearly. When she completed graduate school, Hope was offered a job at a prestigious management consulting firm. Not wanting to "start off on the wrong foot," she accepted the firm's initial salary offer without asking for more. Although she feared that negotiating her salary would damage her new bosses' impression of her, the opposite occurred: She later learned that her failure to negotiate almost convinced the senior management team that they'd made a mistake in hiring her.

Similarly, Ellen, 44, a senior partner at a large law firm, was checking the references of an experienced paralegal named Lucy whom she wanted to hire. One of Lucy's former supervisors described a long list of Lucy's strengths and recommended her highly. But when Ellen asked about Lucy's weaknesses, the supervisor said that Lucy could be more assertive. Ellen asked if she meant Lucy needed to be more assertive on behalf of the firm's clients. The supervisor said no, Lucy was terrific at tracking down any information that could benefit a client's case. What she meant, the supervisor explained, was that Lucy needed to be more assertive on her own behalf. "She could be a lot more assertive when it comes to her own professional needs and rewards," the woman explained. This supervisor felt that not asking for more on her own behalf was a professional weakness in Lucy—and a serious enough weakness that she mentioned it when providing an otherwise glowing reference.

Women also make sacrifices in their personal lives by not asking for what they need more of the time. Miriam, 46, an architect, is also married to an architect. But whereas her husband works for an internationally known firm and travels regularly for his job, Miriam works for herself. And because they have two children, she restricts herself to residential projects in her home state. When her children were small, her husband was out of town two to five days a week, and she was taking care of the children pretty much by herself. Although she enjoyed a lot of artistic freedom in her work and built up a successful practice constructing two- and three-million-dollar houses (houses that won awards and were featured in design maga-zines), the demands of her family life felt crushing. "I just felt like this is the way that life is for me and there is not anything that I can do about this." Now she wonders "if there would have been ways of asking for more help" instead of "working and working until I fell apart." The problem was that "asking didn't really seem like a possibility, but I'm sure that it was."

Missing the Chance

Besides not realizing that asking is possible, many women avoid negotiat-ing even in situations in which they know that negotiation is appropriate and expected (like the female students in the starting salary study). In an-other one of Linda's studies, 20 percent of the women polled said that they never negotiate at all.[17] Although this seems unlikely (perhaps these women think of their negotiations as something else, such as "problem-solving" or "compromising" or even "going along to get along"), their statement conveys a strong antipathy toward negotiating among a huge number of women. (In the United States alone, 20 percent of the female adult population equals 22 million people.)

That many women feel uncomfortable using negotiation to advance their interests—and feel more uncomfortable on average than men—was confirmed by a section of Linda's Internet survey. This part of the survey asked respondents to consider various scenarios and indicate whether they thought negotiation would be appropriate in the situations de-scribed. In situations in which they thought negotiation was appropriate, respondents were also asked to report how likely they would be to negoti-ate in that situation. Particularly around work scenarios, such as thinking they were due for a promotion or a salary increase, women as a group were less likely to try to negotiate than men—even though they recognized that negotiation was appropriate and probably even necessary.[18]

These findings are momentous because until now research on negoti-ation has mostly ignored the issue of when and why people attempt to ne-gotiate, focusing instead on tactics that are successful once a negotiation is underway—what kinds of offers to make, when to concede, and which strategies are most effective in different types of negotiations.[19] With few exceptions, researchers have ignored the crucial fact that the most important step in any negotiation process must be deciding to negotiate in the first place.[20] Asking for what you want is the essential first step that "kicks off" a negotiation. If you miss your chance to negotiate, the best negotiation advice in the world isn't going to help you much. And women simply aren't "asking" at the same rate as men.

A New Perspective

Our goal in this book is to explore the causes of this difference between men and women, using "asking" as a lens through which to examine how women negotiate life in the broadest sense. In the following pages, we will examine why many women often don't realize that change is possible— why they don't know that they *can* ask. We will look at the social forces that school women, from the time they are very young, to focus on the needs of others rather than on their own needs. And we will show how our shared assumptions, as a society, about what constitutes appropriate female behavior can act as a kind of psychological straitjacket when a woman wants to assert her own wishes and desires.

Despite recent gains made by women in many realms and the comparative openness of Western democracies to progress, our society still perpetuates rigid gender-based standards for behavior—standards that require women to behave modestly and unselfishly and to avoid promoting their own self-interest. New generations of children are taught to abide by and internalize these standards, making them less likely as adults to rebel against these common beliefs. In addition, women who do rebel against these standards by pushing more overtly on their own behalf often risk being punished. Sometimes they're called "pushy" or "bitchy" or "difficult to work with." Sometimes their skills and contributions are undervalued and they're passed over for promotions they deserve. Other times, they're left out of information-sharing networks. Experiencing this treatment themselves or seeing other women treated this way, many women struggle with intense anxiety when they consider asking for something they want—anxiety that can deter them from asking at all or interfere with their ability to ask well.

In addition, even when women do negotiate, they often get less than a man in the same situation might get. Sometimes this happens because women set less aggressive goals going into their negotiations than men set and sometimes it happens because both men and women in our society typically take a harder line against women than they take against men in a negotiation. They make worse first offers to women, pressure women to concede more, and themselves concede much less. This doesn't simply limit the results women produce when they do negotiate. If the benefits from negotiating are likely to be small and the process promises to be difficult, many women feel less incentive to ask in the first place.

By exposing the social forces that constrain women from promoting their own interests and limit them from getting more when they try, we hope to make it easier for women to do things differently. We're convinced that for behavior to change, women must understand, at a very deep level, the forces that shape their beliefs, attitudes, and impulses. Simply telling women what they should do differently without helping them understand the root causes of their behavior will make women feel anxious and inadequate, we suspect, but won't help them achieve meaningful change. So in the pages that follow we explore the many causes and ramifications of this newly recognized problem.

Working from this foundation, we also describe in every chapter ways in which women can resist and even retool their early social training, reframe their interactions with others, and overcome the low sense of entitlement, fear, or extreme caution that can keep them from taking full advantage of their talents. We don't mean to imply that this problem has a simple solution, however—that women just need to wake up and ask for things more of the time and the problem will go away. Women tend to hesitate before asking for what they want not because of a silly blind spot that's entirely their own responsibility but because they are taught early on that pushing on their own behalf is unfeminine, unattractive, and unwelcome—not to mention ineffective.

So we want to be clear: This book is not simply a study of an inexplicable female failing that can easily be corrected. It is not about ways in which women need to "fix" themselves. It is an examination of how our culture—modern Western culture—strongly discourages women from asking for what they want. (The situations of women in other parts of the world bear many similarities to those of women in the West, but they're beyond the scope of this book.) We hope it will help individual women improve their circumstances and increase their happiness. But even more, we hope it will provoke social change on a larger scale by inspiring everyone—in the workforce and at home—to think differently about how women can and should behave. To this end, we also include suggestions for how managers in the workplace and adults both at work and at home can change their behavior toward the women around them. Until society accepts that it is a good thing for women to promote their own interests and negotiate on their own behalf, women will continue to find it difficult to pursue their dreams and ambitions in straightforward and effective ways. And we'll show that preventing women from doing so involves substantial social and economic costs for us all.

Affirming the Right to Ask

Can women learn to recognize more hidden opportunities in their circumstances—and can the world learn to accept women who ask? Can women overcome their anxiety and find effective ways to negotiate—and can people stop taking a harder line when they negotiate with women? Luckily, the answer to all of these questions is yes. Recognizing more opportunities for negotiation in your circumstances is a skill that can be learned—in many cases quite easily. In the three years we spent writing this book, we discussed our ideas with many women who went out and applied them in their lives, with dramatic results (many of their stories appear in the chapters that follow). Research also shows that certain kinds of training can help women become more effective negotiators (and can substantially decrease their anxiety) by increasing their sense of control over the negotiation process and teaching them to anticipate roadblocks, plan countermoves, and resist conceding too much or too soon. Rather than merely imitating men (which often doesn't work), women can learn to ask *as women.* They can find their own "negotiating voices," develop more ambitious goals—and get good results.

Society can also change. Malcolm Gladwell, in his book *The Tipping Point*, describes how New York City dramatically reduced its crime rate in a very short time by making crime seem less permissible in the streets of New York. The city did this by cleaning up those streets—eradicating graffiti, replacing broken windows, removing garbage—and by cracking down on even the most minor crimes, such as fare-jumping in the subways. Through these seemingly small changes, the city was able to achieve a profound cultural shift: It was able to change people's behavior. People with the same deprived backgrounds or bad motives—whatever drives people into crime—stopped committing criminal acts simply because small changes in their environment signaled that such behavior was no longer appropriate there. As Gladwell writes, "We like to think of ourselves as autonomous and inner-directed, that who we are and how we act is something permanently set by our genes and our temperament."[21] Instead, he shows, "We are actually powerfully influenced by our surroundings, our immediate context, and the personalities of those around us."[22]

Similarly, changing the context and the cultural environment in which women live and work can change the behavior of the people who live and work with them, making certain ways of responding to women seem less permissible. This type of change can be achieved by a few people in a group consciously deciding to treat men and women more equally—and by their example influencing the behavior and beliefs of others. It can be achieved by men in positions of power making a commitment to mentoring talented women. It can be achieved by a lot of people paying closer attention to the different ways in which they treat men and women and raise their male and female children.

Gladwell calls rapid, large-scale social changes (such as the crime reduction in New York) social "epidemics." As *The Tipping Point* demonstrates, epidemics of social change are rarely the result of a single, unified effort by millions of people. Because subtle adjustments in their circumstances can strongly influence people's beliefs and behavior, even small changes sometimes have a "multiplier" effect. Or, as Gladwell writes, "big changes follow from small events."[23] We hope this book will prompt an

epidemic of small changes and lead to a genuine loosening of the constraints that bind women.

This is not to say that change on a larger scale is not possible as well.
One organization, the international accounting and consulting firm of
Deloitte and Touche, which employs about 29,000 people in the United
States and a total of 95,000 worldwide, has already demonstrated that with
hard work and commitment large-scale cultural change is also possible. In
1991, Deloitte and Touche decided that it had a problem concerning
women. Only 5 percent of the firm's partners were women, and even
though it had been hiring large numbers of women since 1980, by 1991
only 8 percent of the new candidates for partner were female.[24] A task force
formed to look into the problem discovered that so few women were coming up for partnerships because most of them were leaving before they
qualified for partner. The average annual turnover rate among female
managers was huge: 33 percent. The task force also calculated that every
percentage point in turnover translated into an estimated 13 million dollars for costs such as recruitment, hiring bonuses, and training. Although
the members of the task force assumed that women were leaving Deloitte
and Touche to stay home and have children, they quickly learned that this
was not the case. Women were not leaving to stay home but were moving
to other firms. When polled, women cited Deloitte and Touche's male-
dominated culture as a big reason for leaving: The company was just not a
comfortable place for women to work. The task force also found that
within the firm, both men and women wanted the freedom to balance
work and family better. No one wanted what was then the standard 80-
hour work week.

The task force set about fixing these problems by conducting a series
of workshops—attended by more than five thousand people in groups of
24—to talk about gender issues in the workplace. As a way for them to
identify common assumptions made about women in the workplace, the
teams were given scenarios to discuss. For example, in one, a man and a
woman both came late to a meeting. Although the team members ignored
the man's tardiness, they automatically assumed that the woman was having child-care problems. In discussing the impact of this discrepancy in
their responses, the team members realized that assumptions like this can

negatively influence how a woman is evaluated. This led them to look more closely at how men and women at the firm were evaluated, and they discovered that men were typically evaluated on their "potential" while women were more commonly evaluated on their performance. The net result was that men were being promoted much faster than women. Other common practices looked at by the teams included a firmwide tendency to give men and women different work assignments (which make a big difference in who advances) based on unexamined and often unfounded assumptions. These included assuming that women wouldn't be comfortable in manufacturing environments or that women wouldn't want to travel too much—the latter a particularly career-damaging assumption at a company that relies heavily on travel to serve its clients.

Once people at Deloitte and Touche started looking at their assumptions about men and women, they began to see the implications of their beliefs—and how they made the atmosphere at the firm inhospitable to women and limited their advancement. The next step was to make changes. Prompted by the task force, all the firm's offices were required to produce annual reviews documenting how well women were progressing through their portion of the organization. They were also required to track the number of women recruited and retained by each office, and these numbers were widely circulated across offices. This basic accountability changed the way assignments were made and evaluations determined. Individual offices also started networking events and career-planning programs especially for women. Firmwide, the requirements for travel were changed, lessening the time that everyone—both men and women—was expected to be away from the office. The company also advertised that taking advantage of flexible work arrangements wouldn't hinder one's professional advancement within the organization. This dramatically increased the use of these programs by men as well as women.

By the year 2000, the number of female partners at Deloitte and Touche had almost tripled, from 5 to 14 percent—a huge gain in nine years. The firm had also eliminated the gender gap in turnover (now about 18 percent annually for both men and women), and saved close to $250 million in hiring and training costs. Particularly heartening about this story is the evidence that the changes at Deloitte and Touche benefited both men and women—women because they could stay at the company, enjoy working there more, and advance at a better pace, and men because they too could take advantage of flexible work arrangements, reduced travel loads, and a more supportive work environment without negative repercussions. And the bottom line is that rather than costing money, the company actually saved millions of dollars—and stopped hemorrhaging talented people.[25] Building on this success, the company was pushing toward even more ambitious goals by 2005.

The experience of this one far-sighted company provides a wonderful model for how the rest of us, with a little commitment and persistent focus, can change our world. Gender equality, with the benefits it can bring to all of us, our sons as well as our daughters, will not be attainable unless our society has the courage, the resolve, and—perhaps most important—the information and the insight to make across-the-board changes. Harvard Business School professor Rosabeth Moss Kanter explains it this way:

> Individual trickle-up is not enough.... The whole social system must be changed if women in general, not just a hardy, pioneering few, are to gain economic power. The apparent openness of American society to the overachiever from an underprivileged minority group who can pull herself up by the pantyhose and succeed makes it too easy to assume that the problems and solutions are all individual ones. It makes it easy for those in power to point to the token overachiever as an example.[26]

In other words, just because a few women manage to succeed despite the impediments our society erects in their paths doesn't mean that these impediments don't exist or that there's no problem. Kanter also says that "a vision of what is possible, a source of hope and inspiration, is the necessary ingredient for energizing change."[27] We hope that this book, by shining a spotlight on the barriers that prevent women from asking for what they want—and suggesting ways for those barriers to be removed—will play a part in providing that vision of what is possible.

1

OPPORTUNITY DOESN'T
ALWAYS KNOCK

HEATHER, 34, WAS THE PASTOR at a struggling urban church in the Boston area. Heather was also an officer of her denomination's local association council—a group of pastors from around the region that ordains ministers, reviews clergy on disciplinary charges, and helps churches find pastors. At a meeting of the council, another pastor, a man, asked the council to extend the support it had been giving him for the past three years. Heather was unfamiliar with this man's situation and sat up to listen. It turned out that this male pastor had worked for many years at a prosperous Back Bay parish, where he'd been paid a generous salary. Three years before the meeting Heather attended, he'd decided to move to a poor urban parish that was struggling to revive itself. He hadn't wanted to give up the salary he'd made at the rich downtown church, so he'd asked the council to supplement his income—to make up the difference between what he'd been making in the wealthy parish and what he would be paid at his new church. The council controlled a small discretionary fund—a fund very few people knew about—and had agreed to supplement the male pastor's income from this fund for three years. Now those three years were coming to an end, and he was asking the council to renew the subsidy.

Once Heather understood what was happening, she also realized that

the impoverished church this man served was comparable in most re-
spects to her church—and the salary he wanted supplemented was similar
to the one on which she'd been struggling to support her four children for
seven years.

Heather's response revealed a kind of fatalistic dismay:

This fund—I never knew of its existence. I mean, I was on the Association Council! . . . It had never been publicized. . . . There had never
been any discussion about it in any meeting, there had never been any
sort of sense that his time with it was up now, so that it was time for
other churches to apply. . . . There is no application procedure; it's not
like it's a grant that you can apply to get or something. It was really a
matter of this guy being able to somehow finagle this.

Heather's experience perfectly captures one of the major barriers preventing women from asking for what they need more of the time: Their
perception that their circumstances are more fixed and absolute—less
negotiable—than they really are. It also highlights the assumption made
by many women that someone or something else is in control. This
assumption—the result of powerful social influences that go to work the
day a woman is born—has a broad impact on women's behavior. Instead
of looking for ways to improve a difficult situation, women often assume
that they are "stuck" with their circumstances. Instead of publicizing their
accomplishments, they hope that hard work alone will earn them the
recognition and rewards they deserve. Instead of expressing interest in
new opportunities as they arise, they bide their time, assuming that they
will be invited to participate if their participation is wanted. They think
any allowable divergences from the status quo will be announced and offered to everyone. Women expect life to be fair, and despite often dramatic
evidence to the contrary, many of them persist in believing that it will be.

Stephanie, 32, an administrative assistant, illustrates how this belief
can play out in a woman's life. Stephanie told us that she tends to think
that "things will just happen and if they don't there's a reason why they
don't." Because of this attitude, she was unhappy with certain aspects of

her job for some time but never approached her supervisor to see if changes could be made. Finally, Stephanie received another job offer. When she announced that she was leaving, her supervisor asked what it would take to keep her. After her supervisor made every change Stephanie wanted, Stephanie decided to stay. When we asked why she hadn't told her supervisor sooner what was bothering her, Stephanie said, "I tend to think people are pretty fair, so maybe I'm too trusting and expect that I'm getting what I deserve in that I work really hard."

This chapter looks at this barrier and its origins—why it is that many women assume that they must wait to be given the things they want or need and don't realize more of the time that opportunity doesn't always knock.

Turnip or Oyster?

If people's beliefs about the opportunities in life lie along a spectrum, at one end would be the view that "you can't get blood from a turnip." People holding this outlook believe that "what you see is what you get" and most situations cannot be changed. They may also assume, like Heather, that if a situation could be changed, this fact would be advertised to all. At the other end of the spectrum is the view that "the world is your oyster." People with this outlook believe that life is full of opportunities, most situations are flexible, rules are made to be broken, and much can be gained by asking for what you want.

Linda and several colleagues decided to systematically investigate whether men and women differ in their positions along this "turnip to oyster" spectrum. To do so, they developed a scale that measures the degree to which a person recognizes opportunities to negotiate and sees negotiation as critical for realizing those opportunities.[1] Scales are research tools that have been used for many years to measure behavioral and perceptual differences across people. Perhaps the most famous is the Myers-Briggs scale, which maps an individual's personality profile according to where he or she scores on four related scales (extroverted—introverted, sensing—intuitive, thinking—feeling, judging—perceiving). Other scales capture individual differences in beliefs, perceptions, and behavioral tendencies. Not all of these differences are innate or biological, of course. Psychologists believe that behavior is heavily influenced by the situations in which people find themselves—a person may drink more at a party where other people are drinking than he or she would drink if alone, for example. Nonetheless, some stable traits and attitudes do lead to differences in the ways people behave. Scales are used to try to identify those traits and attitudes. People who are rated high on a "shyness" scale, for example, have been shown to talk less and engage in less frequent eye contact than people who rate low on that scale.

Unlike some of Linda's earlier studies, which measured the frequency with which respondents took the lead in starting negotiations, this "recognition of opportunity" or "turnip-to-oyster" scale measured people's propensity to see possibilities for change in their circumstances. This is how it worked: As part of the web survey described in the introduction, Linda and her colleagues presented respondents with a series of statements such as:

- I think a person has to ask for what he or she wants rather than wait for someone to provide it.
- There are many things available to people, if only people ask for them.
- Many interactions I have during the day can be opportunities to improve my situation.

The survey asked respondents to rate along a seven-point scale the extent to which they agreed or disagreed with each statement. Low scorers would be people who see little benefit to asking for what they want because they perceive their environment as unchangeable (these would be the "turnip" people). High scorers would be people who see most situations as adaptable to their needs and regularly look for ways to improve their circumstances (the "oyster" folks).

Confirming our expectations, women were 45 percent more likely than men to score low on this scale, indicating that women are much less likely than men to see the benefits and importance of asking for what they want. Even more telling, we found that a difference of as little as 10 percent on this scale—that is, a score that was only 10 percent higher—translated into about 30 percent more attempts to negotiate (as demonstrated by another part of the survey). The strong correlation between high scores and a much greater tendency to try to negotiate confirmed our hunch that "oyster" people ask for what they want much more often than "turnip" folks—and that many more men than women are "oysters." Since men are more likely than women to believe opportunities can be "had for the asking," or at least that change may be possible, is it any wonder that they're more likely to speak up and let people know what they want?

During our interviews, we found women recounting story after story of not realizing what could be changed by asking—a problem that can arise early and persist well into old age. Amanda, 23, a management consultant, seems to be a very self-possessed and confident young woman. Interested in math and science, she studied engineering in college and was offered an excellent consulting job as soon as she graduated. By her own description, she has always been less like her mother and more like her father, who taught her to be focused and direct, and to go after what she wants. She said of herself "I don't like nonaction." Nonetheless, as a child she assumed that her parents wouldn't let her do all sorts of things—such as going away to camp, or taking trips with friends—that they permitted her younger brother to do. She isn't sure why she made these assumptions, and when as an adult she asked her parents about the different things that they allowed her brother to do, they were surprised. "You never asked us," they said, adding that it would have been fine with them for her to do the things she mentioned.

Kay, 41, a jeweler in Colorado, had worked for many months on a project creating minutely accurate reproductions of ornate antique jeweled boxes. For a year and a half, she and the other jewelers on the project had maintained a schedule that she describes as "insane, inhumane," working nights and weekends without any kind of a break. The pressure was straining Kay's relationship with her partner and her health was suffering. Finally, exhausted, she approached her boss and said she couldn't work nights and weekends anymore. She expected "all kinds of groaning and grumbling," but her boss agreed without a fuss. "I just came in one day and said that, and that was the way it was from then on," she told us.

Renata, 53, a vice president of a cosmetics company, collects art. Once, when she first began collecting, she fell in love with a piece by a particular artist. She loved it so much that she took it home and hung it in her house to see how it looked. She loved it even more, but she couldn't afford it and with great regret she returned it to the dealer. Shortly afterward, the artist who painted the picture died. Realizing that the work's value would sky-rocket, Renata rushed back to the dealer, only to find that the piece had al-ready been sold. "If you loved it that much, you should have asked me to work out a payment plan," the dealer said. "I would have figured out a way for you to have it." This had never occurred to Renata. She assumed that the price was the price, she either had the money or she didn't, and there was no flexibility in the situation.

In stark contrast, the men we interviewed recounted numerous tales of assuming that opportunity abounds—and reaping big rewards. Here are a few of their stories.

Steven, 36, a college administrator, is married to a professor at the school where he works. Shortly after the birth of their first child, Steven's wife was invited to spend a year as a visiting professor at a prestigious uni-versity in another city. Steven's job involved managing a staff of almost 100 people, which is hard to do from another city, but there was no ques-tion about his wife's accepting the invitation—it was a great opportunity. His wife assumed they were in for a year apart, but Steven was unwilling to accept this. Instead, he devised a plan whereby he could do part of his job from out of town and hand off some of his responsibilities to a colleague who would be on-site. In return, he took over several of her duties that didn't need to be done on-site. And he went further: He persuaded this colleague to take on some *extra* duties so that he could reduce the number of hours he worked and spend more time with his newborn daughter. Steven presented the plan to his boss, who was happy to accommodate the needs of a valued employee. Steven and his family enjoyed a wonderful year together, he and his colleague each acquired new skills from trading responsibilities, and Steven's job was waiting for him when he returned.

Hal, 41, owns a small chain of athletic clubs in northern California.

For several years, he'd owned two adjacent lofts in San Francisco, living in one and renting out the other. After his girlfriend moved in with him, he wanted to enlarge his living space by expanding into the loft he'd been renting, but he didn't want to pay the exorbitant prices charged in San Francisco for design and renovation services. Hal had recently joined the board of directors of an Italian furniture and design company, and after a little thought he approached the company's president with the following proposal: "I will pay you to renovate my apartment at cost," he said, "but I will pay you up-front for the work. This will help your cash flow, and it will give work to the employees of your San Francisco store, which has just opened and is not yet busy. You'll also get a local reference and a local project to showcase." The president of the firm agreed, the store's staff took particular care with the project because they wanted to show the San Francisco market what they could do, and for far less than he could have paid any other way, Hal got himself a gorgeously renovated apartment.

Mike, 63, an entrepreneur, attended a New England private school as a boy. After an injury forced him to give up football, he became head cheerleader in order to continue supporting his team. As a big game with a major rival approached, Mike overheard a lot of boys expressing regret that they wouldn't be able to see the game because it would be played at the other school. Looking for a solution, Mike approached the local train company and asked if it would be possible to rent a train! To his surprise, the railway was happy to oblige for a reasonable price, and the entire school was able to ride in style to the football game. At the time, Mike's school sent close to 100 boys a year to Yale. The administrators and college counselors at Mike's school were so impressed by his initiative that they made sure his name was on the Yale list, even though his grades made him a borderline candidate. Going to Yale not only gave him a wonderful education, it provided him with contacts and opportunities that he relies on to this day.

Who's in Control?

Why do men and women differ so much in their propensity to recognize opportunities in their circumstances? Why are men more likely than women to take the chance of asking for something they want, even when there's no obvious evidence that the change they want is possible? A group of psychologists has identified an interesting gender difference that helps answer this question. Using something called a "locus of control" scale, these researchers measure the extent to which individuals believe that their behavior influences their circumstances.[2] The lower people score on the scale, the more they perceive their fate to be influenced by internal rather than external factors. That is, those who have an "internal locus of control" (the low scorers) feel that they "make life happen" whereas those with an "external locus of control" (the high scorers) feel that life happens to them. Research has found that people with an internal locus of control spontaneously undertake activities to advance their own interests more than people with an external locus of control. They're more likely to seek out information in their environment that will help advance their goals and more likely to be assertive toward others. People with an internal locus of control may also be less vulnerable to negative feedback.[3] As it turns out, the average scores for women are significantly higher on locus of control scales than those for men. This tells us that women are more likely to believe that their circumstances are controlled by others while men are more likely to believe that they can influence their circumstances and opportunities through their own actions.[4]

This is not just true of American women. In an unusually far-reaching study, this finding was replicated in 14 countries, including Britain, Belgium, the Netherlands, and Sweden in Western Europe; Bulgaria, Czechoslovakia, Hungary, Poland, and Rumania in Eastern Europe; the former U.S.S.R., India, China, Mexico, and Brazil.[5] The study also controlled for occupational status, meaning that even among senior managers, who might be expected to perceive themselves as having more control over their lives than lower-level, unskilled workers, women still scored higher than men. This indicates that even women who exercise a great deal of control in their jobs still believe that external forces influence their lives more than men in the same jobs believe.

Locus of control issues also help explain the discomfort women feel about negotiations involving money. Martha, 43, a career counselor, described being offered a job and gratefully accepting what her new employer offered to pay her. After she was hired, she learned that she was the only employee who hadn't negotiated her starting salary. But it hadn't occurred to her that she had any control over what she was paid, she said. She assumed the salary for the job was "like a price on an item in a store." Many women, like Martha, go through life thinking that money is something that is controlled by other people, not by themselves.

That women feel as though their lives are controlled by others should not surprise us, perhaps. As the psychiatrist Linda Austin notes in her book *What's Holding You Back?*, "the lives of women have been largely controlled by men until quite recently."[6] A few facts explain what she means. Although women were given the right to vote in Wyoming in 1869 and in Utah in 1870, no nation-state gave them national voting rights until New Zealand in 1893, little more than a hundred years ago. The United States followed in 1920 and Britain in 1924. Switzerland didn't give women this essential form of control over their lives until the astonishingly late date of 1971. No woman was allowed to earn a Bachelor of Science degree anywhere in the British Empire until 1875; the first Bachelor of Arts degree awarded to a woman followed two years later. Battling for other forms of control—such as the right to own property, make free and informed choices about procreation and birth control, and work in any profession of their choosing—occupied women in Western culture for much of the twentieth century.

Even today, men control both the economic and political environments in which women live and work. In 2001 in the United States, only 10.9 percent of the board of directors' seats at Fortune 1000 companies were held by women.[7] Although women now own about 40 percent of all businesses in the United States, they receive only 2.3 percent of the available equity capital needed for growth—male-owned companies receive the other 97.7 percent[8] (a statistic that helps explain Martha's widely shared feeling that "other people" besides women control the money in the world). In politics, no woman has ever been elected president or vice president of the United States; only 14 out of 100 U.S. senators are women; and only 13.5 percent (59 out of 435) U.S. representatives are women. There have been only two female Supreme Court justices since the United States was founded in 1776 (and both were appointed in the past 25 years), despite the fact that women represent more than 50 percent of the population. (Women are not the only group with good reason to feel as though their lives are controlled by others, of course. Many cultural and ethnic minorities suffer a similar "outsider effect," seeing themselves closed out of most positions of political and economic power.)

The situation is not much different in other English-speaking countries or in Europe. Britain had a woman prime minister, Margaret Thatcher, for 11 years (1979–1990), but membership of the House of Commons remains strongly tilted in favor of men (only 18 percent of the 659 members are women). In the judiciary in England and Wales, only 4 percent of the high court judges and only 6 percent of the circuit court judges are women. Women occupy similarly low percentages of the top jobs in government and at major corporations in Australia, New Zealand, and the countries of Western Europe. Although parts of Northern Europe, particularly Scandinavia, have made significant strides in this area over the past two decades, the representation of women in positions of political and economic power in all of these countries remains far below 50 percent.[9]

Long barred from access to formal education and denied the right to vote, own property, and control their own bodies, women were in very material ways dependent on the will and whims of others to decide their fates. Women's collective identity, as Austin writes, "for millennia . . . rested on the accurate acknowledgment that our lives were indeed controlled by external forces."[10]

The impact of this legacy can be enormous, influencing women's actions in their private lives, at school, and in the workplace. In the personal realm, for example, it has long been customary in matters of the heart for women to leave the "asking" to men. Until quite recently, women were taught that they needed to wait for men to ask them to dance, to go out on dates, and to marry them, and the influence of this idea persists to this day. For LaKetia, 23, a sergeant in the U.S. Army who has a two-year-old child, this assumption produced drastic consequences. Unmarried when she became pregnant, LaKetia wanted the father of her child to marry her. But he never offered, so she assumed he was unwilling. Only much later, after her daughter was born and relations with the father had deteriorated, did she discover that he'd been willing to marry her and would have if she had asked. But even though LaKetia is extremely capable, professionally ambitious, and accustomed to exercising a high degree of control over both men and women in her job, she thought control of this particular decision—about whether or not they would marry—rested outside of her. Because the father of her child didn't offer, she concluded that she had no alternative but to raise her daughter on her own.

Another good personal example—less life-determining but still telling—comes from Emma, 36. A social science researcher with a doctorate in education, Emma is extremely successful and makes more money than her husband, a musician. She kept her own name when she married, and pays particular attention to the different ways in which her two children, a boy and a girl, are treated by teachers, family members, and friends. Despite this awareness, however, she found herself taking a "vacation from hell" a few years ago at a ranch in the Southwest. For a week, she and her children (both under four) shared a cabin and rudimentary bathroom facilities with 20 other guests. This happened, she told us, because it was her husband's turn to choose their vacation destination. Since it was his turn, Emma had assumed that his choice was final and nonnegotiable, although he is not an inflexible man. Only later did she realize that she could have exerted some control over the decision by saying "these are the things I'll accept, these are the things I won't accept, and...No, really, if I go on vacation, I need a bathtub for the kids."

The belief that control over their lives rests with others can have a big impact on women's experiences in school as well, as Linda learned from the female graduate students who complained to her because they weren't teaching courses of their own. Since then, Linda has encountered numerous other examples of this problem. One year, a female student asked why two male students had been allowed to participate in the university's May graduation ceremony even though they weren't going to complete their degree requirements until late summer. The female student would have liked to be part of the ceremony too but assumed she needed to finish her degree requirements first. She never asked if she could participate (Linda would have said yes); both the male students had asked. Another time, a woman student asked Linda why she'd given a male student permission to use department resources to print up business cards and had not offered the same opportunity to her. Once again, the answer was the same: The male student had asked; the woman hadn't. Once she did ask, Linda readily approved her request.

The conclusions are obvious: The women believed that control over what they could teach, when they could celebrate their graduations, and which department resources they could use rested entirely with others; the men thought they might be able to exert some control over these issues—and tried.

Examples of women ceding control over their lives in the professional realm also abound. Susannah, a 29-year-old political strategist for a child advocacy organization, was hired by a think tank studying children's rights shortly after she graduated from college. Initially, Susannah willingly "paid her dues" by getting to know the organization and working through its ground-level departments. But after 18 months, she had identified the particular area in which she wanted to work and spotted an open job she thought she could do well. Although she mentioned her interest in the area to her boss more than once, she never named the job she wanted or asked directly to be considered for it. As a result, she spent two more years grinding away at a low-level job far below her capabilities. As soon as she realized that she could exert some control over her future in the organization and asked directly for the higher position (which had remained unfilled for two years), she got the job.

Why This Difference in Perceptions?

As we've already shown, women's continuing lack of political and economic power ensures that much of the control over their lives does in fact remain in other hands. This basic reality of life—the unequal balance of power between men and women—determines adult perceptions about who is in control and influences the developing beliefs of children. Keen observers, children study the different ways in which men and women act, the different roles they play in society, and the different preferences and abilities they display. A central part of their development involves arranging this information into an organized understanding of what constitutes maleness and femaleness—a mental catalogue of the physical attributes, tastes, interests, abilities, and modes of behavior that characterize the different sexes. Psychologists call this understanding a "gender schema."[11]

Research has shown that children begin formulating their gender schemas at a very young age.[12] By around the age of two, children can distinguish the gender of adults. They also learn early that boys and girls play with different types of toys, play in different ways, and wear different clothing. Children learn that adult men and women hold different types of jobs and learn to categorize the "gender" of household objects (such as ironing boards and tool boxes). By the age of six, psychologists believe, "children are experts at gender schemas,"[13] able to recognize and understand the multiple gender cues all around them.

Observing that much of the world is controlled by men, children incorporate this information into their gender schemas and conclude that this is not merely the way things are, but the way things should be. Often, despite parents' best efforts to the contrary, the patterns of family life bolster this point of view. At the dinner table, men often remain seated and women serve, suggesting that men are the "bosses" and women are the "workers" in the household—men are in control and women do their bidding. When both parents are in the car, men drive more than women, suggesting that men control the family's movements and safety. Men rarely change their names at marriage but many women do, and children are usually given the father's rather than the mother's surname, indicating that men determine a family's name and by extension its collective identity.

Even families that consciously strive for gender equality can send unintended messages to their children about control issues. Linda, for example, has always made considerably more money than her husband, who is a university administrator. Nevertheless, when the two of them went out together, or when they went out as a family with their young daughter,

Linda rarely carried cash and deferred to her husband to pay for whatever they needed. Once, when their daughter was three, Linda stopped in a drugstore for something and the child saw a stuffed animal she wanted. "Do you have enough money to buy that for me, Mommy?" she asked. "Do girls have money, or is it just boys that have money?" Linda was horrified. Their family habits had unwittingly communicated to their daughter that men control money, not women. She and her husband now make sure that their daughter sees Linda paying for things frequently; they also bought their daughter a piggy bank so that she can have money of her own.

Similarly, in Sara's household, her husband was the person who usually fixed things when they broke—screen doors, electronic equipment, toilets, toys. He'd recharge exhausted batteries, replace light bulbs when they burned out, and pound down nails that popped up through the floorboards of their front porch. Although Sara is perfectly capable of doing most of these things, her husband enjoyed taking care of them and she got into the habit of leaving them to him. Then, when their older son was four, he broke a toy when his father wasn't around. Sara told him to bring it to her and she'd see what she could do. "No," said her son. "Daddy will fix it. Daddy knows how to fix things." Sara realized that she and her husband had been teaching their son lessons about the limits of female competence. They had also been teaching him that men can control the physical world and the proper functioning of objects in ways that women cannot. (Sara now fixes toys, recharges batteries, and changes a lot more light bulbs.)

Incorporating lessons like these into their gender schemas, children adapt their behavior accordingly. Boys develop a belief that they are or should be in control and act on this understanding, seeking out ways to get the things they want and assert their needs. Girls learn that they will not control their own lives and learn not to behave as if they do. This "learning," a response to strong social pressures, is often subconscious.[14]

Children learn about control issues in other ways as well. Research has shown that many parents encourage boys to be more independent than girls, for example.[15] One study even found that parents perceive their boy and girl babies differently in the hospital (within the first 24 hours of their birth) even though research can discover no differences in objective measures. Both parents tend to see boy babies as more alert, stronger, and more coordinated than girls, whom they perceive to be smaller and more fragile.[16] A child who is perceived to be stronger would also presumably seem more capable, whereas a child who is perceived to be more fragile would seem more in need of care and therefore more dependent. One of the ways in which parents transmit these skewed perceptions is through the types of chores they assign to their male and female children. In an extensive summary of research on children's household chores, the developmental psychologist Jacqueline Goodnow observed that boys are typically given more independent tasks, such as work that must be done on their own outdoors (mowing the lawn, shoveling snow) while girls tend to be assigned indoor tasks that must be supervised and therefore controlled by others (helping to prepare food, caring for younger children).[17] Believing that girls are more vulnerable than boys, many parents are more protective of their daughters as well, controlling their movements and restricting their activities, but allowing their sons more freedom. Some psychologists speculate that it may also be easier for mothers to help their sons separate from them, forge their own identities, and become independent during adolescence, but harder for them to let their daughters go.[18] These types of behavior teach boys that they can and should take control of their lives; girls become accustomed to having their fate directed by others.

The journalist Peggy Orenstein, in her book *Schoolgirls: Young Women, Self-Esteem, and the Confidence Gap*, describes observing a sixth-grade classroom in which the teacher asked her students to think about how their lives would be different if they'd been born the opposite gender. With a lot of giggling, the students compiled two lists. Items on the boys' list included: "I'd have to help my mom cook"; "I'd have to stand around at recess instead of getting to play basketball"; "I'd worry about getting pregnant." Examples from the girls' list included: "I could stay out later"; "I'd get to play more sports"; "I wouldn't care how I look or if my clothes matched." As Orenstein observes, "Almost all of the boys' observations about gender swapping involve disparaging 'have to's,' whereas the girls seem wistful with longing. By sixth grade, it is clear that both girls and boys have learned to equate maleness with opportunity and femininity with constraint."[19]

We heard many stories of how parents communicate this difference to their children. Martha, the career counselor, described a conversation she had with her husband about "how his father had taken the boys out and . . . taught them how to tip—basically, taught them how to slip the maitre d' money for good tables or give some money to the guys who were in the band to play a good song." She'd never met a woman who'd had a comparable experience, she said, in which a parent or other authority figure took her out and showed her, as Martha put it, "how to circumvent the system" to get what she wanted. Where Martha's husband and his brothers were taught that they could change many situations to suit their needs, girls are taught a different lesson, she believes: "I think we teach little girls to be deeply invested exteriorly—that everybody's a stakeholder, that everybody gets to have an opinion about them. . . . I think we raise men to let go of that, and . . . be much more inwardly functioned—'What do you think? Be a man about it.' . . . We still, in some ways—in many ways—train women to be that to whom things are provided."

Learning very early that "everybody gets to have an opinion about them," girls learn to abide by this external social authority, which decrees not only what is permissible behavior for them, but what is not. (We look at the ways in which women can be punished for defying this authority in chapter 4.) They may also learn that this external authority will control decisions about their worth or value—and that these are decisions they must accept rather than question or try to change.

Ellen, the senior partner at a law firm, remembers:

> The very first job I had, I think, was baby-sitting. I was in maybe the sixth or seventh grade. The people who I was going to be baby-sitting for asked me how much money I wanted for baby-sitting and I had no idea so I got off the phone and asked my mother what I should be paid. She said, "Tell them to pay you whatever they are comfortable with." I think I got 35 cents an hour. That was my first lesson in salary negotiation.

In this brief transaction, Ellen learned that it was not appropriate for her to consider what she wanted or needed, and it was not okay for her to ask for what she felt her time and work were worth. She learned instead that she should accept what she was given and be happy with that.

Research in organizational behavior sheds a bright light on the impact this type of experience can have on women. In a study involving salary negotiations for a job (with experienced recruiters playing the employers and business students playing the job candidates), professor of management Lisa Barron carried out detailed post-negotiation interviews with the participants to understand their thinking. She found two distinct groups in terms of how the participants thought their "worth" should be determined. The first group assumed that they determined their own worth and that it was up to them to make sure the company paid them what they were worth. The second group felt that their worth was determined by what the company would pay them. In a striking disparity, 85 percent of the male participants but only 17 percent of the women in the study fell into the first group. In direct contrast, only 15 percent of the men but 83 percent of the women fell into the second group, the group that believed their worth was determined by others.[20] Clearly, the perspective held by most of the men reveals their confidence in their own talents as well as their strong belief that it is their responsibility to make sure that they get what they deserve (they believe that they can exert some control over what they are paid). The perspective held by most of the women reveals their expectation that others will decide what they are worth and determine what they are offered (they assume they have no control over what they are paid). The implications for asking for what you want are obvious. If a woman believes that forces outside herself will decide what to give her based on her performance and value, the possibility that she *can* ask may not even occur to her.

Christine, a 30-year-old investment banker from Columbus, Ohio, noticed after six months at her first job that she was doing very well, and far better than a man who had started at the same time. She was therefore surprised a few months later when the man was promoted before she was. Mystified, she asked her supervisor why someone whose performance was inferior had been promoted sooner. The answer taught her what she felt was a crucial lesson: The man had spoken up and asked for the promotion, while she had waited for her good work to be noticed and rewarded.

Even though by all objective criteria she probably deserved the promotion more (and would do better work for the company in the higher-level job), he was promoted because he asked—and she wasn't because she didn't ask. Her expectation, she reported, was, "I'm doing my job, I'm working hard, so they should recognize that and move me along." Because she assumed that only her supervisors could exercise control over the progress of her career, she failed to realize that an opportunity for constructive action was passing her by.

Liz, 45, a senior analyst at an influential government agency, had always been one of the hardest-working people in her department. For several years, she had been producing high-visibility work and powerful policy makers frequently asked for her by name to brief them. Nonetheless, she found herself waiting and waiting for a promotion she believed she deserved, but never asked for. Eventually, she grew tired of waiting and put out feelers for another job. She was quickly offered a position in which she would net $10,000 more per year than she was currently grossing. Before she quit, she mentioned the situation to her father. He insisted that she tell her current boss about the other offer first. Her boss immediately gave her the promotion she had wanted and a substantial raise. Liz's mistake had been in believing that a promotion was something her boss controlled and would give her as soon as he decided she'd earned it—not something over which she could exert any influence. She didn't understand that what she wanted was something for which she could ask.

Why Can't Life Be a Meritocracy?

Research suggests that Christine and Liz are not alone. The linguist Deborah Tannen, in her book *Talking from 9 to 5: Women and Men in the Workplace: Language, Sex, and Power,* has shown that women are much more likely than men to think that simply working hard and doing a good job will earn them success and advancement.[21] This, too, relates to women's perception that external forces control their lives. They expect that these forces will hand out rewards and opportunities in a reasonable way and that it's reasonable for hard work and good work to be recognized. They expect life to be fair, and they often don't realize that it's up to them to make sure that it is. Of course, the belief that merit will be rewarded is fundamental to the American Dream—in this country if we're talented and work hard, we believe that recognition and rewards will follow. Although both men and women are raised with this idea, evidence suggests that women hold tighter to the conviction that hard work alone is—or should be—sufficient.

Even enormously accomplished and successful women often retain a strong wish for the rewards of their success to be dispensed by others. Louise, 37, a high-ranking power company executive, routinely negotiates deals worth millions of dollars. But when it comes to her own compensation, she would rather be given what she deserves and spared the necessity of asking for it. In a well-managed company, she believes, senior management should recognize everyone's individual contributions and give them what they're worth. "They ought to just deal with those inequities," she said. "And it shouldn't be always on the employee to ask."

And even though Christine learned early that she needs to promote her own interests on the job, she persists in feeling that when an industry is moving ahead and pay levels are increasing, valuable employees shouldn't be forced to ask for their salaries to be adjusted accordingly. "My own feeling," she said, "was and still is that [if you're doing superior work] you should be identified, and your salary should be identified by what the market will bear. I think it's up to the people that you work for, whether it's H.R. or your management, to identify that and keep current with what's in the industry."

In contrast, men seem to be socialized—both on the playing field and in the workplace—according to a scrappier paradigm. Part of doing your best, they learn, is being aggressive in pursuit of what you want. Ben, 42, president of a financial management company, said his parents drummed into him as a kid that the most important thing was to do his best. When he first started out in business, he thought that would be enough. He assumed that his good work would bring him all the advantages and opportunities he deserved. But in the competitive world in which he moved, he quickly realized that he couldn't wait for people to recognize his ability. He had to "hustle," sell himself, collar the attention of clients he desired, advertise his achievements and good ideas, and ask for the plum assignments and advantageous postings he knew would propel him forward. Initially, like many women, he dreaded asking for what he wanted because he feared rejection. But he forced himself to do it, and he quickly learned that it was less difficult than it seemed; in fact, he discovered that most people were grateful to know what he wanted. His bosses, colleagues, and clients regarded knowledge of his desires as useful and important information. They often couldn't give him what he wanted, but when the resources were available and they agreed that his requests made good business sense, they tried to accommodate him. Women's greater reluctance to ask for what they want often prevents them from learning this lesson—or means that they learn it more slowly.

Following Rules

Girls who are raised to believe that external forces control their lives may also be more reluctant than boys (who are taught that they control their own fates) to question rules—and by extension situations—that are not of their own making. The developmental psychologists Jan Carpenter and Aletha Huston have shown that adults encourage boys and girls to play together in different ways.[22] Although no one has yet identified all the causes for this phenomenon, girls tend to engage in more "structured" play activities while boys gravitate toward "unstructured" forms of play. In structured activities, children follow rules and guidelines set by adults; in unstructured play they act more independently, develop their own rules, attempt to lead, and behave more aggressively.[23] Girls' more structured forms of play teach them compliance behavior and accustom them to doing what they're told rather than deciding for themselves what they want to do. Boys' more unstructured forms of play teach them the opposite—to make their own rules and assert themselves more.

Curious about whether these differences in the ways children play are simply natural expressions of their gender or whether the types of play prompt the behavior differences, Carpenter and Huston, with Wilma Holt, another psychologist, designed an experiment to try to find out. For the experiment, they randomly assigned groups of preschoolers, both boys and girls, to structured or unstructured play activities. They observed that the kids' behavior changed with the activity and was not determined by their gender.[24] This tells us that children's forms of play determine how they behave. So if adults are guiding girls toward more structured activities, they're actually training them to follow externally imposed rules, let others control their circumstances, and assert themselves less. They're teaching them to accept the status quo and go along with it, rather than question it. If they're directing boys toward more unstructured play, they're helping them become good at different things, such as exercising independence and acting as leaders. They're also allowing boys to learn that taking control of a situation and trying to adjust it to suit their needs or wishes can be a good strategy. They're teaching them that they don't have to accept the limits of every situation—that alternatives often exist.

Practicing these different types of behavior as children leads girls and boys to behave differently as adults. Geri, 36, the director of a day care center and preschool, said, "Men, for some reason, are more trained from an early age to express themselves.... As a girl I was not encouraged to ask for things. And I was not encouraged to speak up." Geri was trained in compliance behavior—she was taught that control over her life was retained by someone else and it was not appropriate for her to ask for something other than what she was given. As an adult, Geri still feels reluctant to push for what she wants or to make her own needs a priority.

Is There Anything We Can Do?

Some obvious changes can help women recognize more opportunities in their circumstances and take greater control of their fate. Parents can give their female children chores that emphasize independence, guide them toward unstructured rather than structured play, resist the urge to overprotect them, and demonstrate in their own lives that women as well as men earn and spend money, fix things, and exercise other essential forms of control over their own and their families' lives.

In the workplace, people who mentor women can encourage women not to accept the status quo. They can teach them that the world is more "negotiable" than it often seems, and they can demonstrate that seeking out opportunities to improve their circumstances can be an effective and often necessary strategy for getting ahead. Managers who supervise both men and women can take a more active approach to ensuring that their employees are all treated fairly, enjoy the same advantages, and have access to the same opportunities. They can do this by paying attention to what men and women ask for and by extending the same benefits to female employees that male employees request. Otherwise, even if they're committed to treating men and women equitably, the men they supervise will probably end up with more resources simply because they ask for more. This is especially important when women are a minority in the work force, as Linda's experience when she was the director of her school's Ph.D. program illustrates.

Linda, with the best intentions in the world, believed that helping students was a central part of her job. Whenever one of them came to her with a request, she did her best to grant it. She didn't realize that the men were asking more than the women because she wasn't tracking the gender of people who came to her with requests. And since women made up only 30 percent of the students at her school, the fact that fewer women were making requests didn't stand out. As a result, Linda presided over an inequitable distribution of resources, with men getting more than their fair share of opportunities. This led to several unintended consequences. First, while they were in school the male students earned more money than the females because teachers get paid more than teaching assistants. Second, when they completed their studies the men looked like better candidates on the job market (and probably got better jobs) because they had real classroom experience and the women did not. These differences paved the way for even greater disparities—both in income and professional opportunities—as these early disadvantages accumulated over the course of her students' careers.

We know that every time one person asks for a promotion, managers can't promote everyone else they supervise. Each time one person asks for a raise, managers can't raise everybody else's salary too. But we're convinced that whenever a man asks for and receives some significant reward or opportunity, a really good manager will consider doing the same for his or her female employees with the same qualifications. And the best managers will investigate whether any of the women they supervise have skills and experience that aren't being fully used because those women haven't asked to do more. This can achieve several important goals: It can compensate for women's reluctance to ask, reward deserving employees (thereby building loyalty), and boost efficiency and productivity by making the most of the organization's "human resources." Susannah, the political strategist, waited two years before asking for a promotion. Not only did she lose out, but her employer lost out because that job went unfilled for such a long time. In her case, a truly astute manager might have spotted the opportunity to reward a talented and committed employee while producing benefits for the organization at the same time—a classic "win/win" situation.

In addition, people often ask for smaller things, such as flexible schedules or tuition stipends or computer upgrades or even just better titles—and many of these things cost relatively little. Granting this type of request in a consciously equitable manner can increase productivity by building loyalty to the organization. It can also save turnover costs by encouraging people to stay in a place where they feel that they are treated fairly and their contributions are recognized.

From Turnip to Oyster

Women can also change from "turnips" into "oysters"—they can learn how important it is to go after what they want. Susannah told us:

> Over time I've learned that actually asking for what you want is the first big step. I sat for a long time in that one job thinking that people would see that I deserved more and just give it to me because they saw it when actually you really have to . . . make yourself known and ask for it bluntly—and repeatedly—at times. That was a very difficult lesson and I think I'm still learning that lesson, but it does work. I think it's like [political] message work. . . . You have to tell people [what you want] three times for them to hear it.

Christine, too, has realized that whether she likes it or not she needs to speak up on her own behalf. She said: "Nobody's a mind reader. And, as bad as it sounds, you're the only one who's going to look out for you in a business-type atmosphere. So if you don't speak up, you only have yourself to blame if something goes wrong."

Kim, 43, a radio news anchor in a large Southwestern city, described her gradual realization that there's much more you can get for yourself in life just by asking:

> It never occurred to me that you could, for instance, ask a credit card company for a lower interest rate, you know. Or, if there's a late fee, if you're a good customer, you can ask them to waive the late fee because you usually pay your bills on time—that people will extend some kind of a courtesy to you. And it only occurred to me after I had read that somebody had done it, or heard about somebody who had done it. Somebody told me once that you can negotiate the price of any hotel room, anywhere. Number one, I never even thought of that. Number two, I wouldn't necessarily do it, but if I needed to, it sure is good to know that this is how the game is played outside of my little world.

The other good news is that gender differences around perceptions of negotiability *may* be changing. On the "recognition of opportunity" scale (the turnip/oyster scale), the scores of women in their twenties were about the same as those of men in their twenties. Women in their thirties, forties, fifties, and sixties, in contrast, scored lower than men of the same age. This suggests that younger adults of both sexes seem to recognize to an equal degree the importance of taking an active approach to promoting change.[25] Several factors may explain this finding. One theory posits that increased awareness of gender inequities has led parents, schools, and the media to treat children in a more gender-neutral fashion than they did in the past. Another explanation may be that women are making real gains in our society even though they still lag behind men in terms of status and power. Greater representation of women at the higher levels of an organization has been shown to help entering women advance and prosper. In this context, the success of older women may be teaching younger women important lessons about the existence of opportunities in apparently static situations—and about the importance of pursuing those opportunities.[26] If this continues to happen, women will not only begin to control their own lives and the workings of the world far more than they have in the past, they will also be *seen* to be in control to a far greater degree than ever before. As a result, children growing up today and young adults starting out in the world will internalize gender schemas that differ significantly from those of a few decades back.

The least heartening interpretation of the similar scores earned by men and women in their twenties is that young men and women have always had similar attitudes about the existence of opportunity in their lives (this has never been measured before), but as they age men and women learn different things about opportunity. In other words, it's possible that men become more "oysterlike"—more prone to see opportunity everywhere—as they grow older because in fact the world of opportunity opens up more easily to men than to women. While men advance in power, social status, and prestige, women may experience far fewer situations that teach them how much of life is amenable to change. As a result, women's scores on the "turnip-to-oyster" scale may remain essentially unchanged while men's increase.

But even if the scores of women and men in their twenties do not tell of a shift already underway, there is hope in the rapidity with which women seem able to change their "turniplike" attitudes once they recognize them. In the process of writing this book, we met dozens of women who described having a "light-bulb" experience when they heard about our ideas. For the first time, they said, they recognized the reasons for their behavior and the price they paid for not asking for what they wanted more of the time. We heard many stories of women making changes that they previously thought were out of reach. We even heard stories like this from women we hadn't met. Judi, 58, is a psychologist and the mother of one of Linda's male Ph.D. students, whose name is Josh. One day Josh told Linda that his mother wanted to thank her. It turned out that Judi was working part-time for a start-up company. She'd had some ideas about new areas the company could pursue and when she explained her ideas to her boss, he told her to get started on them right away. But Judi wasn't working enough hours to pursue these new areas and still complete her other job responsibilities. She confided in her son that she wished she could work more hours so that she could do a good job on both. Josh suggested that she ask her boss if this was possible. Judi's first response was that she couldn't do this—it would feel awkward and not right and might even damage her relationship with her boss. Josh explained Linda's research and encouraged his mother to try. When she did, her boss was thrilled that she wanted to work more hours and said, "I'm glad you asked!"

Asking for what you want doesn't always guarantee you'll get it, of course. As we will show, our culture often discourages women from saying what they need and responds badly when they do. Nonetheless, until now the average man has approached life both inside and outside the workplace with a powerful advantage over the average woman simply because he suspected that life holds more possibilities than those publicly announced and widely available. What Judi's story reveals (and the experiences of Susannah and Christine and many more women confirm) is that women possess a wonderful capacity to learn this lesson, a lesson that can change their lives in ways both large and small.

2

A Price Higher than Rubies

One of Linda's graduate students—a young woman who had taken her negotiation class—visited Linda in her office to share some good news. The student had just accepted a job offer from a great company and couldn't wait to begin her new career. When Linda asked how the negotiations had gone, the student seemed surprised. Her new employer had offered her so much more than she'd expected, it hadn't occurred to her to negotiate. She simply accepted what she was offered.

This story points out an obvious truth: Before we decide to negotiate for something we must first be dissatisfied with what we have. We need to believe that something else—more money, a better title, or a different division of household chores—would make us happier or more satisfied. But if we're already satisfied with what we have or with what we've been offered, asking for something else might not occur to us. Ironically, this turns out to be a big problem for women: being satisfied with less.

Expecting Less

In 1978, psychologists discovered that women's pay satisfaction tends to be equal to or higher than that of men in similar positions, even though women typically earn less than men doing the same work.[1] Four years later, a broader study looked at many different types of organizations and reached a similar conclusion, which the author of that study, the social psychologist Faye Crosby, called "the paradox of the contented female worker."[2] Seventeen years later, in 1999, a study by two management researchers confirmed this finding again.[3] Even at the turn of the twenty-first century, in other words, with all of the gains made by women during the previous four decades, women still feel at least as satisfied as men with their salaries, even though they continue to earn less for the same work.

How to explain this strange phenomenon? Why would women be just as satisfied as men while earning less? Many scholars believe that women are satisfied with less because they expect less: They go into the work force expecting to be paid less than men, so they're not disappointed when those expectations are met.[4] To test this theory, the psychologist Beth Martin surveyed a group of undergraduate business students. After presenting them with information about salary ranges for the different types of jobs they would be qualified to take after graduating, she asked them to identify which job they expected to obtain and what they thought their starting salary would be. Working from the same information, women reported salary expectations between 3 and 32 percent lower than those reported by men for the same jobs. There was no evidence that the men were more qualified for the jobs they chose—just that women expected to earn less for doing the same work.[5]

In another study, two social psychologists, Brenda Major and Ellen Konar, conducted a mail survey of students in management programs at the State University of New York at Buffalo. In this survey, students were asked to indicate their salary expectations upon graduation as well as at their "career peak"—how much they expected to earn the year they earned the most. They found that the men expected to earn about 13 percent more than the women during their first year of working full-time and expected to earn *32 percent more* at their career peaks. Major and Konar ruled out several potential explanations for these differences, such as gender differences in the importance of pay or in the importance of doing interesting work, gender differences in the students' perceptions of their skills or qualifications, and gender differences in their supervisors' assessments of the students' skills or qualifications.[6]

Another study also found similar gender differences in ideas about how much money was "fair pay" for particular jobs. Using college seniors at Michigan State University, researchers discovered that women's estimates of "fair pay" averaged 4 percent less than men's estimates for their first jobs and 23 percent less than men's for fair career-peak pay.[7] These three studies suggest that women as a rule expect to be paid less than men expect to be paid for the same work.

Our interviews bore out these findings. One standard question we asked was "Are you usually successful in getting what you want?" To our initial surprise, almost every woman we talked to said yes. When we probed further, however, it turned out that many of the women we talked to felt as though they were successful at getting what they wanted in part because they didn't want very much. Angela, 28, the marketing director of a community development bank, said she's usually successful at getting what she wants because "I don't think I ever want something that's that far out of my reach." Julianne, 36, a graphic designer who is now a full-time mother, said she usually gets what she wants because "I have pretty realistic expectations in my life, both professionally and personally." Cheryl, 45, the owner of a small toy store, said she's good at getting what she wants because she's not very demanding and "readily pleased." These women, like so many others, hold modest expectations for what will constitute appropriate rewards for their work and time. Since lower expectations are more likely to be filled than higher ones, the odds are better that these women—and most women—will be satisfied with the rewards that life sends their way.

But this doesn't make sense, you may say. Why would a woman who is poorly paid be satisfied with her salary under any circumstances? Surprisingly, extensive research has documented that pay satisfaction correlates with pay expectations, and not with how much may be possible or with what the market will bear. In other words, satisfaction depends not on whether your salary is comparable to what others like you are paid, but on whether it falls in line with your expectations. People are dissatisfied with their pay only when it falls short of what they expected to get, not when it falls short of what they could have gotten.[8] And most women don't expect to get paid very much, so when they don't get much—as so often happens—they are less likely to be disappointed.

No Value to Women's Work

What leads women to undervalue the work they do and set their expectations so low? The Old Testament says that a good woman is worth "a price higher than rubies."[9] But because most women until recently devoted much of their lives to unpaid labor in the home they're unaccustomed to thinking of their work in terms of its dollar value. Many factors play into this problem, with perhaps the most obvious being our historical predisposition against recognizing the economic value of what society deems to be women's work. The economics journalist Ann Crittenden, in her book *The Price of Motherhood*, explains: "Two-thirds of all wealth is created by human skills, creativity, and enterprise—what is known as 'human capital.' And that means parents who are conscientiously and effectively rearing children are literally, in the words of economist Shirley Burggraf, 'the major wealth producers in our economy.' "[10]

A society's education system also makes a huge contribution to the creation of "human capital," of course—by training children, guiding their creativity, and helping them direct their skills toward productive forms of enterprise. But children who do not grow up with attentive caregivers in safe, stable homes tend to derive far less benefit from their education system and only rarely grow up to become "major wealth producers." Schools can only do so much to compensate for deprivation or neglect at home.

Despite the demonstrated economic importance of child rearing, however, women who devote themselves either full- or part-time to raising their children are not only thought by many people to be doing nothing ("not working"), they suffer a loss of income that, Crittenden reports, "produces a bigger wage gap between mothers and childless women than the wage gap between young men and women. This forgone income, the equivalent of a huge 'mommy tax,' is typically more than $1 million for a college-educated American woman."[11] Looked at this way, doing "women's work" not only means working at an occupation with no recognized monetary value, but working at one that is perceived to have *negative* value. Rather than being paid to do this terribly demanding and important work, in other words, women must pay—with lost earnings, missed opportunities, and, in many cases, radically diminished financial security.

Lest we think that all this has changed since the women's movement propelled so many women into the work force, and that these statistics refer to what is now a relatively small group of women, Crittenden reports that "homemaking ... is still the largest single occupation in the United States. ... Even among women in their thirties, by far the most common occupation is full-time housekeeping and caregiving."[12] Even the most advantaged and best-educated women fall into this category: "The persistence of traditional family patterns cuts across economic, class, and racial lines. ... The United States also has one of the lowest labor force participation rates for college-educated women in the developed world; only in Turkey, Ireland, Switzerland, and the Netherlands does a smaller proportion of female college graduates work for pay."[13]

The cumulative impact of these realities on women cannot be exaggerated. Accustomed to laboring without pay at work that is devalued by every objective financial measure, and to seeing most other women devote a huge proportion of their adult lives to unpaid work, women enter the traditional work force unaccustomed to evaluating their time and abilities in economic terms.

Our interviews produced many examples of this handicap. Angela, the marketing director for the community development bank, had a college degree from Princeton, five years' experience as a successful lobbyist on Capitol Hill, and a year of working on a presidential campaign. When her candidate lost, she began looking for another job and quickly identified two that she found attractive. But neither job matched exactly the work she had been doing before, making her fear that she wasn't qualified for either. As a result, when one of the firms made her an offer, she was so surprised and grateful that she just accepted it. When she called the other company to withdraw her name, she learned to her surprise that they had been planning to make her an offer as well. If she had waited before accepting the first offer, the existence of the second offer would have put her in a better negotiating position. But because she undervalued her skills and her appeal, she accepted the first offer she received—and a salary that was less than she had been making before and less than she almost certainly could have gotten.

Similarly, Joan, 41, a magazine editor, described being sought after to serve as the editor of a new magazine targeted at working women. At one point during the hiring discussions, her future boss asked what she wanted to be paid. "In hindsight," she said, "I was so naïve and clueless, and I just had never really made a lot of money in my life, and I didn't need a lot of money, so what I asked for seemed like a lot of money. And it was just not a lot of money." After she was hired and spoke to other people in similar positions, she discovered how "pathetic" her salary was. Her explanation for her naïveté was that she "hadn't been in the work force for a lot of years of her working life" and was "very young in the world of business"—an explanation that might accurately describe the lives of many, if not most, women.

Like many of their female peers, Angela and Joan were suffering from a limited understanding of their market power. That is, they didn't realize that a market existed for their particular skills and talent and experience— and that this market could help them establish what they were worth to prospective employers. Evidence from our interviews suggests that this is a common problem among women. Kim, the radio news anchor, admits with embarrassment that at one job her immediate boss (who did not control salary decisions) laughed when she discovered what Kim was paid, it was so little. The station's most prominent "on-air" talent, Kim hosted the morning "drive-time" news program at the leading station in an intensely competitive radio market. Although she was widely admired by her colleagues and audience, she later discovered that her peers and even many people who were junior to her in both rank and public prominence—most of them male—were paid far more. She probably could have drummed up an offer from a competing station in short order and might even have been able to double her salary, but at the time she had no idea what her work was worth—or that she could use the market to her advantage in this way.

Even when they recognize their market power, many women feel uncomfortable about using it as leverage in a negotiation. Stephanie, the administrative assistant, didn't ask for an increase in her salary even when she had another job offer and her boss asked what it would take to keep her. "I thought it would be taking advantage of an opportunity but an unfair advantage," she explained. Stephanie understood that she had some market power, but she didn't think it was right to use that power.

The Stanford linguist Penelope Eckert traces women's lack of awareness about their market value to traditional labor divisions between men and women. A man's personal worth, she notes, has long been based on his "accumulation of goods, status, and power in the marketplace," while a woman's worth was until recently based largely on "her ability to maintain order in, and control over, her domestic realm."[14] Because this historical legacy makes men more accustomed to evaluating their worth in the marketplace, they also seem more comfortable using their market power to get what they want—by researching average salaries for comparable work, bringing in competing offers, and emphasizing that they have objective value outside their organizations.

For Love, Not Money

In her review of research on children's household chores, Jacqueline Goodnow observed that, in addition to being given chores that emphasize their dependence, girls are also assigned chores that must be performed on a more routine basis, such as cooking and cleaning. Boys' chores, while encouraging their independence, also tend to involve less frequent tasks such as washing the car, shoveling snow, and taking out the garbage.[15] Goodnow surmises that girls rarely earn money by performing the housekeeping chores they shoulder at home (such as cleaning, cooking, and washing dishes) for their neighbors, because those jobs are identified as female responsibilities and are typically performed by the woman in each house. In contrast, more infrequent tasks, such as lawn-mowing and shoveling snow, tend to be identified as male responsibilities, but the man in each house, instead of performing them himself, often pays a neighborhood child—usually a boy—to fill in for him.[16]

Virginia Valian agrees with this analysis: "Because parents see infrequent tasks as ones that call for payment, they are not likely to pay a daughter, for example, for washing the dishes, but they will pay a son for washing the family car."[17] Valian believes that this "gendered" approach to chore assignments teaches children not only that there is a difference between "men's work" and "women's work," but also that the appropriate rewards are different for each. "Children have reason to think that boys labor for payment, while girls labor 'for love,'" she writes.[18]

As a result of this early training, many women struggle when they must assign a value to their work. Lory, a 30-year-old theater production manager, said, "I have a hard time putting a monetary figure on the work that I do." Although she manages three productions (in three cities) of a long-running hit show and works punishing hours, including most nights and weekends, she "feels weird" asking for more money because she thinks she should be working for "the love of the theater." Emma, the social science researcher, said that at the beginning of her career she didn't have many reference points to help her evaluate her work, and she actually worried that she was making *more* money than she should: "I genuinely thought that I was overpaid. And I also thought that I was working on social service issues, where there's this sense of 'How can I be making all this money when I'm working on issues related to improving services for low-income people? It's not really fair or appropriate.'" If women believe that doing important work—work that they care about and even love—means that they can't place a value on their time and contribution, or that their time and contribution therefore have a lower value, it's no wonder that they have trouble gauging what their work is worth.

Having been trained to think that they should work "for love" rather than money also makes gratitude, strangely enough, another limiting factor for women. Grateful to be paid at all, many women accept what they are offered without negotiating. Angela feels that she made only a half-hearted attempt to negotiate a higher salary for her current position in part because "I was glad to get this job. . . . I really, really wanted the job and I knew I was going to take it no matter what." Emma described a similar experience in which gratitude held her back from asking for more than she was offered:

> I talked to people in Personnel, and they said, "Well, this is the high end of the salary range, and this is all we can do." And so I just accepted that. And then after my son was born, my costs were so high for child care and other things that I went to the person responsible for administration and said, "I have to have a substantial increase." And I got it. And I realized after that that I could have really negotiated for much more. I could have negotiated for fewer hours; I could have negotiated for a signing bonus; there were a lot of things I could have negotiated for, but I didn't. Because I accepted, "Oh, I want to tie in with the range. I should feel lucky I have this job."

Barbara, 59, a human resources consultant, told us about being hired by a consulting firm to create and head a whole new division. Brought in at what the company called "Level 2," she quickly realized that as a division head she should have been at "Level 1." But there were practically no women at Level 1 in the company, and, she said, "at the time I was kind of grateful," so she didn't fight it.

We're not saying, of course, that any of these women should have pushed so hard for more that they jeopardized jobs that they obviously wanted and liked. We're simply saying that an exaggerated sense of gratitude should not have prevented them from gathering information about what was fair and available—and using that information to get more of what they needed or deserved.

Sometimes, women feel grateful simply for being paid enough to live well. Louise, the power company executive, explained that she never pushes too hard for higher compensation, even though she knows she is paid significantly less than her peers. "I think it is this whole thing about feeling like I have a lot and . . . I'm pretty grateful for what I have," she said. This highlights another reason women have trouble estimating what their work is worth: Rather than thinking about their value in the marketplace, they instead focus more narrowly on what they need. This may be because until quite recently women in western culture worked at jobs outside the home only if they "needed" to—if their spouses weren't bringing in enough to support the family, or if they had no other source of income because they were orphaned, unmarried, divorced, or widowed. Even now, when a woman is divorced, many judges determine her financial settlement from her husband based on what the judge decides she "needs"— not based on any objective evaluation of her contribution toward the accumulated assets in the marriage.[19] As a result, women have learned to think of their incomes in terms of what they need rather than in terms of what their work is worth. As Angela explained, another reason she didn't negotiate for a higher salary at her current job was that "It would have been difficult for me to even make the case that it was an issue of what I needed."

Wrong Comparisons

Even when women do collect information about the market value of their work, they often make the mistake of comparing themselves to the wrong people. Research has shown that people typically compare themselves to others whom they consider to be similar, meaning that men are more likely to compare themselves to other men and women to other women.[20] As a result, rather than looking at everyone performing a comparable job who has comparable training, experience, and skill, male or female, women tend to compare themselves only to other women[21]—women who are still paid 76 cents to every man's dollar.[22] Women therefore compare themselves only to people who are likely to be underpaid—and men compare themselves to people who are typically paid more. In addition, since professional networks tend to be gender-segregated, as we describe later in the book, women often have fewer opportunities to compare themselves to men because they know fewer men and have less access to information about what men earn.

Eleanor, 34, a literature professor and biographer, has been reluctant to push for more pay and better "perks" (such as a larger office and adequate funding for her research) because compared with her female peers of the same age, she has "way more." "The people who have more than I do are not my peers," she said. "They're people who are more senior than I am." A committed teacher with a high professional profile and an excellent reputation, Eleanor had already written two highly regarded books that were published by a prestigious publisher and won several important prizes. She confidently declared to Sara that she was far more valuable to her department and to her university than many more senior people who were better paid and enjoyed more perks. But when it came to concrete rewards for her contributions, she didn't compare herself to them; she compared herself to her female friends from graduate school, few of whom had been as successful as she.

Angela, the community development bank marketing director, told us how, in the early years of her career as a lobbyist, she worried that she was "getting away with something" or fooling her employers because she was making such a good salary. Eventually, she traced her concern to a misplaced comparison. "I was comparing myself to my peers age-wise. But when I began to compare myself to my peers professionally, what other lobbyists were making, and even though I was very junior, I was a lobbyist and I was out there, you know, spending the same time and energy. I thought, 'yeah, I deserve this.'"

Once she learned this lesson, she was able to go to her boss and say, "Hey, I'm a bargain to you right now." He agreed, and immediately gave her a raise to keep from losing her. The critical change, for Angela, came when she began "spending more time professionally with my peers versus my personal buddies." She didn't compare herself to lobbyists who had 25 more years of experience than she had, but she compared herself to other lobbyists of *both* sexes with experience comparable to hers. This is a lesson from which many women can learn: In order to judge their worth more accurately and develop a well-founded idea of what the market will pay them, women need to learn how to make the right comparisons by seeking out information about their professional peers of both sexes.

Unsure of What They Deserve

Women may also expect less and feel satisfied with less because they're not sure that they deserve more. Liliane, the electrical engineer, described feeling as though she didn't deserve to be interviewed for an engineering job despite her impressive college record. This lack of self-confidence made her so thrilled when she was offered a job, she didn't care what she was paid—and didn't negotiate her starting salary. Later on in her career, despite notable success, she is still struggling with this issue of what she deserves. Although she feels well compensated in many ways for her work, she hasn't negotiated for a higher title that she wants and that more accurately describes her role. When asked why, she explains that other people might deserve the title more, although she also admits that many less talented and productive people have already been awarded the higher title. Liliane is struggling with what social scientists call a low sense of personal entitlement—a problem that research has shown to be rampant among women.

Before deciding to negotiate for more than you've got, then, you don't just need to feel dissatisfied. You also need to feel sure that you deserve the change you want. Here, too, women struggle with a powerful disadvantage—a disadvantage that they often manage by waiting to be offered what they want rather than asking for it directly. When we interviewed Lory, the production stage manager, she told us that for the past several months she'd worked hundreds of hours of overtime and was waiting for her bosses to notice. She wanted them to recognize her dedication and reward her. Having them acknowledge her work without her needing to ask would make her feel good, she said, and asking for the recognition was not going to feel nearly as good—even if she got it.

Being given a reward (a raise, a promotion, access to an opportunity, even just praise and thanks) without asking not only spares a woman the discomfort of announcing her belief that she deserves that reward, it can also relieve her uncertainty about whether in fact she does deserve it. Julianne, the graphic designer, said that her approach when she wants something is to "work harder so it will be clear I deserve it. I tend not to ask. Because it's a little more rewarding . . . because what that means is that the people who are giving it to me think I deserve it." This testimony is particularly telling because neither Lory nor Julianne is particularly shy or lacking in self-confidence. Nonetheless, both of them felt that being rewarded for their hard work without having to ask would confirm the value of their contribution and boost their self-esteem.

These examples highlight the importance of external factors to a woman's sense of entitlement. Although all of us feel better when we receive praise and approval, extensive research has shown that the average woman's feelings of self-worth tend to fluctuate in response to feedback— whether positive or negative—more than the average man's.[23] One study found that women's positive feelings about their abilities and their work performance increased significantly in response to positive feedback and plummeted dramatically in response to negative feedback. In comparison, men's feelings about the quality of their work changed very little in response to either type of feedback.[24] Being rewarded for their accomplishments (as opposed to asking for recognition) may not only increase a woman's pride about her work, it can also enhance her sense of entitlement. Many women wait to be rewarded for their efforts, in other words, because they don't know whether they deserve something unless someone else tells them that they do.

In one of the first studies on entitlement, the psychologists Charlene Callahan-Levy and Lawrence Messe recruited students to write a series of opinions about campus-related issues. Half of the students were instructed to decide how much money to pay themselves and half were instructed to decide how much to pay someone else for the work. The researchers found that women paid themselves much less than men paid themselves—19 percent less. Furthermore, women paid others, including other women, more than they paid themselves. The researchers found no gender differences in the students' evaluations of how well they had performed the task, meaning that women were not paying themselves less because they believed their work was inferior to the work of men or other women. They simply lost their ability to accurately evaluate what the work was worth when they were the ones performing the task.[25]

In a study by the social psychologists Brenda Major, Dean McFarlin, and Diana Gagnon that followed up this research, men and women were asked to evaluate the application materials of incoming freshmen and predict their college success. They were then told to pay themselves what they felt was fair for their labor. Although the researchers expected gender differences, the disparity they uncovered was dramatic: Men paid themselves *63 percent more on average* than women paid themselves for the same task. Once again, the researchers asked the subjects how well they had performed the task and found no gender differences in their performance evaluations.[26]

In another study, Major, McFarlin, and Gagnon gave male and female research subjects four dollars to perform a "visual perception task" in which they counted the number of dots in a sequence of pictures. They instructed the subjects to keep working until they had "earned" their four dollars. They found that women worked 22 percent longer than men and counted 32 percent more pictures of dots. This result occurred even though privacy was maximized—the students were not being observed by the experimenter and were instructed to put identification numbers, not names, on their materials. But even though women worked longer and faster, the men and women were equally satisfied with their pay and did not differ in terms of how they evaluated their performance.[27] The results of these three studies suggest that women can correctly evaluate and set expectations for others—their low sense of entitlement is reserved for themselves.

A few examples illustrate how women struggle with this issue of what they deserve. Susannah, the political strategist, said that pursuing something she wants makes her uncomfortable because "I don't always feel that I deserve it." She said she often doesn't ask for things "because I get nervous about asking or I don't think I deserve it so I sort of talk myself down from going toward it." Lisa, 46, the receptionist-manager of an animal hospital, said that as a child, "my training—what is really engrained in me—is that you're never quite deserving of what you might want."

When we asked men how they feel about what they deserve, we got very different answers. Brian, 32, an intensive-care nurse, gave an answer that suggested that he thought this was a strange question, with an obvious answer. "Um, sure," he said. "I deserve the things I want—yeah." This is a confident answer, while the answers we heard from many women tended to be far more tentative about what they deserved. Mike, the entrepreneur, responded to this question with what amounted to confusion, saying, "Interesting question! ... The sense that I deserve something is not a sense that I carry with me, generally. Do I deserve this, or deserve that?" Where women are often preoccupied with ascertaining what exactly they deserve, it doesn't really cross Mike's mind to consider whether he deserves something or not—this approach isn't relevant to his thinking.

Another study looked at this question of entitlement in a different way. Lisa Barron asked MBA students to negotiate for a hypothetical job with an actual job recruiter; afterward, she interviewed the students about their experience. To explore entitlement issues, she asked whether the students thought they were entitled to a salary similar to or greater than that offered to other job candidates. Of the subjects who thought they belonged in the "entitled to more than others" category, 70 percent were men and 30 percent were women; of the subjects who fit into the "entitled to the same as others" category, 29 percent were men and 71 percent were women.[28]

Hoping to further illuminate this issue, Linda and her colleagues created an entitlement scale to ask men and women directly about their sense of entitlement. Using the web survey described in the introduction, they presented people with a series of statements about what they thought they might or might not deserve and asked them to rate, on a seven-point scale, the extent to which they agreed or disagreed with each statement. Not surprisingly, men scored significantly higher on this scale than women.[29] What was surprising was the extent of the disparity: More than half the women respondents and almost twice as many women as men turned out to be suffering from a low sense of entitlement (52 percent of the women and only 29 percent of the men). Only 6 percent of the women displayed extremely high levels of entitlement, whereas almost twice as many men (11 percent) fell into this category. In addition—and this is important, because the younger people we interviewed insisted that this would not be the case—the gender differences in entitlement for people in their twenties and early thirties were just as large as the gender differences for older people.

All of these studies, using different approaches, go a long way toward explaining why women are less likely than men to ask for more than they already have: *Women are not sure that they deserve more.* As a result, even when women can imaginé changes that might increase their productivity at work, their happiness at home, or their overall contentment with their lives, their suppressed sense of entitlement creates real barriers to their asking. Because they're not dissatisfied with what they have and not sure they deserve more, women often settle for less.

Where's the Problem?

But if women are satisfied with the personal and professional rewards they receive, where's the problem? Who are we to decide that people shouldn't be satisfied with what they have? Does it do anyone a service to persuade satisfied people to be unsatisfied? We think it does. We're convinced that as a society we are paying a substantial price for leaving women undisturbed and unaware of how much they may be missing. We wouldn't be comfortable with a system that consistently paid people born on even-numbered days less than it paid people born on odd-numbered days—such a suggestion sounds preposterous. But women make up half of our society, just as people born on even-numbered days do. Why should we tolerate a society in which half our citizens are arbitrarily undervalued and underpaid? Fairness as a principle doesn't work if applied only in response to demand; it must be safeguarded and promoted even when its beneficiaries don't realize what they are missing.

Let's start with the social costs. Undervaluing themselves and being undervalued by society can be bad for women's health. The close link between a positive "self-perception" and psychological good health is well known.[30] More recent research now indicates that the opposite is also true. A negative self-evaluation combined with stress can lead to depression,[31] and two-thirds of all depressed adults are women.[32] Depression is not only a problem in itself but can lead to other health problems. As reported in the January 20, 2003, issue of *Time* magazine, "Each year in the U.S., an estimated 30,000 people commit suicide, with the vast majority of cases attributable to depression." *Time* also points out that depression makes "other serious diseases dramatically worse," such as heart disease, cancer, diabetes, epilepsy, and osteoporosis.[33] Unfortunate for each individual, depression often represents a real cost to society as well—to provide care for the uninsured or underinsured at a time when health-care costs are skyrocketing. (And most people are underinsured for mental health care.) Then there's the question of lost productivity due to depression, which *Time* estimates "costs the U.S. economy about $50 billion a year."[34]

We're not claiming, of course, that persuading women to ask for what they want more of the time, and convincing society to accept and encourage this, will do away with depression and increase production. But, as one set of researchers put it: "Because of the potentially serious implications of negative self-perceptions for achievement behavior and psychological health, more attention should be devoted to discovering factors that produce inaccurately negative self-perceptions. A better understanding of the causes of negative self-perceptions may enable us to prevent or at least alleviate these biases, which presently may hold back some females and males from achieving their full potential."[35]

There are other social costs as well from women as a group being unequally rewarded for their work. With many types of benefits (such as social security, disability insurance, unemployment insurance, and pensions) linked to one's salary, paying women less means apportioning inadequate amounts of these "rainy day" guarantees to huge numbers of the populace. As a result "American women over sixty-five are more than twice as likely to be poor as men of the same age."[36] In addition to forcing so many women to struggle at the ends of their lives, leaving this situation uncorrected imposes substantial economic costs on society to support all of these indigent female elderly.

The phenomenon that Faye Crosby has called "the denial of personal disadvantage" also contributes to the social costs we all pay for underestimating the value of women's work and time. Since, as Crosby has shown, "people typically imagine themselves to be exempt from the injustices that they can recognize as affecting their membership or reference groups,"[37] a woman may see that other women earn lower salaries than comparable men and yet believe herself to be exempt from this problem. This is unfortunate for several reasons. First, at a personal level, because this woman doesn't recognize the reality of her situation, she may take no action to fight it. Second, at a broader societal level, people are more likely to push for changes in which they have a personal stake—changes from which they themselves will benefit. The longer women labor under the misapprehension that they personally are doing okay, the longer it will take for the system as a whole to adjust this fundamental and counterproductive inequity.[38]

There are real market costs as well. As we already reported, in the year 2000, women owned 40 percent of all the businesses in the United States (a total of 9.1 million female-owned businesses) but received only 2.3 percent of the available venture capital dollars.[39] How to explain this? Although there are undoubtedly many contributing causes, Joanna Rees Gallanter, a venture capitalist herself, has observed, "Women are often not comfortable talking about what they're worth. They'll go in to pitch a project and naturally put a lower value on it than men do."[40] You may think—well, that's too bad, that's business. Businesses go under every day. But sheer scale puts this problem into perspective. If 40 percent of the businesses in this country may be undercapitalized, this puts far more than the long-term survival of a few businesses at risk. It puts at risk the employees of those 9.1 million businesses, the fiscal health of the communities those businesses serve, and at some level the health of our national economy.

What are some other costs? Just as a person who decides to buy a bottle of wine usually assumes that a higher-priced bottle will be of better quality than a more inexpensive one, employers tend to assume that applicants with better compensation records are more capable than those who have been paid less. Because women's salary histories don't always accurately reflect their true capabilities, employers sometimes fail to hire the most talented people for the jobs they need to fill, and their companies as well as the female applicants lose out. With this happening in every type of business at every level, we as a society are inevitably misusing our resources—our human capital. We may also be limiting potential business growth and related gains in productivity (a major index of economic health), if more than 50 percent of our citizens are not making full use of their talents or being given the opportunity to do the best work of which they are capable.

Finally, businesses suffer when managers don't know what their employees need to do their jobs well. Influential management texts, such as *The Human Equation: Building Profits by Putting People First*, by Jeffrey Pfeffer, stress that being a good manager means keeping your employees happy and productive.[41] An employee who doesn't realize that changes in her working conditions could improve the quality of her work makes her manager's job that much harder. An employee who doesn't communicate to her boss that her work performance is being undermined by financial strain, a conflict with a coworker, or a mismatch between her talents and the needs of a particular project prevents her boss from managing her most effectively. This is not just theoretical. Many senior people we interviewed said that it helps them to know what their people want. Rather than frowning on employees who ask for more money, new opportunities, or different "perks" and benefits, these managers appreciate knowing what they can do to make their employees' lives easier and their work better. The trap of low expectations combined with a depressed sense of entitlement doesn't merely punish women by preventing them from recognizing and pursuing changes that might improve their situation. It deprives their bosses, colleagues, friends, and intimates of valuable information about them. In its worst manifestations, it wastes women's talents and prevents them from realizing their full potential.

As the sociologist Cynthia Fuchs Epstein has written, "it is in the nature of human motivation that when people are not appropriately rewarded for their efforts and contributions, they cease to aim high."[42]

She also points out that "women, like men, find that when others honor their contributions, listen to their ideas, and acknowledge their [work], they perform at higher levels."[43]

Managers also don't want to lose good people because their employees don't ask for what they want and then get lured away by better offers. In many cases, departing employees might have saved themselves the trouble of changing jobs simply by telling their managers what they needed to improve their working conditions and increase their job satisfaction. The responsibility goes the other way too. Managers need to realize that women are less likely to ask for promotions or raises that haven't been given to them. If managers don't take steps to correct the resulting wage inequities, they leave their organizations open to lawsuits when such discrepancies are discovered. They also risk souring morale in their organizations and seeing talented women leave for better-paying jobs when they realize that they've been treated shabbily. Worker turnover costs businesses millions of dollars every year—and much of it could be avoided if managers made a point of finding out what their employees want and need, and workers felt free to tell them.

Here's an example from Linda's own experience. Two male colleagues became eligible for promotion at the same time she did. Although all three of them were equally qualified for promotion, the two men were promoted and Linda was not. Linda had an excellent relationship with her dean and couldn't understand how he'd failed to recognize her significant professional accomplishments and her contributions to the school. She felt angry and unappreciated, and she thought the dean should know how she felt and want to do something about it.

Linda was lucky because she knew she was unhappy, she could clearly identify what she wanted (the promotion), and she felt confident that she deserved the promotion she wanted (perhaps because she was comparing herself to both male and female colleagues). So she spoke to her boss. The colleagues who'd been promoted, it turned out, had received offers from other institutions. They'd threatened to leave unless they were promoted. The dean wanted to keep them, so he gave them what they asked for. Because Linda hadn't asked to be promoted, the dean never even thought of her—she was off his radar. Once she asked, he readily agreed to promote her too.

As Linda left the dean's office, the words "I'm glad you asked" rang in her ears. The dean made it clear that knowing what she wanted was useful information: He wanted to take good care of his people and be a good manager; Linda was a valuable employee, and asking for what she wanted helped him do that.

Greater Expectations

Fortunately, women can learn to avoid the trap of low expectati̶̶̶ Research has identified situations in which gender differences in entitlement
disappear—situations that help us think about ways in which women can
overcome their tendency to underestimate what they deserve. In the 1984
study mentioned earlier in which people were asked to review application
folders and predict the success of incoming college freshmen (the study in
which men paid themselves 63 percent more on average than women did),
the researchers, Major, McFarlin, and Gagnon, also ran a variant condition that produced interesting results. In this condition, they left a bogus
list at the students' desks that listed what earlier participants in the study
had paid themselves. This list contained eight names (four male and four
female) along with the amount each subject had paid him- or herself. The
average amounts male and female subjects had paid themselves were
about the same. In this condition, they found, male and female subjects
paid themselves about the same amount, which corresponded to the average of this list. The researchers also ran two other conditions. One used a
bogus list in which the men paid themselves more on average than the
women and the other used a list in which the women paid themselves
more than the men. Both of these conditions produced no gender differences in what men and women paid themselves.[44] A similar study published eight years later (in 1992) by Brenda Major and another colleague,
Wayne Bylsma, reached the same conclusion—gender differences disappear when men and women receive the same information about the "going rates" for given jobs.[45]

These studies tell us that in unambiguous situations that provide
women with appropriate comparison information, knowledge of what the
market will pay for their skills and time can help override their inaccurate
sense of self-worth. But situations like these are rare. More common are
situations in which information about prevailing salary rates is not readily
available—situations in which women's low sense of entitlement makes
them most vulnerable to unfair treatment (or simply to the natural tendency of the market to reward people no more than they require).

One of Linda's studies confirms that ambiguous negotiating situations, in which comparison information is hard to come by, can produce big gender differences in outcomes. Using data collected by the career services department of an Ivy League business school, Linda and two colleagues, Hannah Riley and Kathleen McGinn, both negotiation experts at Harvard, found that the women's starting salaries for their first jobs after graduation were 6 percent lower on average than the men's—even adjusting for the industries they entered, their pre-MBA salaries, their functional areas, and the cities in which their jobs were located.[46] This is a pretty big difference. But even more striking was that the guaranteed yearly bonuses negotiated by the women were *19 percent smaller* than those obtained by the men (again, taking into account significant differentiating factors). When Hannah Riley discussed these findings with the career services counselors at the school, an interesting detail emerged: Reliable guidelines about starting salary ranges exist for many industries and jobs, but few guidelines exist for standard bonus amounts.

These results suggest that bonus negotiations represent a more ambiguous situation in which women's impaired sense of entitlement makes them more likely to price themselves too low. They also suggest ways for women to reduce their vulnerability in these ambiguous situations—by tracking down the information they need for themselves. How can this be done? The first step involves tapping one's networks—both personal and professional connections—to find out as much as possible about what people in similar positions earn and about the titles or job grades, office assignments, levels of administrative support, workloads, travel requirements, bonuses, vacation time, and benefits that go along with those positions. In a hiring or promotion situation, this type of information can become a valuable resource. Someone who wants more vacation time to spend with her kids might offer to trade her bonus for an extra two weeks off, for example. Someone else who wants more administrative support might offer to do more traveling. The first step in doing this kind of research is to make sure to collect information from both women and men. The second step is to collect information from outside sources that compile salary ranges for particular jobs, such as Internet sites, trade journals, and career counseling offices at colleges, universities, and professional schools. Web sites that contain information about salary ranges for particular jobs include www.salary.com, www.careerjournal.com, www.jobstar.org, and http://content.monster.com/. Detailed information about salaries in various types of businesses and lines of both public- and private-sector work can often be found on industry- or sector-specific sites as well. These resources can provide women with hard data to back up their requests—and give them a concrete idea of their market power.

Gillian, 52, a rehabilitation counselor, had been working on a contract basis at a large hospital for 12 years. She put in a lot of hours, but because hers was not a permanent position, she was paid by the hour and paid poorly—only $16.37 an hour, despite 29 years' experience in her field. When the hospital finally offered her a full-time position, she wasn't sure whether she could also request a higher salary or she should just be grateful to have the security of a permanent job. Her friends told her that she should definitely ask for more money, but she was so uncertain that one of her friends, a colleague of Linda's, suggested that she talk to Linda. Linda told her that her hourly wage was very low and that full-time hourly wages tend to be much higher than those paid to part-timers. Linda encouraged Gillian to research the salaries paid to other people doing comparable work (both men and women), and Gillian discovered that these ranged from $20 to $25 an hour. Encouraged by Linda and her other friends, and with this data in hand, Gillian asked for $23 an hour and got it—a raise of 41 percent. This is a perfect example of how much more women can get for themselves when they question their low sense of entitlement, research appropriate goals, and get the kinds of support they need to ask for what they deserve.

3

Nice Girls Don't Ask

The research we presented in the last chapter suggests that women's low sense of personal entitlement—uncertainty about what their work is worth or how much they deserve to get for what they do—often deters them from asking for more than they already have. But what causes this depressed sense of entitlement? Why does the average woman have more trouble than the average man believing that she deserves more than she's been given? And why is she less comfortable asking for changes that would improve her working conditions, enhance her job satisfaction, or help her run her household more efficiently? In this chapter, we draw on research in sociology and psychology to explore the roots of this problem. We look at the ways in which we as a society school children in gender-appropriate behavior and pressure adults to abide by conventional notions of how women and men should behave.

Society's Messages

We as a society take it for granted that men and women usually behave differently and exhibit different types of traits—this has been well documented.[1] Men are thought to be assertive, dominant, decisive, ambitious, and self-oriented, whereas women are thought to be warm, expressive, nurturing, emotional, and friendly.[2] These are gender stereotypes, and in every branch of the social sciences, from psychology and sociology to organizational behavior and linguistics, researchers have shown that they hold sway over people's perceptions.[3] Because gender is a physical characteristic and immediately apparent, we all draw a wide range of conclusions about the people we meet—as soon as we meet them—based on their gender.

Ideas about gender *roles* go even further. Not merely beliefs about what men and women are like, these shared ideas represent our expectations for how men and women will behave. For example, it's widely believed that women tend to be "communal," or less concerned with their own needs and more focused on the welfare of others. Men, in contrast, are thought to be "agentic," an awkward term that means focused on their own aims and interests and more likely to act independent of others' needs or desires.[4] In common language, women are thought to be more "other-oriented" and men are thought to be more "self-oriented."

The pressure to put the needs of others first manifests itself in a variety of ways in women's lives. Lory, the theater production manager, summed up her other-directed approach to life in this way: "If it's something that's just for me, only for me, then I go back to, 'do I really need it?' More, it's really, 'how does it affect people around me?'" Describing her job, in which she manages the production staffs of three shows in three cities, she said, "really, my needs are group needs.... Which actually fits pretty well into my regular life, too, because I'm not usually too concerned about me. You know, I'm much more outward. I think the purpose in life is to make things nice for everybody." Lory's attitude is especially noteworthy because she's not a 70-year-old grandmother who came of age in the 1950s. She's young and self-confident, she works in a competitive and demanding field, and she's very successful.

In a completely different professional realm, Ada, a lawyer in her early fifties with a distinguished career as a litigator behind her, now serves as inspector general of a high-profile government agency. And like Lory, Ada is extremely successful and outwardly self-confident. But, although she has no trouble asking for things on behalf of her clients, her employees, or her children, she said, "I find it really hard to ask for things for myself." Comfortable being aggressive and capable in her "communal" role, when she is working on behalf of others, she pulls up short when she needs to ask for something on her own behalf.

Of course, no one is completely "other-oriented" or "self-oriented"; we all possess both of these qualities to varying degrees. But many studies have shown that as a society we expect women to be more oriented toward the needs of others and men to be more oriented toward their own needs and ambitions. And this is where problems arise, because the ideas we share about gender roles are also normative—they involve qualities and behaviors that we believe men and women *should* have. So a man who is not especially ambitious risks being called a "wimp" or a "loser." And an assertive, ambitious woman runs head-on into society's requirement that she be selfless and communal. Wanting things for oneself and doing whatever may be necessary to get those things—such as asking for them— often clashes with the social expectation that a woman will devote her attention to the needs of others and pay less attention to her own.[5]

In addition to holding strong ideas about how men and women should feel and behave, we as a society feel confident that everyone else shares these ideas—an assumption that usually turns out to be true. In the "pay allocation" studies by Major, McFarlin, and Gagnon described in the last chapter, for example, both men and women predicted that men would pay themselves more than women. In the "time worked" studies, both men and women predicted that women would work longer than men for the same pay. This tells us that both sexes recognize women's lower feelings of entitlement and assume they will play out in predictable ways: leading women to expect smaller rewards for the work they do and motivating them to work harder for the rewards they get.[6]

Evidence that women are conditioned not to get what they want can be seen all around us in popular culture. Women's magazines exhort women month after month to believe that they're entitled to happiness, self-confidence, and success. (Here are a few cover lines from 2001 and 2002 issues of Oprah Winfrey's magazine, *O*: "Self-Esteem: The 'O' Guide to Getting It"; "Dream Big"; "Success: Define It for Yourself.") *O* and magazines like it publish articles like this precisely because they know that women struggle with entitlement and self-esteem issues—and that offering to help women with these issues sells magazines.

Even something as seemingly basic as sexual satisfaction seems subject to this differential analysis. Studies reporting the percentage of time women reach or fail to reach orgasm are a staple in women's magazines, but similar studies of men rarely if ever appear. This suggests both that the importance of sexual fulfillment for men is generally understood and that we take for granted that women will not have their needs met in this most basic area of life a surprisingly large percentage of the time. It may also suggest that during intimate relations, as in other parts of their lives, women tend to fulfill their expected gender role and focus on the needs of their partners while men, trained to be "self-oriented," are more likely to focus on their own needs.

We don't mean to suggest that men don't also struggle with self-esteem and entitlement issues, of course, but whether they struggle to a much lesser degree or they worry that it's unmanly to admit how much they struggle, men's magazines do not hawk many articles designed to bolster men's self-esteem. And given how much more likely men are to ask for the things they want and need, it's clear that entitlement issues don't constrain men in the same ways that they constrain women.

The Origins of Norms

Where do these ideas about appropriate and "natural" behaviors come from? In the early years of our social development as a species, researchers suspect, biological factors first pushed men and women toward different roles. Women's ability to bear and nurse children gave them clear advantages in the domestic realm while men's superior strength gave them work advantages. So for hundreds of thousands of years, women took care of the children and the housework while men felled trees to build houses, hunted for food, protected their families (even going off to war), and devoted themselves to other tasks that involved physical strength.[7] Once scientific and technological advances eased the pressure of these biological factors, the influence of cultural tradition kicked in—men and women continued to play the historical roles they'd always played because this allocation of roles, being familiar, seemed correct and appropriate. As a result, even today, "domestic" roles (in the home) are still filled over-whelmingly by women and "employee" roles are still filled more by men (although women have made substantial gains in this realm).[8]

At work, the different jobs men and women typically perform also per-petuate traditional ideas about gender roles. As recently as 2001, 98 percent of child-care workers, 82 percent of elementary school teachers, 91 percent of nurses, 99 percent of secretaries, and 70 percent of social workers in the United States were women. In the same year in the United States, 87.5 per-cent of the corporate officers of the 500 largest companies, 90 percent of all engineers, 98 percent of all construction workers, and 70 percent of all fi-nancial managers were men.[9] In addition to perpetuating old notions about what constitutes "women's work" and "men's work," this heavy iden-tification of certain jobs with one gender or the other also suggests that it takes stereotypically "male" or "female" qualities to succeed in those occu-pations. A 1999 study by the social psychologists Mary Ann Cejka and Alice Eagly proved this point by asking college students to rate the attrib-utes necessary to succeed in various occupations. For occupations more heavily dominated (numerically) by men, students felt that male physical qualities (such as being athletic and tall) and masculine personality char-acteristics (such as being competitive and daring) were important for suc-cess in those occupations. For occupations more heavily dominated (numerically) by women, students felt that female physical qualities (such as being pretty and having a soft voice) and female personality characteris-tics (such as being nurturing and supportive) were important for success in those jobs.[10]

The steady inroads women have made into male-dominated occupa-tions in recent years might give us the impression that strict job segrega-tion by gender and the ideas this segregation perpetuates have become things of the past. The percentages of men and women in different profes-sions noted above were drawn from 2001 data, however, and Cejka and Eagly's study was completed in 1999. Another study from the 1990s calcu-lated that for women and men to be equally distributed into similar types of jobs, 77 percent of the women working today would need to change jobs.[11] In other words, for a long time to come, the jobs that men and women typically do will continue to teach us lessons about the jobs men and women "should" do.

There's another dimension to this problem: Western society's historical habit of "assigning" men and women to certain types of work can actually function as a kind of self-fulfilling expectation—exerting pressure on men and women to develop the characteristics and skills needed to perform the jobs to which they've been assigned. As Alice Eagly demonstrated in her influential book *Sex Differences in Social Behavior: A Social Role Interpretation*, being given certain types of jobs forces women to develop the skills those jobs require.[12] The same is obviously also true of men, who in many cases must develop more male-identified skills and cannot make use of the more female-identified traits in their personalities.

But we've become so self-conscious about gender roles and gender stereotypes in recent years, you may say, how can we still be perpetuating them? How do well-loved little girls, given every material advantage and offered opportunities never dreamt of by their female ancestors, grow up to display the same lower sense of entitlement felt by their mothers and grandmothers? That we do perpetuate it is inarguable: Our research observed gender gaps in entitlement for men and women currently 35 and younger that were equal to those for older generations.[13] This means that younger women are just as likely as their older peers to feel unsure about what they deserve—and to feel uncomfortable asking for more than they have.

Two major social forces seem to be responsible for the stubborn persistence of gender-linked norms and beliefs. The first involves the socialization and development of children and the second involves the maintenance of gender roles by adults.

The Socialization of Children

A line of child development research has identified a process of "sex-typing," through which each new generation of children is taught roles and beliefs by previously socialized members of the society.[14] The developmental psychologist Eleanor Maccoby describes the presumed sequence of events: "Adult socialization agents and older children treat children of the two sexes somewhat differently, using reinforcement, punishment, and example to foster whatever behaviors and attitudes a social group deems sex-appropriate. Socialization pressures are also applied to inhibit sex-inappropriate attitudes and behavior. The result of this differential socialization is that boys and girls, on the average, develop somewhat different personality traits, skills, and activity preferences."[15]

We heard many stories about the powerful pressure that gender stereotypes exert on women's sense of entitlement. Adele, 65, a retired financial consultant, said that she was "taught from a very young age that asking for anything was like begging and that 'good girls' didn't beg." As a result, Adele never once in the course of her long career asked for a raise. Instead, she taught herself to avoid thinking about the things she wanted. This protected her from disappointment, but it also impaired her ability to judge what her work was worth—her sense of personal entitlement was almost totally suppressed. Needless to say, not thinking about what she wanted also made her considerably less focused and effective at getting promotions, rewards, and opportunities that she might have deserved and enjoyed.

Lisa, the animal hospital receptionist-manager, says that when she was growing up, "girls were really taught to defer to people, to—you know—be polite, be kind, be compassionate, be considerate. You're always taking second place to the needs of others.... The messages are so strong, and you're so absorbent of them when you're so young that I fight that second nature a lot."

Miriam, the architect, said, "I've been told all of my life . . . that if I have something then I should give it to someone else. I think that is what women and girls are taught—to be generous and give—and boys I think are taught to defend themselves and keep and ask." Brian, the intensive-care nurse, agrees: "I think I'm better, generally [as a negotiator].... I almost think part of that's a sort of societal conditioning, that as a man I have been raised with this sense of entitlement, that I should get what I want. And I almost think that societally women are conditioned that you don't always get what you want."

One of the things men are conditioned to think they should get is money. Becky, 50, a journalist, recalls that when she was a child her brother was given gifts of stocks but she was given dresses. This taught her brother very early on that the world of money and high finance were his rightful home, while she received the message that this was not to be her territory. This is a message—that money is outside their provenance—that girls and women get from all directions. They get it at home (remember Linda's daughter asking if girls have money or if it's just boys who have money?). They get it at school from teachers who let them know (often without realizing it) that girls are not expected to do well at math. And they get it from the media.

A 1999 study revealed, for example, that the percentage of women used as experts in business and economic newscasts on the three major television networks that year averaged a mere 18 percent (CBS used women as financial experts only 11 percent of the time); only 31 percent of all business and economic news stories on the networks were filed by female correspondents. The print media were no better. That same year, in *Time* magazine, only 11 percent of the authors of business and economic news stories were women, in *Newsweek* male sources cited in financial news articles outnumbered female sources seven to one, and in *Business Week* financial articles about influential individuals focused on men 92 percent of the time.[16] Even a child who is not interested in pursuing a profession in the financial world cannot avoid the none-too-subtle message that money is a man's business. This may make her feel less entitled as an adult to ask for more money than she's offered because she does not see herself as a part of the world in which people make a lot of money.

Girls learn other lessons about what they can do from popular culture. A few years ago, the Sesame Workshop, creators of *Sesame Street* and other educational children's television programming, launched a cartoon called *Dragon Tales* aimed at preschool children. The show follows the adventures of a young brother and sister who regularly visit a fantasy place called Dragonland to play with a group of friendly dragons. Their adventures are designed to help children learn how to work and play together, share, and solve problems. In one episode, the sister, Emmy, discovers on her arrival in Dragonland that her girl dragon friends are all members of the Dragon Scouts. Emmy wants to become a scout, too, but for reasons that go unexplained she avoids the obvious route of simply asking her friends if she can join. Instead, she lingers while her friends work on various scout projects, trying to help them and being coy about what she wants. Finally, at the end of the show, her friends invite her to join them, which the show presents as a victory for her approach. The message to little girls could not be clearer: Being coy and indirect about what you want and waiting rather than asking is an effective strategy—more than that, it is the appropriate strategy, and superior to directly articulating your wants and wishes.

Other messages come from children's books and movies. The classic *Make Way for Ducklings*, beloved by generations of children, tells the story of Mr. and Mrs. Mallard, a pair of "married" ducks. After much searching, the Mallards find a spot to nest, lay their eggs, and molt on an island in Boston's Charles River. Once the ducklings hatch, Mr. Mallard decides he wants to explore the river and departs for a week, leaving Mrs. Mallard behind to "raise the kids." While he's gone, she teaches them how to swim, dive for food at the bottom of the river, and walk in a line. From stories like this, children learn that men are free to pursue their own interests and satisfy their personal desires, but communal responsibilities must dominate women's actions.

A more recent example comes from the two *Toy Story* movies, much favored by moms and dads because they are imaginative, they include little violence, and, unlike many movies for children, they don't start with the death of a parent. In both movies, a toy is stranded outside the security of the child's home in which the community of toys resides. In each case, rescuers venture out to retrieve the lost toy, and in each case, male toys embark on the rescue mission while the female toys wait behind. The behavior of the female toys conforms closely to gender role norms for girls in other ways as well. Bo Peep, in the first movie, remains loyal to Woody (the "head" or alpha toy in the group because he has been the child's favorite) even though Woody appears to have purposely flipped a new toy, Buzz Lightyear, out the window because he threatened his status. In *Toy Story 2*, after Woody has been stolen by a greedy toy collector, Mrs. Potato Head packs up supplies for Mr. Potato Head to take on the rescue mission, fussily including all sorts of things he may need to stay well fed and safe. The message is clear: Men get to be the self-assertive risk-takers, while women are relegated to more secondary, other-directed roles. The second movie does include a feisty female character, Jesse, a cowgirl doll, but even she needs to be rescued by the male toys in the end.

A few powerful female characters have appeared on children's television in recent years, such as Xena: Warrior Princess, and the Powerpuff Girls. Nonetheless, recent studies report that of the 123 characters girls who watch children's programming on Saturday mornings may encounter, only 23 percent are female. Of the major characters, only 18 percent are female.[17] This tells girls that they are not the principal "actors" in life's dramas and that it is boys or men who take center stage in the world and make things happen. Girls play bystanders or supporting characters. This lesson is not likely to encourage girls to step forward and grab what they want for themselves; instead, it teaches them to watch and wait and accept whatever comes their way.

Computer and video games—many more of which are designed for boys than for girls—also promote gender-appropriate attitudes by cultivating "agentic" skills such as competitiveness, aggression, and self-interest at the expense of others.[18] In most of these games, the action figures are boys and the few girls appear as scantily clothed props.[19] This distribution of roles reinforces the notion that it is appropriate for boys to strive for success (by "winning" or achieving the highest score) but girls should remain decorative and passive. "Old-fashioned" toys are sex-typed as well—and widely recognized as such. "Girls' toys" include dolls and kitchen equipment (play ovens, tea sets, dishes); "boys' toys" include vehicles (cars, trains, planes) and construction sets (blocks, trucks, Lincoln Logs). Adults not only prefer to see their children play with "sex-appropriate toys" like these, they communicate this message so effectively that even when children are unconstrained they choose sex-typed toys the majority of the time.[20] Girls learn from the toys they receive that it is important for them to take care of others—bathing and dressing their doll "babies," serving "tea" to friends, preparing food and cleaning up after meals. Boys learn from their transportation toys that they can move freely through the world and from their construction toys that they can define the earth around them by constructing buildings, roads, and complicated machinery. The net effect of this "toy-coding" is to teach girls to subordinate their needs to the needs of others and to teach boys to take charge of their environment.

Through these and related forms of socialization, stereotypes and gender-role ideas take hold very early in a child's consciousness. In the "pay allocation" studies described in chapter 2, for example, the researchers consistently replicated the adult gender gap in entitlement among schoolchildren. Using first, fourth, seventh, and tenth graders (with Hershey's kisses instead of money for the first graders), the researchers found that in every grade, girls paid themselves less than boys paid themselves—between 30 and 78 percent less. Again, the researchers found no gender differences in the children's evaluations of how well they thought they'd performed the set task.[21] Even more to the point, perhaps, the amounts girls paid themselves correlated positively with the perceived "masculinity" or "femininity" of their occupation preferences. Girls who indicated that they preferred "male-dominated" occupations such as firefighter, astronaut, or police officer paid themselves more than girls who indicated that they preferred "female" occupations such as secretary, nurse, and teacher. This suggests that the extent to which girls identify with traditional female roles influences their level of perceived entitlement.

The different messages boys and girls receive growing up may also affect their self-esteem, with research suggesting that women as a group have lower levels of self-esteem than men do.[22] Scholars have proposed numerous causes for this, with some sources blaming a bombardment of anti-female messages in the media. Whatever the causes, they don't seem to be genetic: After an extensive review of the existing literature on gender and self-esteem, the psychologists Kristen Kling, Janet Shelby-Hyde, Carolin Showers, and Brenda Buswell concluded that the different socialization messages boys and girls receive from our culture seem to be responsible. Boys are "expected to develop self-confidence," they write, "whereas displaying self-confidence has traditionally been a gender-role violation for girls."[23] Believing that you're good at what you do, assuming that you deserve to be amply rewarded for your good work, and asking for more—having a strong sense of entitlement and showing it—would clearly be displaying self-confidence, and would therefore be a gender-role violation for a girl.

The social importance of abiding by gender roles was illustrated by a recent study of adolescence and self-esteem. Researchers found that boys in late adolescence (between the ages of 17 and 19) who had "agentic" or self-oriented conceptions of themselves showed significant increases in their self-esteem when they reached young adulthood a few years later (between the ages of 21 and 23). Similarly, girls at the same stage of late adolescence (between 17 and 19) who held "communal" or other-directed conceptions of themselves showed significant increases in their self-esteem when they reached young adulthood.[24] This tells us that abiding by the strictures of prevailing gender roles can have a positive impact on self-esteem, presumably because other people respond positively to boys and girls—and men and women—who behave according to expectations. It also tells us that behaving in ways *inconsistent* with gender roles may have negative consequences for self-esteem, because such behavior often elicits critical responses and negative feedback. The link between self-esteem and a sense of personal entitlement is not hard to see: If you have a low sense of self-worth, your sense of what you deserve is likely to be similarly depressed—and you're not likely to feel especially comfortable asking for more than you've already got.

The Expectations of Adults

Because we all subconsciously adjust our behavior in response to other people's expectations, many researchers believe that the behavior of adults also helps to perpetuate society's gender-role restrictions.[25] A famous and sobering study demonstrates the power of expectations. In this study, two Harvard psychologists, Robert Rosenthal and Lenore Jacobson, administered two tests to a group of children at an elementary school (every child in the study took both tests).[26] One test evaluated each child's general ability. The other, Rosenthal and Jacobson told the children's teachers, could predict which children were about to experience an "intellectual growth spurt"—a substantial leap forward in their capabilities. The psychologists explained to the teachers that "all children show hills, plateaus, and valleys in their scholastic progress," and that they had developed the Harvard Test of Inflected Acquisition (or the Harvard TIA) in order to identify those children who were about to "show an inflection point or 'spurt' in the near future."[27] After administering both tests, Rosenthal and Jacobson gave each teacher a list of the children in his or her class who they said were about to experience a leap forward in their learning abilities.

A year and a half later, the psychologists returned to the same school and readministered the test of general ability. When they compared the new results with the results from the general ability test administered at their previous visit, the children the researchers had said were about to "spurt" had improved more than the others. While the "nonspurters" had gained an average of only 8.42 points on the test, the preidentified "spurters" had gained an average of 12.22 points in general learning ability—a difference of 50 percent. In addition, the teachers gave the "spurters" higher grades in reading and reported that they were "happier and more intellectually curious" than their peers.

The significant detail here is that the Harvard TIA was not a real test. It was designed to convince the teachers that the kids were taking a real test. But the researchers never scored the test or processed any results from it. Instead, they randomly chose 20 percent of the children and gave their names to the teachers. The change in the children's scores on the real test, the test of general ability, revealed the huge impact of the teachers' expectations on the performance of those children whose names were on the list. Because the teachers expected those children to "get smarter," they did.

The researchers speculated that the teachers paid more attention to the targeted students, expressed more enthusiasm when they did well, encouraged them more, and generally made them feel special—all behaviors that built the students' confidence, increased their motivation to do well, and led to the leap forward in their achievement.[28] When children whose names were not on the list did well, the teachers were less likely to notice or respond with special encouragement, thereby missing opportunities to build their self-confidence and motivation.

Since this landmark study (which would probably be considered unethical if administered today), a large body of psychological research has confirmed that people typically comply with the expectations others have of them—expectations that can be expressed in both overt and subtle ways.[29] And several studies have confirmed that expectations based on gender can be particularly powerful.[30]

Elaine, 55, a U.S. District Court judge, provides an example of how adults unthinkingly communicate their differing expectations of women and men. Elaine and two other women were appointed at the same time to her district court, which has a total of 13 judges and had previously been all-male. During her first week on the bench, Elaine and one of the other female judges participated in a meeting with several of the male judges. As Elaine tells it, "It was a very important meeting, and everybody was talking, and we were talking, raising our hands and contributing to the conversation, and the chief judge was summarizing what everyone said. And he said, 'Well, Judge Josephson said this, Judge Harris said this, and Phoebe said this, and Elaine said that.'" Elaine and the other female judge at the meeting exchanged looks—they both noticed immediately that the chief judge was calling the men by their titles and the women by their first names. She said, "I don't think he meant to demean us, but it was clear that he thought of us in different ways, and that comes across. And we thought of *ourselves* in different ways. I think it's hard not be treated that way without having it rub off." The chief judge had inadvertently revealed that, like most people, he thinks of men as "assertive, dominant, decisive, ambitious, and instrumental," and therefore deserving of being called "judge," a title that confers the right to assert oneself and exercise personal power. He also showed that he probably thinks of women as more "warm, expressive, nurturing, emotional, and friendly," and therefore more appropriately addressed by their "friendlier" first names.

In Elaine's experience, this was only one of numerous times in her career when she realized how other people's beliefs could influence her behavior. Struggling with this reality, she learned that there was "a range of roles that I could play, and I had to work with not only what I looked like physically [as a woman]; I had to work with the roles that society was going to ascribe to me . . . and they changed over time, . . . modified both by my age and by society's expectations of who I was. You could push to a point, but you couldn't go beyond that if you meant to be successful in the world."

Simply ignoring a stereotype or refusing to behave as expected doesn't solve the problem, in other words. Suppose, for example, that a man believes that women make bad leaders. This man may express doubt and distrust whenever he encounters a woman in a leadership position. His response may range from rolling his eyes to disobeying her outright; in either case, his expectation, thus communicated, may shake her confidence. Understanding that she's not "supposed" to be a good leader, she may behave in more uncertain, less capable ways, stumbling over instructions she gives to subordinates, questioning her own decisions, and "leading" less capably.

If she doesn't let him "shake" her and persists in leading capably and well, this may actually antagonize him, with unpleasant consequences (we discuss how women can be punished for violating gender stereotypes in the next chapter). Psychologists have also shown that when people encounter evidence inconsistent with their beliefs, they tend to ignore it.[31] So, the man who thinks women make bad leaders may completely disregard a situation in which a woman conducts herself effectively as a leader. (Similarly, the expectation that women won't push on their own behalf can make people ignore or undermine them when they do.)

Even memory can be affected by stereotypes, causing this man to remember every instance of poor leadership by a woman and forget events inconsistent with his belief, such as a woman leading exceptionally well. The man might even "remember" events consistent with the stereotype that did not actually occur because people often "create" memories that conform to their beliefs, memory researchers have found.[32] A final factor is that this same man might shy away from putting women in leadership roles, thereby limiting his opportunities to observe women behaving in ways inconsistent with his belief, as well as limiting women's opportunities to work on their leadership skills. All of these processes reduce the chances that his belief will be challenged and revised.

Regardless of the mechanisms by which these gender roles are perpetuated, it seems unlikely that our conceptions about gender roles will change quickly. Although the last 30 years have seen a marked rise in the proportion of women in the paid labor force, perceptions of women as other-oriented and men as self-oriented have remained fairly stable.[33] One study by the negotiation researchers Laura Kray, Leigh Thompson, and

Adam Galinsky, published in 2001, asked undergraduates to write essays discussing who has the advantage in negotiations, men or women. By a large majority, the students' responses confirmed prevailing gender stereotypes, describing men as assertive, strong, and able to stand firm against compromise, and women as emotional, relationship-oriented, accommodating, and attuned to feelings.[34] In other words, young adults today hold many of the same beliefs about typically male and female behaviors that their parents and grandparents held. Before these beliefs can be changed, it would seem, we will need to find ways to change both the roles women play in society and our widely shared ideas about acceptable behavior for women. Teaching women to assert their needs and wishes more and teaching society to accept women who ask for what they want may be one of those ways.

Why Don't Women Resist These Norms?

Existing gender roles and stereotypes hardly work to the material or economic advantage of women. Why, then, don't women rebel against them? One explanation, perhaps the most straightforward, contends that socialization does such a thorough job of teaching little girls their proper role that by the time they reach adulthood, they believe that their gender-appropriate impulses and behavior—such as being nurturing, friendly, and selfless—are intrinsic expressions of their personalities rather than learned behaviors.[35] They may also believe that these behaviors are attractive and valuable, which of course they are. But so are many behaviors that boys are taught, such as exercising initiative and sticking up for themselves.

Elaine, the judge described earlier, is unusual in her awareness of the impact of gender stereotypes on her behavior and her sense of herself; most women, researchers suspect, don't realize how much they are influenced by social expectations. The Stanford social psychologist John Jost suggests that "women in general are relatively unaware of their status as an oppressed group," and consequently, "hold many beliefs that are consonant with their own oppression." He also suggests that what he calls "gender socialization practices" are "so thorough in their justification of inequality" that girls and women end up believing that the existing system of inequality and discrimination is appropriate and right.[36] In other words, "members of oppressed groups internalize aspects of their oppression, coming to believe in the legitimacy of their own inferiority."[37]

To understand how this works, consider a girl who has been taught that girls don't make good scientists. Believing this, she may try less hard at science in school (to avoid failing at something in which she has invested her energies—and her ego). Or she might become interested in other subjects at which she feels she can excel. In this way, she never encounters evidence to dispute what she's been taught—and she never learns that she can be good at science if she chooses to be. Since research suggests that evidence inconsistent with a previously held belief is frequently ignored or underweighted,[38] her belief that she is not good at science may even persist in the face of disconfirming evidence. If she does well on a science test, for example, she may ascribe this to luck rather than talent, or find some other excuse (such as dismissing it as an easy test). Thus, traditional beliefs are passed down, generation to generation.

Linda had almost this exact experience, except that she was lucky enough to stumble into a situation that tested her unfounded beliefs about her abilities. As a child, like many girls, she thought she wasn't very good at math. She can't identify any specific comment from a parent or a teacher, or any other experiences that might account for this assumption, but being a girl she assumed that math just wasn't her subject, and no one tried to convince her otherwise. In high school, when some of her friends took calculus, she thought it would be too difficult for her. She started out in college planning to become a dancer, but after an injury forced her to stop dancing she became interested in economics. Economics at the undergraduate level, at least at her school, didn't involve much math, and Linda found that she was very good at it—good enough to go to graduate school in the subject. In graduate school, however, she discovered that economics at the Ph.D. level is almost *all* math, and very challenging math at that. But, it turned out, Linda was good at that too—she just didn't know this until circumstances disproved her conditioned assumptions about her own limitations.

The power of what John Jost calls "gender socialization practices" to convince women of "the legitimacy of their own inferiority" also manifests itself in what has been termed "the imposter syndrome." Many women who have ventured into fields that were previously closed to them suffer from "a deep sense of inadequacy that is objectively unfounded," the sociologist Gerhard Sonnert reports in *Who Succeeds in Science: The Gender Dimension*.[39] Among a large group of former doctoral-level fellows, all of whom won prestigious postdoctorate awards early in their careers, Sonnert reports that 70 percent of the men but only 52 percent of the women considered their scientific ability to be above average. This discrepancy has been documented in other fields as well.[40] Studies of women graduate students show that they have much lower levels of self-confidence than their male peers even when their grades are just as good or better.[41] Having advanced far up the rungs of a ladder that women are not supposed to climb, or achieved significant success in an area in which women aren't supposed to excel, many women secretly harbor the feeling that they're just "faking it" and that their inadequacy will soon be discovered.

In *Schoolgirls: Young Women, Self-Esteem, and the Confidence Gap*, Peggy Orenstein describes this feeling shared by so many women: "In spite of all of our successes, in spite of the fact that we have attained the superficial ideal of womanhood held out to our generation, we feel unsure, insecure, inadequate." As early as her college years, she writes, "I became paralyzed during the writing of my senior thesis, convinced that my fraudulence was about to be unmasked. Back then, I went to my adviser and told her of the fears that were choking me. 'You feel like an impostor?' she asked. 'Don't worry about it. All smart women feel that way.' "[42] Secretly convinced that generalizations about women's abilities are true, women refrain from rebelling openly against those generalizations for fear that their weakness and inferiority will be exposed if they do.

Women also don't resist gender norm constraints because, in many cases, they are oblivious to their power and believe these norms have no impact on their own behavior. Faye Crosby and Stacy Ropp have shown that "it is difficult for most people to recognize personal injustices."[43] They also report that women are not likely to take action when they see their group—women—discriminated against but don't feel personally mistreated themselves. A woman might think, "Why should I rebel against something that doesn't affect me or how I behave?" A selection of quotations from short profiles of women lawyers in an issue of the *New York Times Magazine* devoted to "Women and Power" illustrates this point well: "I'm absolutely against blaming any type of failure on outside circumstances. I believe that you create possibility for yourself. I think the way people are treated follows naturally from how they perceive themselves"; "I don't have any obstacles, so if I don't get to the top, it will be because of my own personal choices. There's no discrimination except for the kind we face within ourselves"; "I think if you know your stuff you're going to be fine."[44]

Although the self-confidence of these women is admirable and will surely serve them well, their optimism is misplaced for two reasons. First, as we discussed earlier, other people's beliefs and stereotypes color the ways in which they see the world. So people around these capable and confident women are going to interpret, process, and respond to their actions through the lens of their stereotypes about women—often without realizing that they're doing so. As a result, the work these women do may be rated as inferior to comparable work by men even when the actual work product is identical. (We explore this phenomenon in the following chapter.) Their work may be "devalued simply because they are women," the social psychologist Madeline Heilman has shown.[45]

Second, it has been demonstrated that expectations and stereotypes can subconsciously influence a person's behavior even when those stereotypes are not embraced or internalized.[46] An area of research termed "stereotype threat" pioneered by the psychologist Claude Steele and his colleagues has shown that merely "activating" a stereotype by asking about it—that is, eliciting the information that someone belongs to a particular group—can have a significant impact on that person's behavior.[47] For example, asking about a student's race before a test of verbal ability can cause African-American students to perform significantly worse—25 percent worse—than they perform when they are not asked about their race beforehand.[48] On the other hand, asking an Asian student about his or her race before a mathematics test can actually improve that student's performance, because Asians are thought to have superior skill at mathematics. Similar results have been found in research that examined gender stereotypes.[49] In a study at the University of Michigan, undergraduate students were given a difficult mathematics test. One group of participants was told that there were usually no gender differences in performance on the test they were about to take, and among this group men and women performed equally well on the test. Another group was told that the test usually produced gender differences in performance (but they weren't told whether men or women tended to perform better). Among this group, presumably because men are believed to have superior math skills, women's scores dropped sharply—by more than half—while men's scores increased by about 33 percent.[50]

Scholars do not yet fully understand the psychological processes that influence performance in these situations, but most researchers suspect that "activating" the stereotype either evokes a surge of positive self-esteem that enhances performance, if the stereotype is a flattering one, or rouses concern about confirming the stereotype (concern that may not even be conscious), if the stereotype is an unflattering one. This concern, they suspect, increases a person's performance anxiety while also adding to the number of things he or she is thinking about—leaving less room in his or her head for doing other things, such as concentrating on complex math calculations. The result is a degradation of performance.[51]

Here's an example from Sara's own experience. When she was 28, Sara left a job as a publishing executive and decided to take some time to figure out what she wanted to do next. While she considered her options, she took a job in a bookstore to help pay her bills. It was a small store, and most of the time she worked closely with the owner. This man had gone to business school and prided himself on the speed with which he could do calculations in his head. He also made no bones about the fact that he believed women were no good at math. The store was equipped with an old cash register that frequently forced Sara to do simple calculations in her head to save time. Sara had also always been good at math, and she considered herself fast and accurate at making calculations in her head. In her previous job she had been responsible for the details of complex contracts, and she always figured out the tip in restaurants when she was out with friends. Nonetheless, whenever the bookstore owner was standing by and she had to complete calculations in her head, she made mistakes or felt sufficiently unsure of her answers that she would repeat the calculations on paper to convince herself that she was being accurate. Although she knew this made no sense and felt exasperated with herself for what she perceived as a weakness, she was unable to combat the power of the owner's conviction that she could not do these relatively simple mental tasks.

This area of research suggests that stereotypes with negative connotations about the abilities of women may influence a woman's behavior even if she repudiates the stereotype or feels herself to be immune from its damage. While the studies described above found performance deficits when a person's race or gender was explicitly identified, stereotype threat can also occur in a multitude of situations that simply make a person's gender noticeable. For example, a recent study investigated how "tokenism" can affect performance.[52] The researchers in this study asked students to take a test of mathematical ability (from the GRE) in groups of three. Some of the groups were composed of three women; others were made up of one woman and two men. In comparing the results of the all-female groups with those that included two men, the researchers found that women in the "token" groups (women who took the test with two men) performed 21 percent worse than the women in the all-female groups. They concluded that when a person's "token" status becomes salient—when the makeup of a group highlights an individual's difference from the dominant group—this creates a self-consciousness in the "token" individual that can interfere with performance.

Linda had an experience that illustrates this clearly. One year, she was asked to serve as interim dean of her graduate school while a full-scale search was launched to fill the position permanently. Shortly after she took up the post, Linda found herself at an important meeting with the university president, the provost, and the rest of the deans, all of whom were men. Although Linda had never observed any behavior to suggest that her colleagues were sexist and they had always been enthusiastic about her work, Linda felt acutely conscious of the fact that everyone else in the room was male. At this meeting, Linda was scheduled to present a strategic plan she'd developed for the school. She remembers thinking that she really needed to do a great job to show that women can be successful leaders and deserve to be "at the table." Yet she felt herself growing uncharacteristically nervous. By the time it was her turn to speak, she was petrified. Afterward, she acknowledged to her own chagrin that self-consciousness about her gender had interfered with her performance.

This suggests that even if a woman believes that society's gender-role requirements are inappropriate and even offensive, the mere knowledge that these beliefs are held by others may be enough to influence her behavior. If she is unaware that this is occurring, she may take no action to counteract it. And even if she does realize what's happening, like both Sara and Linda, she may have trouble fighting it. By causing women to perform less well under pressure, stereotype threat helps perpetuate negative generalizations about women's capacities and helps reinforce the very ideas that have caused them. And by making women more uncomfortable about demonstrating their abilities, damaging their self-confidence at crucial moments, and seemingly confirming the expectations they have been resisting, it may become an important force in pushing women's behavior into line with prevailing gender-role ideas. In this way the stereotype that women make bad negotiators, for example, may hamper women from discovering how good they can be.

Prospects for Change

Change can begin at home, with parents examining their reflexive responses to their female and male children and the lessons they teach their children through their behavior. It can begin in schools, with teachers making sure that they don't send unintended messages to girls and boys about what is expected of them—and what is not permitted. It can begin with individual managers examining the beliefs they hold about women and men and trying to be more self-conscious about how they interpret the behavior of their female employees, evaluate their work, and make decisions regarding compensation and advancement.

Deloitte and Touche, the firm we described in the introduction, demonstrated that large-scale change is also possible—and Deloitte and Touche's success has already inspired other companies to follow suit. According to Sue Molina, a Deloitte and Touche tax partner and the national director of the Initiative for the Retention and Advancement of Women, other companies contact the firm regularly for information about the initiative. In addition, D&T's "human capital" group is beginning to consult for other companies seeking to improve the status of women in their organizations.[53]

Change is underway elsewhere as well. Accenture, a management consulting and technology services company, launched a "Great Place to Work for Women" initiative in the United States in 1994 (and expanded to the rest of the world in 2000), which seeks to "attract, retain and advance women by recognizing, fostering and maximizing their performance." To achieve these goals, the program "is customized locally to offer information, networking opportunities, policies and programs specific to each of the countries in which the program has been implemented. The company uses a variety of innovative processes such as geographic scorecards, global surveys and performance appraisals to ensure that company leadership remains accountable for the initiative's success."[54]

Accenture's program aims for more thorough change at all levels of the organization by making the company's leadership accountable for achieving success, which research has shown to be especially effective in bringing about real change.[55] Catalyst president Sheila Wellington singled out the Accenture program for praise because of "the scope of the initiative combined with the ease by which it can be replicated worldwide" and called it "a truly innovative effort."[56] (Catalyst is a nonprofit research and advisory organization concerned with the professional advancement of women.)

Ernst and Young, an international accounting and professional services firm with 110,000 employees worldwide, launched a series of "women's development initiatives" in 1997 that increased women in executive management positions from 0 to 13 percent by 2002. During the same five years, the percentage of women promoted to partner at Ernst and Young doubled. The firm's commitment to making its corporate culture more hospitable to women earned it a spot on *Working Mother* magazine's "100 Best Companies for Working Mothers" list for five consecutive years, landed it on *Fortune* magazine's "100 Best Companies to Work For" list, and made it one of three firms in 2003 to win Catalyst's award for "companies and firms with outstanding initiatives that result in women's career development and advancement." And, as at Deloitte and Touche, improving the firm's culture for women made a difference for men as well. Approximately 1,000 Ernst and Young employees had babies in 2002, and 949 of them took advantage of the firm's parental leave benefit—almost half of them men. In addition, both men and women have made use of the firm's flex-time options, including partners, principals, and directors, without suffering any slow-down in their professional progress.

The huge increase in firms applying to be considered for *Working Mother*'s "100 Best Companies for Working Mothers" award since the program began in 1986 shows that American companies have begun to recognize the value of promoting women's professional progress. According to Amy DiTillio, a senior associate editor at *Working Mother*, as more firms apply, winning requires truly meaningful change, continually "raising the bar."

Most of the initiatives undertaken by these companies involve so-called "work/life" benefits, such as child-care services, flexible work arrangements, and elder-care and adoption assistance programs. Mother-friendly policies make it possible for these companies to retain talented employees in whom they've invested substantial resources. Steve Sanger, the CEO of General Mills, who won *Working Mother*'s "2003 Chief Executive of the Year" award for demonstrating extraordinary commitment to creating a family-friendly workplace, explained why these policies make good business sense: "You know what's really expensive? Turnover. If we've invested in recruiting and developing good people, then we want them to stay."[57]

In addition to their positive impact on the bottom line, family-friendly initiatives can remove barriers to women's advancement by transforming women's "communal" impulse to take care of their families into a gender norm for both sexes. In response, men in these companies are flocking to take advantage of these programs.

Unfortunately, however, most of these companies have not gone as far as Deloitte and Touche in looking at the entrenched attitudes, unthinking responses, and unseen roadblocks to women's advancement that lurk throughout our culture. These companies—and many more—still need to remove many of the barriers that can prevent women from asserting themselves, asking for what they want, and getting what they deserve. Change of this sort is not only possible, it's necessary—because another reason women don't resist the constraints of gender roles and stereotypes involves the consequences for violating those expectations. As our culture currently functions, women sometimes find themselves punished for behaving in ways that go against prevailing gender norms. Promoting their own interests by asking for what they want may be one of those ways. We explore this last reason in depth in the next chapter.

4

SCARING THE BOYS

IN THE LATE 1990s, Jean Hollands, founder of an executive coaching firm in California called the Growth and Leadership Center, recognized a new need in her field: Someone had to teach tough, capable women in business to tone down their act. Women with enormous passion for their jobs and little tolerance for incompetence were intimidating their subordinates, coworkers, and even their bosses. As a result, these women's careers were stalling. A "tough" personal style, often an advantage for men in business, had emerged as a liability for ambitious women.[1]

In response, Jean Hollands started the "Bully Broads" program, which charges around $18,000 (almost always paid by a woman's employer) to "modify" or "reform" tough women by teaching them how to be "nicer."[2] Does she acknowledge that there's a double standard? Absolutely. "Many of the things these women do would not be as inappropriate in a man," Ms. Hollands says.[3] Her son-in-law, Ron Steck, a vice president of the Growth and Leadership Center, goes further: "With a male executive, there's no expectation to be nice. He has more permission to be an ass. But when women speak their minds, they're seen as harsh."[4] To counteract this impression, Bully Broads teaches these women to speak more slowly and softly, hesitate or stammer when presenting their ideas, use self-deprecating humor, and even allow themselves to cry at meetings. They need to "become ladies first," Hollands says; they also need to appear vulnerable and use what she calls "foreplay"—elaborate apologies and explanations to soften bad news or unwelcome directives.[5]

How big a "problem" is women's overly tough behavior? Whereas the majority of the men who go to the Growth and Leadership Center are sent by their companies to learn how to delegate work or handle stress better, a full 95 percent of the women are sent because their firms say their coworkers find them scary. This doesn't mean that the world is suddenly being overrun by bitchy women. It means that an assertive personal style can be a gender-norm violation for a woman. As the psychologist Roberta Nutt, former chair of the Psychology of Women Division of the American Psychological Association, noted, "When women first entered the workplace they often tried to do things like men, but it didn't work. We don't accept from women what we do from men."[6] This is true of objectively aggressive and dominant types of behavior, such as pointing at others, speaking with a stern expression on one's face, and making verbal and nonverbal threats.[7] It is also true of nonverbal behavior that could be seen to express a dominant attitude, such as making a lot of eye contact while speaking.[8] Sadly, it has even been shown to be true of behavior that could be characterized as simply assertive and self-confident, such as speaking without the use of disclaimers, tag questions ("don't you agree?"), and hedges ("I'm not sure this will work, but it might be worth trying").[9] It can be true of simply disagreeing with another person as well—we accept this behavior from a man much more readily than we do from a woman.[10]

Unfortunately, many of these behaviors can be effective in a negotiation—but they carry risks for women. Marti, 28, who worked on sound design for toys at a recording studio and is now the registrar of a theater company and acting school, told us that she learned pretty early "that if a woman picks that hard-edged negotiation style she can often...come across as a bitch to people. And, still, I think, society looks at a woman who is a successful businesswoman and a successful negotiator, and somehow looks down upon her because she's not as soft as she's supposed to be."

Gender norms limit the behavior of men, too, of course: Men aren't free to cry or show weakness in most situations, for example. It isn't, therefore, just that women must be more concerned than men about creating a good impression: It's that particularly in the realm of negotiating, women's behavior is more rigidly restricted than men's. And an extensive body of research has found clear evidence that when women stray—or stride—across those boundaries they face penalties (what social scientists call "social sanctions") for violating society's expectations for their behavior. These penalties can range from resentment for "acting like men"[11] to a devaluing of their skills and job effectiveness[12] to outright hostility and censure.[13] Their fear of these penalties makes many women hesitate to pursue their goals too directly. It can also be a major cause of anxiety for women when they need to negotiate on their own behalf because they've learned that by doing so they risk being punished in both subtle and overt ways. (Being sent to Bully Broads would be one of the more overt ways, especially since many women are told by their employers that if they don't go they'll lose their jobs). As psychologist Mary Wade writes: "Women do not frequently make requests for themselves, because they have learned that they may ultimately lose more than they gain.... Women have learned their social normative lessons all too well."[14] Many women decide, in other words, that the gains to be had from asking for what they want are not worth the price they may have to pay.

In this chapter, we look broadly at society's double standard for judging the behavior of men and women in order to understand why women frequently feel punished for asking for what they want. We examine some of the constraints society places on women's behavior—constraints that have persuaded many women that asking is not an effective strategy for achieving their goals. We then look at ways for women to ask for and get what they want without provoking hostile responses. And we look at ways in which society can change to make "asking" by women more permissible and effective.

The Likeability Factor

For women who want to influence other people, research has found that being *likeable* is critically important—and that women's influence increases the more they are liked. Since negotiation is all about trying to influence

people, this means that women must be likeable in order to negotiate successfully. You might think that women also need to be assertive to negotiate
successfully—able to present strong arguments, defend their interests and
positions, and communicate confidence in their points of view. Unfortunately, research has revealed that assertive women are less well liked than
those who are not assertive.[15] This means that an assertive woman, no matter how well she presents her arguments in a negotiation, risks decreasing
her likeability and therefore her ability to influence the other side to agree
with her point of view. In contrast, whether or not they are liked does not affect men's ability to influence others, and there is no connection between assertive behavior and likeability for men. Men are equally well liked whether
they are assertive or passive.[16]

This research is buttressed by studies showing that women are penalized far more than men for boasting.[17] In one study, researchers gave a
group of students a "boasting" statement and another group a "non-
boasting" statement. Some members of each group were told that the
statement they'd received had been made by a man and some were told it
had been made by a woman. They were all asked to rate the "likeability" of
the person who made their statement on a scale of one to seven. The researchers found that the likeability of men fell when they boasted, but that
women's likeability fell much further—42 percent more.[18]

The special pressure on women to be likeable can sometimes discourage them from asking for anything at all. Adele, the retired financial consultant, said she was raised to believe that being liked is of paramount
importance for a woman. Afraid she would be disliked if she pressed for
what she wanted, she would "never negotiate for anything" and taught
herself to "ask for things very covertly." Melissa, 39, a social worker, said
that in any type of negotiation, regardless of whom she's negotiating with,
she's likely to ask for less than she really wants because her primary concern is for the other person to like her: "It sounds really kind of silly, but I
don't want to ruin it somehow by being demanding in some way. And not
being liked is something that's hard for me, and so I think that sometimes,
if I feel like people are going to think, 'Oh, she's demanding,' I don't
know—it's hard. Because ... I want to fit into what they want."

The "likeability" issue can put women in a particularly tight bind, because self-confidence, assertiveness, and asking directly for what you want are often necessary to get ahead in the world. Consider, for example, situations involving hiring and promotion decisions. Since research has found that women are generally perceived to be less competent than men, women who compete against men in job situations need to counter this stereotype by demonstrating their superior capabilities.[19] Self-promotion (describing one's qualities and accomplishments) has been shown to enhance people's perceptions of one's competence.[20] But, as the psychologist Laurie Rudman writes, "self-promotion poses special problems for women." Although self-promotion may educate a woman's superiors about her qualifications, it may make her less likeable—and make her superiors less inclined to give her what she wants. As Rudman writes, "women may be stuck in a Catch-22 in which they are damned if they do self-promote and damned if they do not."[21]

Other studies have shown that men (and sometimes women) react negatively when women adopt styles or communication patterns expected of men, such as acting assertive and self-confident rather than tentative.[22] But research also shows that women fare no better if they don't self-promote because men judge women who restrict themselves to more gender-appropriate behavior as less capable and "unsuited to management."[23]

Marcela, 48, a nuclear engineer, described a supervisor who gave her "feedback at a rating session that I was indecisive or too hesitant, which I thought was complete bologna because I don't see myself that way at all and I don't think that anybody else does either. That was just his perception and it was definitely a male/female thing. We had completely opposite styles of everything and I hated working for him, absolutely hated it!" In other words, using more "feminine" styles or communication patterns often won't get women what they want either, especially when what they want is to be given management responsibilities and the opportunity to rise into the higher levels of their organizations.[24]

Style and Prejudice

Recent research on leadership by Alice Eagly, Mona Makhijani, and Bruce Klonsky confirms that we require different behavior from women in leadership roles than we require from men: Men are judged to be equally effective as leaders whether they use autocratic or democratic leadership styles, but women who use autocratic styles are judged less favorably than women who use democratic styles.[25] Sadly, women managers or "leaders" can be penalized for violating role expectations even when they steer a careful course between the extremes of masculine and feminine styles of behavior. In one study, researchers formed students into groups of four to rank the value of nine items (such as a first-aid kit and a map) to someone who has crashed on the moon. Each group included a confederate of the researchers (either male or female) who was trained to play the role of a cooperative, pleasantly assertive group leader. As each group ranked the items, researchers observed the facial expressions of the "nonconfederates" in response to the behavior of the confederate leaders.

The researchers found that the students responded very differently to identical behavior by men and women. Males playing the leadership roles elicited more positive than negative facial reactions but females playing leadership roles prompted the opposite response—more negative than positive reactions. The researchers later asked the participants to evaluate the personal attributes of the leaders in their groups. Across the board, they rated males who had taken leadership positions as having more ability, skill, and intelligence than the female leaders and rated the female leaders as more emotional, bossy, and domineering—this despite the fact that the behavior of the men and women playing leadership roles was exactly the same. However, when the participants were asked directly about their attitudes toward men and women in leadership roles, they exhibited no sex biases and believed that they held none.[26]

Researchers speculate that many people object to women playing leadership roles because their ideas about leadership behavior clash with their perceptions of how women should behave. To study this phenomenon, in the 1970s the psychologist Virginia Schein developed the Schein Descriptive Index, a list of 92 words and phrases commonly used to describe people's characteristics. Using this index, she looked at the correspondences between the characteristics people attribute to successful managers and the characteristics they attribute to men and women. She found that people chose many more of the same words to describe both men and managers (such as assertive and ambitious) but very few of the same words to describe both women and managers.[27] Later research in the 1980s reached much the same conclusions.[28]

More recently, in the mid and late 1990s, researchers noticed that this correlation has begun to change for female subjects but not male subjects—women have begun to see the characteristics of managers as being similar to the characteristics of both men and women, while men continue to see managers and women as dissimilar.[29] A 1998 study showed that males in particular continue to hold extremely negative beliefs about females with senior professional standing. In this study, a group of undergraduates was given the Schein Descriptive Index and asked to identify words that describe female managers. Although female subjects chose words and phrases such as *able to separate feelings from ideas, competent, creative, emotionally stable, helpful, intelligent, objective, self-controlled, sympathetic,* and *well-informed* to describe female managers, male subjects chose terms such as *bitter, deceitful, easily influenced, frivolous, hasty, nervous, passive, quarrelsome,* and *uncertain.*[30] Research in Germany, the United Kingdom, China, and Japan has produced similar results. In each of these very different cultures, men see a high correspondence between the characteristics of men and the characteristics of managers—and little to no correspondence between the characteristics of women and the characteristics of managers.[31]

Taken together, these studies suggest that people's prejudices can powerfully influence the ways in which they respond to men and women without their realizing it. People may observe that a woman functions adequately or even extremely well according to objective measures—the number of billable hours she has worked or the number of clients she has brought in or the amounts of money she has raised—and still conclude that she lacks desirable personal attributes (she's not as likeable, or she's too emotional, bossy, and domineering, or she's too easily influenced, frivolous, and quarrelsome). This can be particularly problematic in an era, like our own, in which CEOs often become celebrities, as Rakesh Khurana, a professor of organizational behavior at the Harvard Business School, wrote in *Searching for a Corporate Savior: The Irrational Quest for Charismatic CEOs*. In this climate, writes Khurana, CEOs are "no longer defined as professional managers, but instead as leaders," with their ability to lead deriving largely from "their personal characteristics, or, more simply, their charisma."[32] In an atmosphere in which one's "personal characteristics" (pretty vague criteria) qualify or disqualify you for leadership roles, the subconscious prejudices people hold about women and their lack of fitness for management roles can translate into powerful deterrents when women ask to be considered for leadership positions.

As the psychologist Madeline Heilman writes, "Even when she produces the identical product as a man, a woman's work is often regarded as inferior" because often "women's achievements are viewed in a way that is consistent with stereotype-based negative performance expectations, and their work is devalued simply because they are women."[33] A woman may be told that she hasn't been promoted for vague reasons—she "needs more seasoning," "just isn't ready yet," or "needs to be a better team player." The woman may suspect that she has been unfairly evaluated, but because the criteria for evaluation are ambiguous, she can't prove it. She may conclude that something about her behavior has put her in the wrong—and that what put her in the wrong was asking to be promoted in the first place. This may make her reluctant to actively pursue advancement in the future.

Double Trouble

Other research shows that responses to women may be especially distorted by negative stereotypes when they work in areas in which there are few other women. Rosabeth Moss Kanter, in her influential 1977 book *Men and Women of the Corporation*, demonstrated that when women are tokens (when there aren't many of them around) their personal characteristics are more likely to be seen as similar to negative stereotypes about women's characteristics.[34] In a 1980 study, Madeline Heilman confirmed this finding by asking a group of MBAs to rate potential applicants for a hypothetical job. When less than 25 percent of the applicant pool was female, the MBAs rated female applicants lower (and also perceived them as more stereotypically feminine) than they did when larger percentages of the pool were female—showing that women are more likely to be devalued when their numbers are relatively small.[35]

This means that the higher a woman rises in an organization, the more likely she is to encounter stereotyped responses to her behavior—because there don't tend to be many women at the higher levels of most organizations. There are of course exceptions—highly visible and influential women who have achieved enormous success despite the persistent discouragement encountered by so many others. But these women *are* exceptions. A study by the economists Marianne Bertrand and Kevin Hallock, which looked at the top five highest-paid executives in firms of varying sizes between 1992 and 1997, found that women held only 2.5 percent of these posts.[36] In an article in *Fast Company* magazine, Margaret Heffernan, a former CEO at CMGI, an umbrella organization for several different Internet operating and development companies, described encountering a young woman in an elevator when she was at CMGI. After inquiring if she was indeed Margaret, the young woman said, "I just wanted to meet you and shake your hand.... I've never seen a female CEO before."[37] This was not 15 years ago, but in the year 2000, and this woman's experience, Heffernan points out, is not unusual. "Most men and women in business have never seen a female CEO—much less worked with one."[38]

Another problem women encounter is that the more power and status involved in a job, the more "masculine" the job is perceived to be—and therefore, as the Schein Index studies show, the less likely people are to see women's qualities as suitable for that work.[39] As a result, women may be perceived to be doing good work only as long as they are toiling away at less important jobs. Once they qualify for and start asking for more important, and therefore more "masculine," jobs, their work may begin to be devalued and their "personal style" may suddenly become a problem. This could explain why the women who are sent to the Bully Broads program usually hold high positions in their organizations—they're vice presidents, chief financial officers, and senior partners, all jobs that until recently were almost universally occupied by men. Presumably, for a long time these women were thought to be doing a good job, otherwise they wouldn't have been promoted again and again. But because the jobs they were doing were less important, they were less identified as "masculine" jobs—and their presence in those jobs posed less of a problem for their peers. Once they reached positions of significant power in their organizations, positions that are seen to be the province of men, their "style" became a problem.

Until she became CEO of Hewlett-Packard, a staunchly male company, Carly Fiorina's work was highly regarded. Then, all of a sudden, Fiorina's "style" became an issue. As Adam Lashinsky wrote in a November 2002 issue of *Fortune*: "Internally, rumors began to swirl. She had a personal trainer and personal hairdresser at her beck and call. She'd bought a new Gulfstream IV jet. She had her exercise equipment flown on a separate plane. She treated employees imperiously. None of this was true."[40] During the proxy fight that ensued when Fiorina decided to merge HP with Compaq, she was portrayed in the media "as a ruthless decision-maker— haughty and cocky."[41] Yet six months after the proxy fight was settled, Lashinsky followed her around for a few days and found her listening sympathetically to the concerns of a group of employees, teasing a sales manager and his boss, and getting an audience of "6000 sophisticated tech buyers eating out of her hand."[42] The impression conveyed was of an engaged and capable manager, not an arrogant, take-no-prisoners prima donna. Although one might conclude that Fiorina is smart enough to conceal her ruthlessness, hauteur, and cockiness when there's a reporter around, another interpretation also seems possible: that in the almost exclusively male world of proxy fights, where women hardly ever dare to tread, the ugly and inaccurate rumors about her behavior were provoked more by negative stereotypes aroused by her token status than by anything specific that she said or did.

Not Just Your Imagination

Although women may suspect that they've been the victims of negative attitudes toward women, they can rarely prove it and often have no recourse. But a few studies have at least confirmed that women's suspicions are correct. In one, the economist David Neumark sent men and women with equally impressive backgrounds and résumés to apply for jobs as wait staff in the upscale restaurants of Philadelphia. He found that women were 40 percent less likely to get called for interviews and 50 percent less likely to receive job offers if they did get interviews.[43] In an even more dramatic example, the economists Claudia Goldin and Cecilia Rouse looked at symphony orchestra auditions. They found that the use of a screen to hide the identity—and thus the gender—of auditioning musicians increased by a full 50 percent the probability that a woman would advance in the audition process. They also found that the likelihood that a woman would win an orchestra seat was increased by 250 percent when a screen was used. Goldin and Rouse credit the switch to blind auditions as a major factor in the gains women made in the top five U.S. symphonies between 1970, when women filled only 5 percent of the chairs, and the year 2000, when that number had grown to 25 percent.[44]

In *Why So Slow? The Advancement of Women,* Virginia Valian looked at earnings and advancement in six occupations—sports, law, medicine, business, academia, and engineering—and discovered that men earn more money and attain higher status than women in each of these professions. Although Valian conceded that many factors contribute to this "sex disparity in income and rank," she concluded that "gender always explains an additional portion. Women are required to meet a higher standard."[45] This requirement makes it harder for many women to ask for and get what they want as freely and fairly as they should. And given what we know about the "accumulation of disadvantage," this requirement represents a huge barrier to true gender equity.

The "C200 Business Leadership Index 2002," a publication of the Committee of 200, an organization of women in business, includes several statistics that support the theory that women frequently encounter road-blocks in conventional business environments. First, the number of women-owned businesses grew 14 percent between 1997 and 2001—twice as fast as all privately held businesses. Second, during the same period, the average size of women-owned businesses grew at the extremely rapid rate of almost 17 percent a year, compared to 2 percent per year for all businesses. Noting that both of these rates of progress far outstrip gains in the percentage of female Fortune 500 corporate officers, the C200 Index observes that "this comparison indicates a greater ability of women to succeed outside the constraints of the corporate environment."[46] Although several factors probably contribute to this reality, the likelihood that subtle forms of sanctioning deter women's progress cannot be overlooked.

Even though much of the available data in this area can tell us only that a gender gap in earnings exists and not why, this we do know: Women as a group earn less than men, progress more slowly through the ranks of most businesses, and rarely rise as high. Looking at weekly earnings for full-time workers during the years 1994 to 1998, the economists Francine Blau and Lawrence Kahn, in a National Bureau of Economic Research publication, found this to be true not only in the United States, where women's earnings total only 76 percent of men's, but in Canada (where women make 70 percent of what men make), in Britain (75 percent), in Japan (64 percent), and in Australia (87 percent). The gap between the earnings of men and women is narrowest in Belgium, where women earn 90 percent of what men earn.[47] Researchers have yet to identify any country in which women's earnings equal or exceed men's. Using different data and looking at different occupations the answer is always the same—women are paid less.

Margaret Heffernan, the former CEO at CMGI, described her own experience of how gender can influence a woman's career in upper management—and limit how much she is paid—without her knowing it. "For years," Heffernan reported, "I was the only woman CEO at CMGI. But it wasn't until I read the company's proxy statement that I realized that my salary was 50 percent of that of my male counterparts. I had the CEO title, but I was being paid as if I were a director."[48]

When the Punishment Is Hard to Miss

Sanctions such as some of those described above may be difficult to pinpoint and attribute to gender. Women may suspect that they've been unfairly evaluated but can't prove it. They may feel generally discouraged from asking for what they want and yet be unable to say why. But sometimes the sanctioning—the punishment—is hard to miss.

Sandy, 41, a full-time mother who spent part of her career working as a commercial lending officer at a bank, told this story. The bank was interested in persuading an important customer (an aluminum smelting company) to borrow a large sum from the bank. Other banks were also courting the client, and competition was fierce. Sandy had worked with the president of the smelting company, a man in his fifties, for the past year, during which time he had treated her in a condescending manner—tolerating her requests for information but making it clear that he was not happy to be working with her. When Sandy brought up the subject of the big loan, however, he railed against her and said he would not talk to a woman about his business needs. Women were not "business material," he shouted, and he would terminate his relationship with the bank if she were not replaced with a man.

Sandy returned to the bank and described the meeting to her boss, a man in his early thirties, and to his boss, a man in his early forties. Both said they supported Sandy and offered to meet with the smelting company president and sort out the problem. At this meeting, with Sandy present, the president of the smelting company repeated his request that she be replaced in a loud, verbally abusive manner. Sandy said, "I don't recall if he called me a whore, but I wouldn't be surprised if he did because I was so utterly shocked by his behavior—it seemed suited to a back alley brawl!" The two bank managers immediately buckled to his request and said she would be replaced. Afterward, they refused to explain their behavior. Sandy was punished—not merely taken off this important account, but insulted and humiliated without protest from her superiors—simply for asking this man to do business with her. From his point of view, it was outrageous for her to think she could perform an important job, a job that he thought should therefore be a man's job. Sandy observed that "this experience fit into a general prejudice that I had against men in the workplace—that their attitudes and perceptions of women made it difficult to ask for what was fair and right. I definitely had difficulty with the men I knew at the bank in asking for what I felt was fair for me."

The punishment for venturing into "masculine" jobs can be equally severe at the other end of the social spectrum, in blue-collar fields that have long been male-dominated. The journalist Susan Faludi, in *Backlash: The Undeclared War against American Women,* reports the experiences of Diane Joyce, a widow raising four children on her own. Joyce landed a job on a Santa Clara, California, county road crew, coming in third out of 87 applicants on the job test.[49] When she showed up for work, the experienced drivers of the county's bobtail trucks who were supposed to train her gave her unclear, conflicting, and at one point dangerous instructions; her supervisor refused to issue her a pair of coveralls (she had to file a formal grievance to get them); and her co-workers kept the ladies' room locked. "You wanted a man's job, you learn to pee like a man," her supervisor told her.[50] Obscene graffiti about her appeared on the sides of trucks, and men in the department screamed at her to "go the hell away."[51] When Joyce later applied for a more senior road dispatcher's job, they gave it to a man with three years' less experience. She complained and got the job, but the man who lost it sued for reverse discrimination—and pursued the case all the way to the Supreme Court. He lost at every juncture, but this didn't stop Joyce's coworkers from continuing to harass her.

Faludi writes, "Joyce's experience was typical of the forthright and often violent backlash within the blue-collar workforce.... At a construction site in New York...the men took a woman's work boots and hacked them to bits. Another woman was injured by a male co-worker; he hit her on the head with a two-by-four. In Santa Clara County...the county's equal opportunity files were stuffed with reports of ostracism, hazing, sexual harassment, threats, verbal and physical abuse."[52]

Professor of management Judy Rosener offers this explanation for the intensity of men's resistance to seeing women move into realms that have traditionally been male: "The glass ceiling for those below it is the floor for those above it. When we take away our ceiling, we take away their floor, and they have a fear of falling."[53] As a result, high-powered women who are too self-assertive are sent to programs such as "Bully Broads," women working at middle levels of management are paid less and promoted more slowly than their male peers, and blue-collar women are threatened, ostracized, and undermined in their efforts to perform their jobs. All of these forms of punishment discourage women from asking for the same things men want and get and enjoy, whether that is attaining high levels of success in their fields, getting paid the same as their peers, or simply being allowed to do the jobs they want to do.

Although our interviews produced numerous stories of "punishment" similar to those included here, overt sanctioning of this sort has rarely been the topic of systematic analysis, in part because it is less likely to emerge in the bright light of the laboratory. This is especially true because so much research is performed on college campuses, where the populations available for study are particularly sensitive to issues of "political correctness" and have learned to refrain from voicing or acting out their prejudices. But even though many members of our society have become more cautious about expressing their prejudices, this doesn't mean those prejudices have ceased to influence their actions.

Danger! Danger!—The Message Is Everywhere

Even women who have themselves escaped overt forms of punishment for pursuing their ambitions cannot ignore the messages from every side that it's risky for women to try to become too successful. Susan Faludi argues that this is because for many people the core meaning of masculinity is threatened by the improved economic status of women. This view is supported by the results of a 1989 poll, in which most people (men and women) defined masculinity as "being a good provider for your family."[54] One of our society's strongest gender norms for women, in contrast, is that they will be modest and selfless. As a result, many people don't consider being preoccupied by money or attaching a dollar value to their work and time to be proper or attractive for a woman.[55]

Linda Evangelista, one of the first models to be identified as a "super-model," earned an avalanche of derision in the summer of 1990 when she admitted to a reporter that she and Christy Turlington, another "super-model," had an expression they liked to use: "We don't wake up for less than $10,000 a day." Loudly denounced at the time, she has been dogged by the remark ever since. As recently as the September 2001 edition of *Vogue*, an interviewer pressed her again to explain her remark. Evangelista said, "I feel like those words are going to be engraved on my tombstone.... I apologized for it. I acknowledged it.... Would I hope that I would never say something like that ever again? Yes." Keep in mind that Evangelista made this remark in 1990, after a decade (the 1980s) in which everyone from Donald Trump to Michael Milken boasted of his huge income on television talk shows, in the society pages, and in the financial news—a decade in which accumulating wealth and flaunting it amounted to a national obsession. But Evangelista's story tells us that what is good for the gander is *not* good for the goose. When a woman knows what she's worth—and feels proud of her abilities and of what she can earn—she sets herself up to be scorned and chastised.

Caring more about relationships than about personal gain represents another powerful gender norm for women. The media's treatment of an episode at the 2002 Winter Olympics in Salt Lake City provided an object lesson for women on the dangers of violating this norm. Jean Racine, considered the top female bobsled driver in the world and the Olympic front-runner for the American women's bobsledding team, spent most of her career partnered with a friend (many media sources said her "best friend"), Jen Davidson. Racine and Davidson competed in the two-person version of the sport, in which one athlete, the driver, sits in front and steers while the other, the brakewoman, pushes from behind to get the sled started down the course and then stops the sled at the bottom. Brake-women need to be very strong. Racine was the driver and Davidson the brakewoman until two months before the games. Then, feeling that Davidson was not as strong as another player, Racine switched partners—or, as the media reported it, "dumped" Davidson. Shortly before the games, Racine's new partner, Gea Johnson, suffered a hamstring injury, and Racine tried switching partners again, this time asking a relative newcomer, Vonetta Flowers, to join her. Flowers turned Racine down and with her partner, Jill Bakken, eventually won the gold medal. Racine and the injured Gea Johnson did not perform well and failed to win a medal.

This story was widely covered, with everyone from the *New York Times* to *USA Today* to the supermarket tabloids and both network and cable news programs weighing in with their judgments. The reporting, for the most part, reduced this story of personal struggle, hard choices, and disappointment to the realm of soap opera, a trivial squabble among women, with even such august news bodies as NBC dubbing the episode "As the Sled Turns." No one claimed that Jen Davidson was faster than the other brakewomen who made the U.S. team, and a few news sources even conceded that switching partners is extremely common in the sport, among male bobsledders as well as female. Nonetheless, press reports described Racine as "ruthless" and "without remorse," referred to her behavior as "scandalous" and "appalling," and implied that she deserved to lose because she had put her own interests above the claims of friendship. Flowers, on the other hand, deserved to win because she'd been loyal. "Perhaps warmth and sweetness have their place in the cutthroat world of Olympic bobsledding. Loyalty does, at least," wrote the *New York Times*'s reporter.[56]

The thing is: Jean Racine was an Olympic-caliber athlete. Like any athlete, her chances to compete in the Olympics were limited, and she wanted to win. That's what the Olympics are about, after all. And she put her personal ambition and desire—she put what she wanted—ahead of relationship concerns, a major taboo for a woman. For this, she was publicly lambasted. The message to women: If trying to get what you want means violating gender norms for women, don't do it. You may not get what you want, and on top of that disappointment you'll be roundly criticized and publicly shamed.

Faludi believes that men, and many women, combat their fear that masculinity is threatened by women's success by trying to shift the "cultural gears" into reverse. They do this by promoting the idea that the movement of women into the workplace is responsible for many of society's problems, especially those involving families and children.[57] So the media publishes stories with titles like "Feminism Is Bad for Women's Health Care" (from the *Wall Street Journal*)[58] and conservative thinkers produce books such as *A Return to Modesty: Discovering the Lost Virtue*, by Wendy Shalit[59]; *Domestic Tranquility: A Brief against Feminism*, by F. Carolyn Graglia[60]; and *The War against Boys: How Misguided Feminism Is Harming Our Young Men*, by Christina Hoff Sommers.[61]

In demonizing feminists and telling women that they're responsible for society's problems, these reactionary forces teach businesses that it's permissible to penalize women for asking to do jobs typically performed by men—or simply for pursuing their own professional goals rather than deferring to the needs and ambitions of others. They can also make women feel less sure that it's okay for them to want what they want, especially if what they want involves professional success. This can persuade them to scale back their ambitions and to hope for—and ask for—fewer of life's rewards.

Women Have Learned Their Lessons Well

The oppressive but inescapable message—that women will be punished for exceeding the bounds of acceptable behavior—has come through loud and clear, and women have adapted their behavior accordingly.[62] Ariadne, 33, is an MBA who enjoyed a successful career in public relations before becoming a full-time mother. Ariadne has a very direct manner. Although she believes that a similarly direct man would be perceived as a "straight-shooter" or a "no-nonsense guy," her style has prompted people to call her a bitch or complain that she is too aggressive. As a result, Ariadne learned in the course of her career to tone down her personal style and adopt a less straightforward manner. She would even avoid claiming credit for her own ideas (and asking for appropriate recognition) because she found that letting other people think her good ideas were their own helped get those ideas implemented, and backfired less on her.

An extensive body of research confirms that Ariadne's is not an isolated case: Women consistently adjust their behavior between private and public settings—revealing their clear understanding that they may pay a penalty for behaving freely when observed by others. Of course, both men and women behave differently in public than they do at home, but research shows that women adjust their behavior more. In one of the "pay allocation" experiments mentioned in chapter 2, for example, men and women were instructed to work on a task until they had "earned" four dollars. Although women worked longer and harder than men in the "private," unobserved condition (22 percent longer), they worked even longer if the amount of time they worked was monitored by the experimenter (52 percent longer than men). Men did not work longer when they were observed.[63] This tells us that women have learned that they must pay more attention than men to the impressions they make on others, presumably because they fear the penalties for counterstereotypical behavior.

Other research confirms that women conform more to gender roles in public than in private. In one study, researchers asked college students to estimate their grade-point averages (GPAs) for the upcoming semester either privately, on paper, or out loud to a peer. Although there were no gender differences between the male and female students' predictions in the private condition, the female students' estimates were lower in the presence of a peer (the males' estimates did not change).[64] A review of the research in this area concludes that unlike men, women "often limit their displays of achievement-oriented behavior to situations in which autonomy and privacy are assured."[65]

Women have learned, in other words, that asking through their actions to be recognized for their abilities and accomplishments can be a mistake. This self-consciousness about being observed extends to negotiation contexts, in which women request lower salaries when another person is present than they request when they assume no one else is watching. Men's requests, on the other hand, *increase* in the presence of another person.[66]

Do Not Compete

Women don't just modify their behavior in public settings, one study suggests, they may also shy away from competition, especially competition with men. For this study, three economists, Uri Gneezy, Muriel Niederle, and Aldo Rustichini, asked female and male engineering students to work through mazes on a computer. At first, the students worked on their own and were paid a flat rate for each maze they completed (the "piece-rate" condition). In this situation, men and women completed the same number of mazes on average. Then the researchers asked the same students to participate in a "tournament," in which three female students and three male students would compete to see who could complete the most mazes in a set amount of time. The winner would be paid six times as much for each maze solved as he or she had earned in the piece-rate condition, while the rest of the students would earn no money for their work.[67]

Traditional economic theory would expect every participant to complete more mazes in the tournament condition than in the piece-rate condition because the reward for winning would give everyone an incentive to work harder. But Gneezy, Niederle, and Rustichini found that this was true only of the men. Whereas men completed 34 percent more mazes during the tournaments than they'd solved in the piece-rate condition, the number of mazes the women solved did not increase. The men didn't suddenly get smarter—the tournament setting inspired them to compete with each other and try harder. But the tournament did not have the same impact on the women.

One might conclude from this study that women simply don't like to compete. To explore this hypothesis, the researchers organized additional tournaments in which they segregated the groups by gender. They found that the performance of the men in the all-male tournaments was identical to their performance in the mixed-gender tournaments: The incentive of "winning" prompted them to increase their efforts over the piece-rate condition by the same amount no matter who they were competing against. But the most revealing data emerged from the all-female tournaments: The women completed far more mazes in the all-female tournament groups than in either the piece-rate condition or in the tournaments in which they were competing against men.

One explanation for these uneven results could be that women believe that men are better at solving mazes than women. Assuming they won't win in a mixed-gender tournament, they consequently don't try. Or stereotype threat may play a part: If women believe that men are better at solving mazes, this could undermine their performance at a subconscious level. Although the authors could not rule out these hypotheses, we can find nothing to suggest that mazes, which involve pretty basic skills, are in fact gender-defined and perceived to be the province of men. Another possible conclusion is that women just don't like competing against men. Much of what we know about gender norms supports this interpretation: Boys learn that they are expected to compete, that being a good competitor is a defining male trait. They also learn that they are expected to demonstrate superior ability over girls in certain areas (intelligence, physical prowess, business success) and that this superiority is central to our society's definition of maleness. Girls also learn these lessons about males. Because negotiation contains within it a basic form of competition, both males and females in our culture may make the connection that this consequently cannot be a woman's domain. To compete with a man in a negotiation and win—to get him to give you a better raise than he wanted, or a better price for a car, or more responsibility on a project than he intended—may threaten his socially received idea of his own maleness. And women learn that this is rarely a good idea, because such a destabilizing threat will almost inevitably rebound in negative ways, punishing the woman who posed it.

She may pay a price in her private life as well as at work. In *Creating a Life: Professional Women and the Quest for Children*, the economist Sylvia Ann Hewlett reports that "the more successful the woman, the less likely it is she will find a husband or bear a child."[68] Although many men scoff at the notion that they feel threatened by smart women or are less likely to date them, this phenomenon seems to persist. Two female Harvard MBA students interviewed on the television newsmagazine *60 Minutes* in 2002 confessed that they no longer admit to men that they go to Harvard, because men feel too threatened by their success to pursue relationships with them.[69]

The popular cable television series *Sex and the City*, about the personal lives of four New York career women (one of whom quits working to get married), illustrated this dilemma in one episode.[70] Miranda, one of the show's four principal characters, is a successful lawyer and a partner in her firm. Having observed that her career success frightens off many of the men she meets, Miranda pretends that she is a flight attendant to see if men will respond to her differently. This fiction, to her chagrin, turns out to be very successful: Men respond to her far more enthusiastically than before, concisely demonstrating the pressure women feel to downplay their accomplishments in order to protect men from being intimidated—and to protect their own chances of establishing relationships with them.

Marcela, the nuclear engineer, described how she learned this lesson. When she was growing up, she said, "girls being smart was definitely an issue; when you were in your dating years the whole thing was not to let the guys know how smart you were. Because if they ever found out that your SAT scores were a lot higher than theirs then they wouldn't go out with you or whatever." She also said, "There was a point at which which . . . I was told that I shouldn't be so obvious in my accomplishments." This lesson influences Marcela's professional behavior to this day. Periodically, she must write up an assessment of her abilities and accomplishments as part of her firm's "rating" process for awarding raises, bonuses, and promotions. Implicit in the process is the expectation that she will indicate what she feels she deserves for the work she has done—a form of asking. She hates doing this, she said, because she doesn't like "the kind of exercise where you have to either write about your contributions or your accomplishments. . . . Not because I don't think that I've accomplished anything or made contributions but because I don't like writing it down. It just makes me uncomfortable to have to self-promote. I'm not very comfortable being self-promoting."

Marcela knows, in private, that she has accomplished a great deal, but she's aware of the risks entailed in publicly acknowledging this. She also admitted that if she doesn't receive an award or a bonus that she feels she deserves, "I would never ask for it. If it wasn't freely given, I wouldn't ask for it. I might gripe about it at home, but that would be the extent of it."

Ways of Asking and Getting

Ellen, the senior partner at a law firm, told us that when she was a teenager, her father said to her: "Honey, you know you can't act like a tiger. You have to act like a kitten." His point was clear: To get what she wants, a woman can't be too aggressive or direct. Although society has changed in many ways since Ellen was a child, women still need to be careful about "coming on too strong." Fortunately, women can be careful and—some of the time—still get what they want. Recent research has identified ways for women to be influential and effective without making themselves less likeable and bringing social sanctions down on their heads. This research has shown that for women, the key to safely and successfully exercising their influence is to be "nice." Like being likeable, being "nice" is expected of women—it's a gender norm requirement. To be "nice," a woman must seem friendly, act concerned about the needs and feelings of others, and avoid being confrontational. Several studies have demonstrated the efficacy of this approach for women.

The social psychologists Linda Carli, Suzanne LaFleur, and Christopher Lober videotaped male and female research assistants trying to persuade their peers to agree with a particular point of view—in this case, that it would be better not to make any changes in the cafeteria meal plan at their university (an unpopular opinion to hold). The researchers videotaped eight different versions of the same script, four with a man making the argument and four with a woman. The text and the message were the same in all eight versions, but the actors in the videos were coached to use different nonverbal behavior strategies in each: a "dominant style" (making constant eye contact, using a lot of hand gestures, speaking in a loud angry voice, and tightening their face muscles so that they appeared tense); a "submissive style" (avoiding eye contact, making nervous gestures with their hands, speaking in a soft unsteady voice, stammering and hesitating, slouching); a "task-oriented style" (frequently making eye contact, using only calm hand movements, speaking rapidly and with few hesitations); and a "social style" (leaning toward the audience, using unintrusive gestures, acting relaxed, communicating "friendliness and affiliation," smiling). After the researchers screened the videotapes for mixed male and female audiences, they asked them to rate how much they agreed with each speaker's point of view (this served as an overall measure of the speaker's ability to influence); they also asked them to rate each speaker on a number of qualities, such as how likeable, competent, and threatening he or she seemed.[71] The audiences found that male speakers were most influential when they used a "task-oriented style" (rather than any other style) but that a "social style" worked best for women.

Other research by the sociologist Cecilia Ridgeway supports this finding. Placing female confederates in mixed male and female groups that were instructed to make a series of decisions, she found that the women were most influential in the groups when they were "friendly, cooperative, confident, but nonconfrontational, and considerate."[72] They were able to exert far less influence on the group's decision making when they acted merely self-confident and behaved in a self-interested way. This finding and the results of another study led Ridgeway to conclude: "Women seeking to assert authority can mitigate the legitimacy problems they face by combining their assertive, highly competent behaviors with positive social 'softeners.' . . . Using such techniques, highly competent women can overcome others' resistance and win influence and compliance. . . . The positive consequences of such techniques are not trivial. They allow very competent women to break through the maze of constraints created by gender status to wield authority. This begins to undermine the structural arrangements in society that support gender status beliefs."[73]

The psychologists Laurie Rudman and Peter Glick, in a study looking at hiring situations, produced similar results: Women were more likely to be hired when they paired competence with "communal" behavior (such as demonstrating an interest in the needs and challenges of those hiring them) than when they paired competence with more "agentic" behavior (such as focusing more on their own needs and ambitions).[74] As Rudman and Glick write, self-oriented or "agentic" women "are viewed as socially deficient, compared with identically presented men."[75] Being perceived as "socially deficient" may make a woman seem threatening. At the very least, it can make her seem less likeable and reduce her ability to influence others and get what she wants.

All of these studies tell us that when women go into a negotiation, in addition to arming themselves with information, ideas, and resolve, they must also bring along an arsenal of "friendly," nonthreatening social mannerisms; they must be prepared to be cooperative and interested in the needs of others; and they must avoid being confrontational.[76] This does not mean they need to back down or give in. Imagine that a woman who likes her job but feels underpaid receives a job offer from another company for more money. If she goes into her boss's office and says "I've received an offer for $xx,000 more and I'm going to take it if you don't match that salary," he may react badly to her direct approach and tell her to take the other job. Starting out with something like, "Hi, I need to talk to you about my salary; is now a good time?" can set a different tone for the negotiation. Demonstrating that she knows he has many demands on his time shows concern for him and his situation. If he agrees to talk, she could explain that she's been offered the other job and mention the salary that goes with it. Then she might say, "I really enjoy working for you, but I have to consider this offer because it's for so much more money. You've always treated me fairly and I want to be fair to you by letting you know about this offer." She might also say that she'll stay if he matches the salary she's been offered. This will not only reinforce that she cares about the relationship, it will also frame the situation positively (she wants to stay) rather than posing it as a threat (she'll go if he doesn't meet her demands).

Although this approach can often produce better results, many women (including the two of us) may resent that women have to work so hard not to offend in this type of situation. As Ridgeway writes, "there is a price associated with such techniques as well: They inadvertently reaffirm gender stereotypes that require women to be 'nicer' than men in order to exercise equivalent power and authority."[77] Rudman and Glick also concede that this puts an extra burden on women: "Treading the fine line of appearing competent, ambitious, and competitive, but not at the expense of others, is a tall order.... To the extent that women have to maintain a 'bilingual' impression of themselves (as both nice and able) in order not to be perceived as overbearing and dominant, their situation is more difficult and tenuous in comparison to their male counterparts."[78]

The psychologist Janice Yoder goes further: "Relying on women themselves to compensate for structural inequities is inherently unfair, even to successful women, and makes less successful women vulnerable to self-blame and victim blaming from others."[79] Although this is undoubtedly true, more pragmatic scholars prefer to point to the positive aspects of these findings, which can, in fact, help women. Social psychologist Linda

Carli argues that more friendly, social behaviors need not be seen as expressing weakness or an excessive desire to please since studies show that communal behaviors (such as smiling) do not suggest low status.[80] She believes that pairing assertive and communal behaviors can allow women to become more successful and that these behaviors can be a source of real power. And while earlier research has suggested that acting tentative, apologetic, and uncertain (the Bully Broads approach) can also reduce the threat competent women pose in male domains, this type of behavior has the negative side-effect of making women appear less competent.[81] Using a friendly, social style provides a more attractive alternative, since it minimizes the threat posed by a woman in a leadership role while still communicating competence and self-confidence.

Whether or not this advice seems offensive or useful, it appears that successful women have taken heed. Research on the leadership styles of men and women has found that highly successful women do employ more communal types of behavior and a softer style than equally successful men.[82] An article in the June 10, 2002, issue of *Fortune* provides a good example of a woman whose social style has clearly helped her gain great power and influence in her field. The article, about the stock research firm Sanford C. Bernstein, described the personal style of the firm's then-chair and CEO, Sally Krawcheck, 37. Sanford C. Bernstein was famous for making tough calls and never pulling its punches. Bernstein would downgrade a stock every other firm was promoting and put out "buy" recommendations on stocks no one else wanted to touch. And the firm had an excellent track record for making good calls, which turns out to be unusual for securities analysts. How did Krawcheck succeed in running such a hardhitting, uncompromising enterprise without suffering the punishment many women encounter for rising too high in their professions? What allowed her to become such an effective leader in a male-dominated field without being called a bitch or being sent to Bully Broads? Explained writer David Rynecki: "She has a gracious, refined manner that masks her toughness."[83]

Smart Women, Smart Choices

How can the information we've presented in this chapter help women ensure that their work is fairly evaluated and free them to pursue their professional and personal ambitions without fear of punishment? We see three courses.

The first and perhaps most obvious is for women to start their own businesses. As the C200 Index figures demonstrated, many women have already given up trying to get fair treatment in conventional business settings and have decided to strike out on their own.

A second possibility is for women who work in male-dominated industries or organizations to do everything they can to reduce their token status: recruiting other women to their fields and their firms; mentoring younger women and helping them rise to higher levels; and working actively to build networks of women that can provide the same benefits men's networks have traditionally provided. These include serving as conduits for information, providing opportunities to establish strong relationships with peers in related fields, and creating sources of mutual support.

The third course involves choosing wisely. Women can seek out firms where a lot of women already do what they want to do. Even in occupations that are mostly male-dominated, some firms will have more women performing those functions than others. Research has shown that a "lifting of sanctions" begins to occur when the percentage of women in a particular environment reaches about 15 percent; when 35 to 40 percent of the people in a given environment are women, the range of behaviors allowed to women widens considerably and the environment can actually become quite hospitable to women.[84] Women can also choose firms with an organizational culture that supports female advancement, discourages stereotyping, and maintains an open and well-structured system for evaluating people.

A well-structured evaluation system is particularly key, and several aspects of how a firm evaluates its people can make a big difference for women. First, women fare better when an evaluation process is more structured, includes clearly understood benchmarks, and is less open to subjective judgments.[85] A situation in which everyone at a particular level, in a particular group, or performing a particular function must meet similar performance benchmarks can work very well for women, for example. Second, women do better and suffer less harm from negative stereotypes about their competence when they are evaluated for their individual work products rather than for their contributions to the work of a team. When a team performs well or achieves a high level of productivity, evaluators can attribute the team's good performance to any one of the team members—and a woman on the team is least likely to be seen as responsible for the group's success.[86]

Choosing wisely also involves feeling entitled to "shop" for a job by doing plenty of research before you decide where to apply—and then asking questions during the application and interview process. In a "Careers" column in *Fortune*, Matthew Boyle offers this advice: "The first step, often overlooked, is to find out what suits you. . . . Then it's time to find out who offers that specific environment." Once you've done this much legwork and you're considering a particular company, Boyle says, "ask how you'll be evaluated." He quotes Thomas Tierney, former CEO of Bain & Co., who said, "It's amazing how many people don't ask that. . . . You're going to sign up for a game and not know how the score is kept?"[87]

Transforming the Context

We don't mean to suggest that only women need to change. As a society, as managers and coworkers and clients and friends, we all need to examine our responses to women when they behave in ways more typically thought of as "masculine." Managers, in particular, need to recognize that stereotypes can influence how they evaluate people without their knowing it. They need to take strong steps to prevent this from happening when women are performing jobs that have traditionally been performed by men or when the proportion of women doing a particular job is very small. They need to establish transparent evaluation processes and criteria that minimize the impact of subjective responses in performance evaluations. By teaching themselves to react differently to women who assert themselves, and consistently applying fixed and well-known standards to the work of everyone they supervise, male or female, managers will free women to promote their own interests without censure or blame. Doing so will help them retain talented employees in whom their firms have invested substantial resources. But they shouldn't do it just because it's good business. As a result of the courage and persistence of one woman, it's also now the law.

In 1982, Ann Hopkins was the only woman out of 88 people being considered for partner at the accounting firm Price Waterhouse. Hopkins had brought in $25 million in business and billed more hours that year than any of the 87 men, yet she was rejected for partner. "Her style was assertive, task-oriented, and instrumental," writes Virginia Valian. "She had all the qualities that gender schemas dictate successful men should have. Her problem was that she wasn't a man."[88] Hopkins sued, pressed her case all the way to the Supreme Court, and won each time. Instrumental in the case was the testimony of Susan Fiske, a research psychologist and expert on how stereotypes can influence people's judgment. Relying on Fiske's testimony and on an *amicus curiae* (friend of the court) brief filed by the American Psychological Association, the Supreme Court wrote:

> In the specific context of sex stereotyping, an employer who acts on the basis of a belief that a woman cannot be aggressive, or that she must not be, has acted on the basis of gender. . . . We are beyond the day when an employer could evaluate employees by assuming or insisting that they matched the stereotype associated with their group. . . . An employer who objects to aggressiveness in women but whose positions require this trait places women in an intolerable Catch 22: out of a job if they behave aggressively and out of a job if they don't. Title VII lifts women out of this bind.[89]

In other words, it is now illegal for "women who do not have a 'soft, genteel way' about them" to be told "that they should wear more makeup and go to charm school." (This is what Ann Hopkins's supervisors said when they rejected her bid for a partnership.)[90]

Although Hopkins had the self-confidence to fight for what she had earned, and changed the law in the process, many women prefer to avoid this kind of struggle and instead back away from asking for what they've rightly earned. The very real risks involved in displaying their competence, trying to ensure that their work is fairly evaluated, and promoting their own ambitions can cause many women so much anxiety that they choose instead to avoid negotiation altogether. We look at the sometimes crippling impact of anxiety on women's reluctance to ask for what they want in the next chapter.

5

FEAR OF ASKING

CATHERINE, A 43-YEAR-OLD LAWYER from Kansas City, had worked in the public sector for most of her career. She never made much money and after almost two decades of public service she decided to switch to the private sector. Although she anticipated a large boost in her earnings, she took the precaution of consulting Linda—a friend from college—before embarking on her search. With Linda's help, she researched what comparable people in comparable jobs were making, identified the salary she should be able to get, and practiced negotiation tactics. She soon found a job she liked, but the offer she received was significantly lower than she'd hoped. Nonetheless, despite all her preparation, Catherine accepted the offer without negotiating. At the critical moment, she said, she "panicked and caved." The prospect of negotiating made her too nervous to go through with her plan.

Gabriela, 50, serves as the general manager of a leading symphony orchestra. This extraordinarily capable woman routinely negotiates with unions, foundations, record companies, and concert halls on behalf of her company. Despite her reputation as a tough and skillful bargainer, though, she cannot bring herself to ask her own board of directors for what she thinks is a fair raise. Every year at the time of her review, she gives the directors a list of salaries earned by individuals in comparable jobs—and every year she accepts whatever they offer her without asking for more. She says, "I'm annoyed that this last time I did it again...I just said thank you. I'm annoyed because I think they'd respect me more if I said something back. They're probably wondering—how good can she be at negotiating for [the orchestra] if she can't even negotiate for herself?" Even though the benefits of asking are obvious to Gabriela (not just more money but greater respect from her board), her anxiety makes it impossible for her to do so.

What's going on here? Catherine had practiced and prepared to negotiate, but at the last moment she couldn't bring herself to try. Gabriela knows that asking for a raise would probably produce a totally positive outcome—both more money *and* more respect—but still she doesn't do it. Why not? Little research to date answers this question, presumably because until now scholars have assumed that people of both sexes approach negotiation using simple economic reasoning: After calculating costs and benefits, they decide to negotiate when the benefits promise to exceed the costs. But how does this explain the large number of women who say they never negotiate at all? How can the simple economics of their lives be so different from those of men, who as we've shown negotiate much more frequently? Remember Linda's study in which 20 percent of the women respondents (the equivalent of 22 million people in the United States) said that they never negotiate at all? Surely it can't be that some women *never* encounter situations that offer net benefits from negotiating. And the economic explanation barely illuminates Gabriela's predicament: Apparently, in asking for a raise for herself, the cost that far outweighs any possible benefit is the internal cost to herself—the intolerably high level of discomfort created by the process of negotiating on her own behalf. Many men also feel nervous about asking for a raise, but for a variety of reasons more of them seem able to overcome their discomfort and ask anyway.

So what's making women so nervous? What are the sources of Catherine's panic and Gabriela's intense discomfort? Why would huge numbers of women strenuously avoid negotiation despite the very real costs of *not* negotiating? This chapter looks at the broad impact of a problem that consistently plagues women, interfering with their ability to ask for and get what they want: Anxiety.

Real Anxiety, Real Barriers

Although researchers have long speculated that women feel more anxiety around negotiating than men and that their anxiety often prevents them from negotiating, until now there hasn't been much research showing that this is true. But Linda's web survey finally established that women do indeed feel more anxiety and discomfort than men feel about negotiating. In the survey, respondents were asked to indicate their level of agreement with statements such as: "I feel anxious when I have to ask for something I want" and "It always takes me a long time to work up the courage to ask for things I want." Using their answers, Linda's team created a scale to measure each respondent's level of "negotiation apprehension." True to expectations, women scored significantly higher than men on this scale, with 2.5 times as many women as men feeling "a great deal of apprehension" about negotiating.[1] (This survey, you'll recall, included respondents of all ages and from a wide range of backgrounds.)

Another part of the survey measured respondents' "negotiation apprehension" in a different way. Respondents were asked to read several negotiation scenarios and then rate how anxious they would feel in each situation. Women expressed significantly more apprehension about negotiating in all the scenarios except one (negotiating with family members about where to go on vacation). Women felt particularly uneasy about scenarios involving work or activities in which they felt less expert than men (such as getting their cars fixed). In those scenarios, twice as many women as men felt "very anxious" or "extremely anxious" about conducting the negotiation.

Approaching this issue from yet another angle, the survey asked respondents to read a list of words and indicate those that described how they thought about negotiation. Men associated words such as *exciting* and *fun* with negotiation far more than women, who were more likely than men to choose words such as *scary*. In a related study, the organizational psychologist Michele Gelfand asked respondents to read a list of metaphors and identify those that captured their experience of negotiation. Where men chose metaphors such as *winning a ballgame* and *a wrestling match,* women were more likely to pick metaphors such as *going to the dentist* as representative of their experience of negotiation.[2]

Linda has also found in her teaching that women express more anxiety than men about negotiation. Linda frequently asks her negotiation students to write down their reasons for taking her course. While men tend to give answers like "I want to improve my negotiation skills," women often say things like "I hate negotiating and I want to learn how to do it better" or "I tend to avoid negotiating because it makes me so uncomfortable; I hope to change that." The differences between the responses of male and female students are so constant and predictable, Linda can almost always identify the sex of the students from their answers without looking at their names.

Extreme discomfort with negotiating can afflict even extremely powerful and successful women. In 2000, Linda conducted a negotiation workshop with about 20 female physician executives—women doctors in high-level managerial positions such as the chief medical officer of a hospital and the vice president of an insurance company. In the course of the workshop, Linda surveyed these physicians to discover their feelings when they negotiate. A full two-thirds reported that negotiating made them very nervous and a total of 86 percent expressed strong negative feelings about negotiating, such as saying it makes them feel insecure and defensive. Only 14 percent of these accomplished and successful women expressed any positive emotions about negotiating, such as saying that it makes them feel powerful and assertive.

The Consequences of Anxiety

Women's greater anxiety about negotiating doesn't just make the process of negotiating harder for them (although it does that too). It also prevents women from negotiating as much as men do. The survey revealed that similar levels of anxiety prove to be far more disabling for women than for men—more than three times as crippling. When a woman's anxiety jacks up 25 percent, for example, the likelihood that she'll go through with a negotiation decreases by 11 percent. But a 25 percent increase in a man's anxiety decreases the likelihood he'll ask for what he wants only by 3 percent. So women not only experience more anxiety about negotiation, their anxiety presents more of a stumbling block for them than it does for men.[3] Illustrating the different ways in which men and women respond, David, 34, a hedge fund manager, said that he knows he can make progress in a negotiation if he can "endure the moment of discomfort." Martha, the career counselor, in contrast, said that she often avoids negotiating altogether because of "the personal expense psychically and physically." The prospect of that "moment of discomfort" discourages her from negotiating at all.

This urge in women to avoid negotiating is so strong that a man in Pittsburgh has launched a successful business negotiating the purchase of cars for other people. Not surprisingly, most of his clients are women— women willing to pay significant sums of money to avoid the unpleasantness of negotiating. It's not that these women are afraid they'll negotiate badly and end up paying too much for their cars. The fees they pay for the service eat up whatever savings their "professional negotiator" wins for them. They just don't want to have to negotiate. A study by the business professors Devavrat Purohit and Harris Sondak confirmed that saving money is not a driving goal for women in this situation, and that they are willing to pay as much as $1,353 to avoid negotiating the price of a car, compared to half as much, $666, for men.[4] This may explain why 63 percent of Saturn car buyers are women—drawn to Saturn's strategy of not negotiating prices.[5]

Anxiety and the Primacy of Relationships

What causes women's greater feelings of discomfort and anxiety around negotiating? Why are men more likely to concentrate on the issues in a dispute or the advantages they can win for themselves, while women are more likely to amplify the negative side of negotiating? In addition to the reasons we've already discussed, many women worry about their competence at negotiating: They worry that they'll lose control of the negotiation and make mistakes, that they'll concede too quickly or be thrown off guard or become intimidated.

Later in the book, we describe techniques for women to build up their self-confidence around negotiating and strengthen their control over the negotiation process—techniques that have been shown to substantially increase women's negotiating success. But before we explore those solutions, we need to understand one of the major causes of female anxiety around negotiating—women's fear that asking for something they want may harm their relationship with the person they need to ask. This fear often causes women's anxiety to surge, making it much harder for them to step over the "threshold for asking" and try to negotiate.

Extensive literature in virtually every discipline in the social and behavioral sciences concludes that relationships play a more central role in the lives of women than in the lives of men.[6] This has been shown to be true for small children and teenagers as well as for women and men in all walks of life and at every stage of adulthood. What this means is that women see the world—and themselves—through "relationship-colored" glasses. Looking at life through these glasses, they don't separate the relationships involved from the particular issues being considered in working out a business deal, solving a problem at work, bargaining with a merchant, or making decisions with a friend or family member.

Let's look at some of this research. A 1982 study by the psychologists William McGuire and Claire McGuire interviewed 560 children in grades one through eleven. Each child was given five minutes to tell the interviewer about him- or herself. The researchers found that the girls were far more likely than the boys to describe other people in their conceptualizations of themselves.[7] A 1988 study by two researchers at the National Institutes of Health, Robert McCrae and Paul Costa Jr., turned up similar results among elderly people.[8] Other research by the psychologists Jane Bybee, Marion Glick, and Edward Zigler asked people to describe their "ideal self." They found that women were more likely than men to include relationships in their descriptions.[9]

In one fascinating study, the psychologists Stephanie Clancy and Stephen Dollinger recruited 201 college students to take part in a study for extra credit. They instructed these students to collect 12 photographs that "describe who you are as you see yourself." The students themselves could take the photographs, they could ask other people to take the photographs, or they could use photographs that had already been taken. Clancy and Dollinger found that male students were more likely to submit pictures that captured them engaged in an activity (such as playing a sport), displaying prized possessions (such as a car), or alone. Female students were more likely to submit pictures of themselves with other people. The authors concluded that women tend to define themselves more in terms of their relationships, while men tend to define themselves more in terms of their abilities and accomplishments—terms reflective of their individuality, independence, and separateness.[10] Another researcher, Sarah Taylor, repeated this study with a class of ninth graders, with similar results: Girls were almost twice as likely to submit pictures that showed them in connection with others (69 percent of the girls' photos were about connection, compared to only 38 percent of the boys' photos) and 50 percent of the boys' pictures showed them alone, whereas just 18 percent of the girls' pictures were solo shots.[11]

Although researchers disagree about the role of genetics in the different importance of relationships to men and women, the treatment of male and female children by adults at the very least encourages it.[12] Researchers have found evidence, for example, that parents discuss emotions and feelings with their daughters more than with their sons, thereby teaching girls to be more attentive to the feelings of those around them and, by implication, to take more responsibility for those feelings.[13] This is a lesson that girls may also be explicitly taught. Sandy, the former commercial lending officer, was a talented gymnast when she was young. Most of the other girls on Sandy's team specialized in one event, but Sandy was talented enough to perform well in several events. At one point, her coach took her aside and told her that Cindy, one of her teammates, was upset because Sandy was so good at Cindy's event. The message could not have been clearer: Sandy's achievements and potential were less important than the feelings of another girl. More generally, Sandy was being told that she needed to curb her own ambitions—she needed to strive and hope for less—in order to protect the feelings of the people around her. It's hard to imagine a coach telling a male athlete to perform less well to spare the feelings of another boy.

Different Views of the Self

Whatever the causes, the different importance men and women place on relationships has led psychologists to conclude that men and women see themselves differently or have different "self-schemas" or "construals of the self."[14] Psychologists define a self-schema as your internal sense of who you are and what you're like—an interior self-portrait made up of how you experience your own personality and how you believe other people see you.[15] Your self-schema influences the ways in which you perceive the world around you—it provides a "filter" through which you process information, understand events, and organize your memories. It is also a prime motivator of your behavior.

In an impressive piece of scholarship that ties together research findings from many disciplines, the social psychologists Susan Cross and Laura Madson argue that men have more independent self-schemas and women have more interdependent ones. People with independent self-schemas—like many men—define themselves in terms of their distinction from others and pay less attention to the impact of their actions on the people around them. They focus on promoting their personal preferences and goals and seek out relationships that tend to be more instrumental than intimate, more numerous, and less personally binding.[16] People with interdependent self-schemas, in contrast, define themselves in terms of their connections to others—"relationships are viewed as integral parts of the person's very being."[17] They see their actions in terms of how they will influence people around them, and one of their primary goals is to develop strong relationships and protect them.

Not surprisingly, men's and women's different self-schemas can have a profound impact on how they feel about asking for what they want.[18] In one study, Lisa Barron observed male and female students as they participated in a job negotiation. Afterward, she interviewed them to understand their goals and strategies. Based on these interviews, she divided the participants into two categories: those who saw the negotiation as a way of advancing their interests and those who saw the negotiation as a way of furthering their acceptance by others (such as the hiring manager or others in the organization). Barron found that men made up 72 percent and women made up only 28 percent of those in the "advancement" category while men made up only 29 percent and women made up 71 percent of those in the "acceptance" category.[19] This strongly suggests that men are more likely to see the "instrumental" side of a negotiation (they see it as "just business") and women are more likely to focus on the interpersonal side, where relationship concerns are salient.

Our interviews produced numerous examples of this different point of view. Becky, the journalist, said, "When I go into a negotiation...I think about the relationship first....I think about maintaining that relationship before I think about my own [needs] really." David, the hedge fund manager, said just the opposite: "I don't worry about hurting feelings in a professional context."

Negotiation Equals Conflict

Women's strong urge to foster and protect relationships can make many of them fear that a disagreement about the outcome of a negotiation— a disagreement about the issues being discussed—actually represents a personal conflict between the negotiators involved. Negotiation scholars Deborah Kolb and Gloria Coolidge write: "Negotiation, conceived as a context in which conflict and competition are important, may not be a comfortable place for many women" because it puts them "in opposition to others."[20] That is, women often feel uncomfortable negotiating even in situations in which this type of controlled conflict is expected and appropriate, because promoting conflict is foreign to their self-schemas and their sense of identity. Men, for the most part, are less likely to believe that a disagreement about issues also means a conflict between the negotiators. They also typically worry less about the damaging effects of conflict.

Researchers believe that childhood socialization and styles of play create these different attitudes toward disagreement and conflict. By about age three, they point out, girls prefer playing with girls and boys prefer playing with boys. This preference intensifies with age—by age six, children play with other children of the same sex about eleven times as much as they do with children of the opposite sex.[21] This is important because boys and girls play differently—and learn different things from the ways in which they play.

Girls tend to play in small groups and form close relationships with one or two other girls. Their most important goals involve increasing intimacy and preserving connection.[22] As a result, girls, much more than boys, engage in activities in which everyone is equal and there are no winners and losers.[23] When there is a dispute during play, girls will frequently end a game in order to protect the relationships among the players.[24] Girls make polite suggestions to one another and prefer to agree rather than disagree. From these forms of play, girls develop a strong preference for cooperation and for avoiding conflict, and they discover that avoiding conflict can be a successful strategy for achieving their important goal of maintaining close relationships.

Boys, in contrast, play in larger groups than girls and their play is rougher.[25] Boys issue direct orders to one another far more than girls do; and boys' play involves more competition, conflict, and struggle for dominance.[26] When boys talk, their agenda is one of self-assertion.[27] If there is a dispute in a game, boys deal with it by implementing agreed-upon rules.[28] Through these types of behavior, boys learn that they can be aggressive in their interactions without really hurting each other or damaging their relationships. They also learn that competition is fun, that those on the opposite sides of a contest can still be friends, and that asserting themselves can be a successful strategy for attaining their goals (such as winning the game they're playing). In the process, they discover that they can interact with others in aggressive ways without harming their relationships.[29] Even more important, they learn *how* to do this—how to oppose others without harming their relationships. In her 1994 book *Talking from 9 to 5*, Deborah Tannen describes the following situation: "A woman told me she watched with distaste and distress as her office-mate heatedly argued with another colleague about whose division would suffer necessary cuts in funding, but she went into shock when, shortly after this altercation, the two men were as friendly as ever. 'How can you pretend that fight never happened?' she asked the man who shared her office. He responded,

'Who's pretending it never happened?' as puzzled by her question as she was by his behavior. 'It happened,' he said, 'and it's over.' "[30]

With fewer opportunities to engage in "friendly competition" and perhaps both a natural inclination and strong social reinforcement to develop and safeguard relationships, girls and women may be slower to learn how to do this. Martha, the career counselor, said: "I do think [for men] there's that sense of 'this isn't personal, we're on the soccer field, this is a battle, but once we step off we will be fine.' That kind of depersonalization of the interaction is something that I definitely don't feel like I got as a girl growing up. I felt like it was instilled upon me that it was all personal." Because women have had more limited experience of conflict than men, they have also had fewer opportunities to learn how to deal with conflict in ways that *don't* threaten their relationships—they don't have those skills.[31]

Lynn, a 25-year-old professional nanny, moved into an apartment with two roommates who had already been living there for some time. Lynn's bedroom was extremely small and she wanted to move a bookcase and a desk into the living room, but her roommates had left no space for her. Afraid that she would be branded a "troublemaker" and that her relationship with them would start off badly, she never asked whether room could be made for her things. "I worry that if a conflict occurs when I'm in a negotiation in any realm it will cause stress in the relationship," she explained. "If the relationship is important... you don't want to hurt the relationship with the people you're negotiating with." Deborah Tannen, in her 1990 book *You Just Don't Understand*, observed that when faced with a choice between holding fast to personal goals and backing down from a request in order to preserve harmony in a relationship, many women will choose the latter.[32] Although men often do this as well, evidence suggests that women do it more.

The strength of women's need to avoid any hint of conflict can influence their behavior even when there's no need for them to care about their relationship with the other negotiator. Martha, the career counselor, tells a story that illustrates how a woman's reflexive impulse to worry about relationships can prevail even when all objective evidence indicates that the relationship at stake is not important:

I remember getting into an awful dispute with somebody who was
handling some money for my mother. He disappeared basically after
he started handling it, and eventually I got it back. But I remember a
friend of mine saying, "Why are you so worried that he's not going to
like you? You know this guy should be in jail." And there was that kind
of mentality that said in addition to getting the money back I also had
to make sure that I kept everybody happy, and that's a real struggle....
He wasn't part of my social circle. I never ran into him. He probably
should have been in jail.

The impulse to pay attention to relationships is so deeply imbedded in
women's psyches that they rarely see any of their interactions as *not* having
a relationship dimension, Deborah Kolb and Gloria Coolidge contend.[33]
So when they find themselves in situations, like Martha's, in which there is
no potential for future interaction and the opinion of the other negotiator
can have no impact on their lives, they don't make the adjustment that
says "okay, I don't need to care about this relationship"—because caring is
the routine way in which they approach things.

Women also worry more about how asking for something may
threaten a relationship because women typically suffer more when their
relationships suffer.[34] This is because the self-esteem of people with interdependent self-schemas depends in good part on the relationships they
have with others, research has shown.[35] As a result, a rocky business interaction or a negotiation from which the other negotiator leaves unhappy
may present a painful challenge to a woman's self-esteem. In her book
Toward a New Psychology of Women, professor of psychiatry Jean Baker
Miller explains that "women's sense of self becomes very much organized
around being able to make and then to maintain affiliations and relationships. Eventually, for many women the threat of disruption of connections
is perceived not just as a loss of a relationship but as something closer to a
total loss of self."[36]

The self-esteem of people with independent self-schemas suffers less
when relationships are threatened. Several studies support this supposi-
tion. One shows that not being forgiven by a friend damages a woman's
self-esteem more than it damages a man's, for example.[37] Another found

that for women there is a positive association between self-esteem and their perceived degree of personal "connectedness" to others—but no association between these for men.[38] No one likes to be rejected, of course, but rejection seems to hit women harder on average than it hits men—and seems to represent more of a deterrent to their asking.

The End of Anxiety

Women's fears are not entirely unfounded, of course. Aggressive negotiation behavior, such as making extreme demands, refusing to concede, and bullying the other side, can stir up a lot of conflict and damage relationships. But this doesn't mean that women should avoid negotiation altogether. Nor does it mean that women should forget about their anxieties, "act like men," and ignore the impact of their behavior on their relationships. Instead, women need to acknowledge that they almost always have dual goals in a negotiation—issue-related goals and relationship goals—and that they need to find ways to achieve both. Fortunately, the past 20 years of negotiation research have shown that everyone, both men and women, can benefit by embracing both of these goals when they negotiate.

From Contest to Cooperation

The first step toward achieving both issue-related and relationship goals in a negotiation—and reducing negotiation anxiety—involves reframing the interaction. This means approaching it not as a contest or a competition, but as a chance to share ideas with the opposing negotiator and work together to solve problems that affect you both. In their book *The Shadow Negotiation: How Women Can Master the Hidden Agendas That Determine Bargaining Success*, Deborah Kolb and Judith Williams, both negotiating scholars, explain that when negotiators "take steps to insure that the negotiation conversation unfolds as a collaborative dialogue rather than an adversarial contest," the process of negotiation can become far more productive and lead to "solutions that would never have occurred to anyone

independently."[39] The influential negotiation book *Getting to Yes*, by Roger
Fisher and William Ury, first introduced this approach to a wider audience
and provides numerous suggestions for how to make it work. One of the
principal strategies recommended by Fisher and Ury involves using what
they call "interest-based" rather than "position-based" bargaining. They
draw on the writings of early management theorist Mary Parker Follett to
demonstrate the difference between the two:

> Consider the story of two men quarreling in a library. One wants the
> window open and the other wants it closed. They bicker back and
> forth about how much to leave it open: a crack, halfway, three quarters
> of the way. No solution satisfies them both. Enter the librarian. She
> asks one why he wants the window open: "To get some fresh air." She
> asks the other why he wants it closed: "To avoid the draft." After think-
> ing a minute, she opens wide a window in the next room, bringing in
> fresh air without a draft.[40]

The key to this example is that the two men were arguing about their
positions (whether the window should be open or closed), which were in-
compatible, rather than about their *interests* (the needs and wishes under-
lying those positions). The librarian, rather than siding with one of the
two positions, instead tried to find a way to satisfy the interests of both
men, and ended up making both of them happy. This can be a great approach for maintaining and even improving relationships because it fo-
cuses the negotiators' efforts on ways to "attack the problem"—figure out
a good solution—without "attacking each other" by fighting each others'
positions.[41] Techniques for doing this include:

- asking diagnostic questions (what problems does opening or
  closing the window create for you?);
- sharing information about your own interests (the stuffiness in
  here is making me uncomfortable; I have a cold and shouldn't sit
  in a draft);
- unbundling the issues or adding issues (is there a way for you to
  get some fresh air without me sitting in a draft?);

- brainstorming about possible solutions rather than defending established positions (Let's try to think of ways to satisfy both of our needs).[42]

These techniques appeal to many women because they don't put relationships in jeopardy—and can significantly decrease their anxiety about negotiating. Women also appreciate this approach because working together and fostering cooperation are already things that many women like to do and do well. Their childhood forms of play make them skillful at these kinds of behavior and—this point is worth stressing—make them comfortable with them. When women need to change their behavior dramatically or act in ways that feel inconsistent with who they are, this tends to ramp up their anxiety, not lessen it. Trying to understand the needs, interests, and concerns of the other side often allows women to get to know the other negotiators better. This doesn't merely produce superior outcomes, it can actually improve their relationships. (We look more closely at the advantages women bring to negotiation and how their cooperative approach can produce better results for all parties in chapter 8.)

But paying attention to the interests of the other side doesn't mean over-identifying with their needs. Susannah, the political strategist, believes that the intense anxiety she experiences going into a negotiation comes in part from an exaggerated identification with the person on the other side of the table. "I just feel so guilty," she said. "I worry that I'm putting them in a difficult situation, especially if I'm asking for something that I think will be hard for them to give to me. I'm just wracked with guilt." Heather, the pastor, remarked that in many cases women have "negotiated themselves out of their position before they even open their mouths. . . . Before even the get-go, we've decided not to ask for something, because we're worried that it's going to be too much to ask." So another means of controlling anxiety when approaching a negotiation is to trust the other negotiators to take care of themselves. Most people have no trouble saying no when they can't or don't want to do something, but they're often eager to say yes if they can—and if they know what you want.

A friend of Sara's named Jane told Sara that she was hesitant to ask for a big raise because she thought it would be hard for her boss to give her so much. Sara asked Jane how she feels when one of her own employees comes to her with a request, even one she can't fully satisfy. Without pausing to consider, Jane said, "Well, it's my job to take care of my employees, do what I can to keep them, and make them happy." When Sara pointed out the inconsistency of her response, Jane recognized the contradiction. She also felt better about asking for as much as she wanted—and got the raise she wanted.

Another useful strategy for women can be recognizing that they don't need to bar emotion from their negotiations completely. Many women worry about becoming emotional in a negotiation and that this will be a mistake. The key to expressing emotion in a negotiation is to use appropriate emotions—emotions that can help achieve your ends. Expressing negative emotions (such as anger or frustration) by banging on a table, yelling at the other side, or becoming defensive are rarely effective in persuading another person to see your point of view. Bursting into tears doesn't usually work well either. But communicating positive feelings (such as cheerfulness) by smiling and speaking in a calm voice can be enormously effective because emotions have been shown to be contagious—one side can actually "catch" the emotions of the other. So communicating a positive, let's-work-together-to-figure-this-out attitude can often reframe an interaction that starts out on a combative note and change both the mood of the other negotiator and the overall tone of the negotiation.[43] Research has also shown that people in good moods think more creatively, are more likely to engage in cooperative strategies such as exchanging information, and find more innovative ways to solve problems. They're also less likely to resort to competitive strategies and contentious tactics.[44]

Using humor can be another effective way to influence the tone of a negotiation. Elaine, the district court judge, described relying on humor both when she was a lawyer and now that she is a judge because "humor has a way of leveling things, not leveling exactly, but . . . it relaxes people." And when people are relaxed, the anxiety of everyone in the room decreases.

Getting Help

There's another way to deal with anxiety about damaging a relationship by asking for too much: Get help when help is available. Eleanor, the literature professor and biographer, negotiated the contracts for her first two books by herself. The editor who bought them was extremely powerful and well regarded, and Eleanor's fear of offending this editor made her hesitate to push for too much money. "When it came down to it," Eleanor said, "I backed down because I didn't want her to hate me." After Sara interviewed Eleanor and talked to her about our research, Eleanor hired an agent to negotiate the contract for her third book, something she'd been reluctant to do because she thought her editor wouldn't like it. Not only was the editor fine with Eleanor having hired an agent, the agent negotiated an advance for Eleanor's third book that was *more than ten times the amount she'd gotten for the second book.* This gives us a pretty good idea of how much money her relationship concerns prompted her to leave on the table in those first two contract negotiations. It also gives us a sense of how much women in general sacrifice because they worry that pressing for what they want will damage a relationship.

Disarming the Tough Guys

But what about when you run into opposing negotiators who resist taking a cooperative approach to the process—a particularly anxiety-producing scenario for many women? Roger Fisher and William Ury then recommend resorting to what they call "negotiation jujitsu," a term derived from the ancient martial art of jujitsu. In jujitsu, combatants "avoid pitting their strength against each other directly and instead try to step out of the way and use their competitors' strength to achieve their own ends."[45] "Negotiation jujitsu" provides a way to defuse a conflict when other negotiators take a competitive approach, stake out an inflexible position, or attack your position or you. In a situation like this, a direct counterattack would most likely lead to an escalation of conflict, with both sides degenerating into personal attacks, negative emotions, and positional bargaining.[46] Far more effective is to meet this type of competitive approach by doing what William Ury calls "stepping to their side."[47] Stepping to their side involves continuing to treat the other negotiators with respect despite their combative attitude. It involves listening to their arguments, acknowledging the legitimacy of their opinions, and agreeing with them wherever you can. In addition to reducing the conflict between you, it allows you to focus on their interests rather than on their positions—and invites them to do the same for you.

Here's an example of how this can work. Suppose you want to reduce your work week and work only Monday through Thursday, with Fridays off. When you ask your boss whether this will be possible, he responds by yelling, "Absolutely not!" Rather than shouting back (as many men might do) or becoming emotional and backing down (as many women might), an effective strategy would be to change the tone of the conversation by responding calmly or with humor: "Wow, you really hate that idea! I guess it would create a lot of problems for you." In this way, you acknowledge your boss's strong feelings and show that you've listened to him. But you haven't conceded; instead you've moved from being an adversary to being on his side—you're trying to see his point of view. This is effective because it is hard to argue with someone who is on your side.

The next step involves reframing the conflict from a "positions" orientation to an "interests" orientation—getting your boss to think beyond his reflexive position ("absolutely not!") so together you can search for a solution that works for both of you.[48] A good way to do this would be to ask a question, such as: "What problems does my absence on Fridays create?" This accomplishes two things: It gives you information and it moves the interaction away from arguing and disagreeing and toward problem solving. Once your boss has explained why he thinks giving you Fridays off is impossible ("no one else with your expertise is in on Fridays if we have an emergency"), a good response would be to acknowledge your boss's situation ("now I understand your reaction"). Then follow up with a question that addresses your interests: "But I want to spend more time with my children (or study for a test that would qualify me for a higher position, or take a course that meets on Fridays). Do you have any ideas about how I could get a little more time away from work without causing you a lot of problems?" This approach continues the process of "stepping to his side" while promoting mutual cooperation and problem solving.

Although these techniques may not always get you what you want (it just may not be possible for you to take time off without really harming your employer), they do protect your relationships while you're negotiating. In this example, both you and your boss can walk away from the negotiation with an increased understanding of each other and the knowledge that together you can try to solve problems cooperatively and creatively. This can give a huge boost to your future working relationship.

Mercy, 51, the director of space management for a large state university in the Southwest, described how this approach has worked for her:

> With a number of vice presidents here on campus...they initially came in demanding and expecting to get instantly whatever they requested, and they'd heard the nasty word "no."...After negotiating with them and finding some sort of solution for them, not nearly what they wanted, but certainly a viable solution, there have been a number of times where they...walked away with a sort of new respect or a different level of understanding of my job, and respect comes with that. They didn't get what they wanted, but they were happy with the outcome.

Sara had a similar experience when she worked at a consulting firm. As the senior editor and writer working on a large-scale training program that included video scripts, case studies, workbooks, and teaching manuals, Sara had to rely heavily on the firm's word processing department for rapid turnaround on several sets of revisions. Shortly before the deadline for the materials to be delivered to the client, the word processing department made a sizable mistake that delayed delivery. After the problem was sorted out and the materials were completed, Sara asked for a meeting with the head of the word processing department and his supervisor. As soon as she entered the room, she realized that the two of them were steeled for a fight, expecting her to blame them entirely for the mishap. Rather than staking out a strong negative position such as "you screwed up and made me look bad," Sara presented her interests in a calm, concil-iatory voice. She needed to understand what had gone wrong so that she could explain it to the consultant who was running the project, she said, and she wanted to figure out what both she and the word processing de-partment could do differently next time in order to avoid making a simi-lar mistake. As soon as the other two realized that she wasn't going to attack them, they relaxed. The three of them talked back and forth about possible process changes and without raised voices or hard feelings reached an agreement about how to do things differently in the future. Not only did this improve the production process, it improved Sara's rela-tionship with the head of the word processing department and made her future working interactions with him more pleasant and productive.

Although taking a cooperative approach to negotiating can eliminate some of the causes for women's anxiety, even when women negotiate well they often get less than a man might get in the same situation. This is be-cause women often don't ask for as much as they can get, and because peo-ple on the other side of the table often resist conceding as much to a woman as they might concede to a man under identical circumstances. We look at these factors impeding women—the pressures that prevent women from setting higher goals for themselves and the limits society places on how much a woman can get in a negotiation—in the next two chapters.

6

LOW GOALS AND SAFE TARGETS

MEN ACQUIRE MORE economic resources than women—they earn higher salaries, own more property, boast bigger stock portfolios, and leave behind larger estates when they die. Women also fare badly when it comes to noneconomic resources, such as leisure time. One study shows, for example, that even when both spouses work full-time, a huge percentage of women do most of the housework and childcare, leaving them little time for themselves.[1] Although we can point to deep historical and sociological reasons for women coming up short both economically and otherwise, we're convinced that negotiation also plays a critical part in this seemingly universal phenomenon. Not only are women less likely than men to ask for more than they have—they usually come away with less than men even when they do negotiate. This is particularly true in single-issue, or "distributive," negotiations, in which only one item, such as a salary increase or the price of a car, is being discussed.[2] Even among Ivy League MBA students conducting negotiations, a group you might expect to include some of the toughest, most capable (and competitive) young women in America, Linda, Hannah Riley, and Kathleen McGinn found that women produce worse results than those produced by men (on average 30 percent worse).[3]

In the introduction, we described how much women can lose over the course of their careers by neglecting to negotiate their starting salaries. But just negotiating isn't always enough—how well they negotiate and how much they're able to get also make a big difference. In a study demonstrating this, the business school professors Barry Gerhart and Sara Rynes looked at the salaries obtained by more than 200 students graduating from an Ivy League MBA program. They found that the men negotiated starting salaries that were 4.3 percent higher on average than the original offers they received while women negotiated increases that were only 2.7 percent higher than their first offers.[4] This means that the men's payoff for this single negotiation was 59 percent greater than the women's (4.3 is 59 percent higher than 2.7). If the men at every stage of their careers consistently negotiate raises that are 59 percent higher than the raises women in the same positions negotiate, by the time they retire the men will have earned far more than the women.

To get a sense of how much more, consider another example: Say a man and a woman both receive identical first job offers at age 22 for $35,000. The man, by negotiating, increases his offer by 4.3 percent to $36,505, while the woman also negotiates but can only increase her offer by 2.7 percent to $35,945. Although the difference between the two figures—only $560—may seem small, let's look at what happens if they both negotiate identical percentage increases every year until they retire at age 65 (the man raising his salary by 4.3 percent each year and the woman raising hers by only 2.7 percent). By the time they retire, his salary will be $213,941, while hers will be only $110,052—about half of what he's making. Even worse, if he banks the difference between their salaries in an account earning 3 percent a year, by the time they retire he will have accumulated $2,120,731. And these calculations don't account for the woman's losses in retirement and pension benefits, which are typically tied to earnings. This is a perfect example of the "accumulation of disadvantage" phenomenon: The difference between a 2.7 percent raise and a 4.3 percent raise doesn't seem that big. But molehills can rapidly become mountains—and small differences add up to huge disparities over time.

This chapter examines why women often get less than men when they negotiate, focusing on their tendency to ask for too little and concede too much or too soon. It looks at women's lack of confidence in their negotiating abilities and explores ways for women to establish—and attain—ambitious goals for themselves when they negotiate.

Goals, Goals, Goals

Delia and John, both medical researchers with Ph.D.s, were hired by the same medical school at the same time, right out of graduate school. They were both offered the same starting salaries and the same basic budgets to set up their labs. Delia negotiated and successfully raised both her salary and her budget a modest amount. John also negotiated for a higher salary and bigger budget, but he asked for more than Delia asked for—and got more. In addition, John asked for a salary for a full-time research assistant. Having both the bigger budget and the regular assistant boosted John's research productivity substantially. As a result, he was promoted more rapidly than Delia, and the gap between their salaries widened even further.

Why do men outperform women in negotiations? Targets—the goals men and women take into negotiations—have been shown to make a critical difference.[5] John went into his negotiation aiming to get more than Delia aimed to get, he asked for more, and he got more. Extensive research on the relationship between goal-setting and performance—for example, among dieters and recovering addicts—has found that setting concrete, challenging goals consistently improves results.[6] Research confirms that this is true for negotiating as well: People who go into negotiations with more ambitious targets tend to get more of what they want than people who go in with more moderate goals. In the Ivy League MBA study mentioned above, Linda and her colleagues observed that a 30 percent increase in a person's goal going into a negotiation produced, at a minimum, a 10 percent increase in the negotiated amount he or she was able to obtain.[7] This means that if one person goes into a salary negotiation with a target of $50,000, for example, and another goes in with a target of $65,000 (which is 30 percent higher), the person hoping to get $50,000 might get $50,000, but the other person, who aimed higher, would have a good chance of coming away with $55,000 (10 percent more).

Higher targets have been shown to improve negotiation outcomes for two reasons: They influence the "first offer" a person makes in a negotiation and they influence how quickly or slowly a person concedes from his or her opening position. A first offer is like an opening move in a chess game—it signals a player's intentions, gives an idea of what kind of player he or she is, and sets the stage for everything that follows. First offers play a critical role in producing good negotiated outcomes because they influence the other negotiators' expectations for what you will accept and provide a starting point for the interaction. They also tend to lead to higher final agreements. The impact of higher targets on first offers was demonstrated by another study Linda conducted with Hannah Riley and Kathleen McGinn in which they found a direct one-to-one correlation between targets and first offers—meaning that each dollar increase in a person's goal translated into an increase in his or her first offer of about a dollar. So the higher the goal, the higher the first offer, and the higher the first offer, the higher the likely negotiated settlement.[8]

Setting high goals is also important because a lack of ambitious goals contributes to another negotiation misstep particularly common among women: conceding too much and conceding too quickly. Someone with relatively modest goals often makes concessions faster than someone with higher goals, who will frequently hold out longer to get more.[9] People who go into a negotiation thinking only about their "bottom line"—the minimum they will accept—may concede as soon as they receive an offer equal or close to that bottom line.[10]

Carol, 38, a doctor, described negotiating with her husband when they bought the house in which they live. "There were two houses that I liked," she explained:

I liked the house that we bought, and I liked another house. I had narrowed it down to the two, and in retrospect over time it's become clear to me that we probably would have been better off in that other house just because of some of the things it offered that ours doesn't have . . . but my husband really didn't like the other house and he really wanted the one that we got, and so we went with it. But you know, I kind of wonder if I should have fought harder for that other house....I did not persist at all....I was happy that he liked one of the five that I had picked.

Carol's goal and bottom line going into this negotiation had been the same: merely for her husband to agree to buy one of the houses she liked. If she had set a higher goal—for him to recognize and consider the comparative virtues of each choice or to understand her reasons for preferring one of the houses over the others—she might not have conceded so quickly. She might also have come away with a superior outcome and been spared, years later, the regret of realizing that they might have made a better choice.

In contrast, people who go into a negotiation focusing on the top amount they'd like to earn or the best possible outcome tend to hold out longer.[11] Kirk, a television producer, moved from Chicago to a smaller city in the Pacific Northwest when his wife changed jobs. Because of his talent and experience, he quickly found himself at one of the major network affiliates talking to the station manager about a job. Kirk had won several prizes for his work in Chicago, but he knew that this was a smaller television market and he might not be able to earn as much as he'd been making before. But he also knew that the station was engaged in a fierce battle for market share with its competitors and that the station manager really wanted to hire him. So he asked for $85,000, thinking he'd probably get $60,000 or at most $70,000. When the station manager seemed to balk, instead of conceding, Kirk said, "That's what the market is telling me I can get right now." The station manager leaned back in his chair, scratched his head, and finally said, "Okay, I'll give it to you. I think you're worth it." If Kirk had asked for less, obviously he would have gotten less, and if he'd backed down when the station manager resisted his original figure, he would have gotten less too. He later learned that he was making $25,000 more than any other producer at the station. Although Kirk's credentials undoubtedly accounted for some of this difference, both the high target he took into his negotiation with the station manager and his resistance to conceding surely made a big difference as well.

Why the Differences?

We know that women typically set less aggressive goals than men, make more modest first offers,[12] and concede more rapidly. One of Linda's studies with Hannah Riley and Kathleen McGinn found male negotiators setting goals that were about 15 percent more aggressive than those of female negotiators in comparable circumstances.[13] Looking simply at the salary realm (although setting high targets produces better results in almost any type of negotiation), the consistency with which women's lower goals limit how much women are paid has persuaded some researchers that the gender gap in wages could be all but eliminated if men and women were to set comparable goals.[14]

But why does this happen? We've already discussed some of the causes: Women frequently feel unsure about what they deserve, worry that asking for too much may threaten a relationship, or fear that the people around them will react badly if they ask for too much. In addition, women tend to be less optimistic than men about what they can get from a negotiation. They also feel less comfortable than men with risk taking and often lack confidence in their negotiating ability—making them ask only for things that will be easy to get.

The Power of Optimism

Angela, the community development bank marketing director, thinks that men ask for more, in part, because "in their heads the pie is a lot bigger than it is in women's heads." Research seems to bear this out. In one study, male and female business students considered a hypothetical job description for a management position and estimated the highest amount the company would pay for this position. Male students estimated this amount to be much greater than female students thought it would be.[15]

In another study, students were given detailed information about the facts of a dispute in a pretrial negotiation and then assigned to play the role of either plaintiff or defendant. As part of the exercise, the students were asked to estimate the amount that a judge or jury would award the plaintiff should the case go to trial. When men were playing the plaintiff role, their estimates of this amount were significantly greater than the estimates of women playing the same role—9 percent higher, on average, which in a large settlement could mean a difference of hundreds of thousands of dollars.[16]

This greater optimism about what is available and possible gives men a powerful advantage at the negotiating table. Because they believe (rightly or wrongly) that they are in a better bargaining position than women feel themselves to be, men often develop more aggressive targets, present more extreme first offers, and make fewer concessions. In many cases, this means they also come away from the bargaining table with a better deal for themselves or for their side of the negotiation.

Why are men more optimistic about available rewards? Not much research has been done in this area, but one area of study called "risk assessment" allows us to speculate a little. Psychologists who study risk assessment measure people's perceptions about the degree of danger posed by a range of substances (nuclear waste, asbestos, tap water), activities (sun tanning, irradiating food, burning fossil fuels, commercial air travel), and public health and security threats (bacteria in food, AIDS, terrorism). In every case but one (the burning of fossil fuels—an odd exception), men see these things as less risky than women.[17] Revealingly, however, whites also see them as less risky than nonwhites. This suggests to researchers that these differences stem from sociopolitical and cultural influences rather than from biological differences between men and women. As Paul Slovic, an expert on risk assessment, explained, "Perhaps white males see less risk in the world because they create, manage, control and benefit from many of the major technologies and activities. Perhaps women and non-white men see the world as more dangerous because in many ways they are more vulnerable, because they benefit less from many of its technologies and institutions, and because they have less power and control over what happens in their communities and their lives."[18]

Similarly, we can wonder whether men's experience has taught them different things about the availability of resources. Since men do accumulate more financial resources than women in their lifetimes, perhaps they learn to expect more. Maybe men believe that more is available to them in part because, in our society at least, more *is* available to them. This general optimism about what they can get carries over into other types of negotiations as well. Elaine, the district court judge, told us that when she was a litigator, "there were men who would come into a negotiation and press a point regardless of whether it made the slightest bit of sense. They were prepared to take more outrageous positions." This could be an advantage because "a man who is seeking out a ridiculous position and sticking to it could force the other side to accept just because he was going to hold on longer." But it could be a disadvantage, too, if she or another opposing counsel was "prepared to litigate to the end"—to go to court, in other words.

This points up the existence of a dark side to men's more optimistic perceptions of how much they can get from a negotiation. Because they more often overestimate their alternatives and occasionally aim too high, men end up without agreements more often than women do.[19] This is undeniably bad for men because in most cases they would be better off with agreements. In this light, women have the advantage—an advantage we discuss in detail in chapter 8.

The Power of Information

Their lack of optimism about available rewards can lead women to predetermine their own fate before a negotiation begins—by asking for too little they limit what they can get in advance. Janice, the receptionist at a health club, was asked by the manager of the gym to take over scheduling and supervising the club's personal trainers. When Janice agreed, the manager asked her what she wanted to be paid. "I totally botched the negotiation process and sold myself way too low," Janice reported. "Personal trainers get paid way more by the hour than I was making as a receptionist so I just asked for the personal trainers' rate, which seemed like a lot to me. I wasn't even sure I could get that." Janice's boss actually said he would pay her a little more than she asked for since her new responsibilities fell into a supervisory category with relation to the personal trainers, and therefore by all rights should be more highly paid. But Janice hadn't thought about the value of the new role she would be filling. She thought only about what she had been earning before as a receptionist. This led her to set a target for the negotiation that was way too low. Although her boss was nice enough to pay her more than she asked for (a pretty rare occurrence), she may well have been able to get even more had she set a higher goal for herself. Before future negotiations, she told us, she will research the going rate for the kind of work she's being asked to do, and use that information—rather than her earnings history or her own sense of self-worth—to figure out what she should ask for.

This is the right tack for her to take. Research finds that using market information and other externally set guidelines to set goals can improve women's negotiation results substantially.[20] Rhonda is the manager of a very successful mutual fund. After running this fund for almost ten years, she concluded that she was being grossly underpaid. But when she asked her boss for a salary increase, he turned her down. Rhonda responded by researching what other top fund managers earned. When she discovered that very few women had achieved her level of success, she contacted several top male managers and asked what they were paid. She then went back to her boss armed with this information. This time, he granted her request. Now she's the highest-paid fund manager at the company.

Another one of Linda's studies with Hannah Riley and Kathleen McGinn suggests that the use of external guidelines not only increases women's goals and helps them achieve better negotiated settlements—it may even eliminate the gender gap in outcomes. For this study, they recruited undergraduates from the Boston area to participate in negotiations and divided them into two groups. They gave one group a bottom line—for sellers the minimum they could accept and for buyers the maximum they could pay. They gave the other group both a bottom line and a goal—an amount they were to shoot for in the negotiation. Among the students who received just a bottom line (the bottom lines given to men and women were identical), female buyers set less aggressive goals than male buyers (10 percent less) and negotiated prices that were 27 percent worse than those achieved by the male buyers. But among those students who were provided with both bottom lines *and* goals, there was no gender difference in negotiated prices.[21] In other words, gender differences in out-comes may be eliminated if male and female negotiators are working toward identical goals.

This has two important implications. First, it points out the critical role played by goals in causing gender differences. Second, it shines a light on one way in which women can improve the results of their negotiations—by spending more time researching aggressive yet potentially obtainable goals *before* they begin.

The Rewards of Risk

If optimism is about how much we believe is available, risk taking is about "going for it"—taking a chance to get as much as we can—and men seem to be more comfortable than women taking risks. Studies that have included subjects from all over the world have shown that women are less likely than men to engage in activities that involve physical risk.[22] Men also score higher on "sensation-seeking" scales. These scales (actually four subscales), developed by the psychologist Marvin Zuckerman, measure: "thrill and adventure seeking" (a desire to participate in physical risk-taking activities); "experience seeking" (wanting to pursue new and different experiences); "disinhibition" (interest in pursuing hedonistic pleasure); and "boredom susceptibility" (a dislike of dull and boring people, activities, or environments).[23] Men score higher than women in each category.

Men and women also approach activities involving social risk differently. Males are "more likely to see a challenge that calls forth participation" in a socially risky situation, according to the psychologist Elizabeth Arch, whereas females more commonly perceive such activities as threatening and try to avoid them.[24] Because negotiation by definition contains the possibility of rejection or failure, it always involves a certain amount of social risk—making it potentially threatening to women. Women's fear that negotiating for what they want can damage their relationships may also make negotiation seem socially risky to women.

Arch argues that women's fear of taking social risks prompts them to behave more cautiously than men. If this is true, their greater sense of caution may prevent girls and women from breaking rules and challenging the status quo while they're growing up. As a result, they may not discover that this kind of risk taking—and by extension any unsanctioned approach to getting what they want (such as asking for something when it hasn't been offered)—can be a successful strategy. Men's greater propensity to take risks may teach them, in contrast, that challenging the status quo and pushing their own agendas can work to their advantage. Many women learn this lesson much more slowly, if at all.

One relatively new line of research suggests that men's biology may actually prime them to feel more comfortable taking risks. Several recent studies have shown a correlation between testosterone levels in men and dominance behaviors, for example. Dominance behaviors are defined as actions designed to improve a person's power, status, and access to desirable rewards (material or otherwise).[25] Men who receive testosterone injections to treat a variety of medical conditions report feeling more confident, aggressive, and ready to take risks immediately after their treatment and for several days afterward—until their testosterone levels sink again.[26] Testosterone levels in male athletes have also been shown to rise before a competition,[27] with some researchers suggesting that this upsurge may increase an athlete's readiness to take risks,[28] and others speculating that these elevated testosterone levels may improve coordination, enhance mental functioning, and aid concentration.[29] Studies have also shown that testosterone levels remain elevated among "winners" but fall in "losers."[30] This suggests that when risk taking is rewarded by success, men experience a biological reaction—a sustained testosterone "high," if you will—that promotes more risk taking. Another study shows that the testosterone levels of men in occupations that involve a lot of personal risk, such as actors, professional football players, and firefighters, tend to be higher than those of men in professions that involve less personal risk, such as ministers and doctors.[31] Women also have testosterone in their systems (in much smaller amounts), but researchers have not yet demonstrated any consistent correlation between changes in women's testosterone levels and their behavior.[32]

Although a great deal of controversy surrounds this area of study, and it's important to remember that "correlation does not imply causation" (there's no proof yet that rises in testosterone under certain circumstances actually *cause* the behaviors observed), the link to negotiation is not hard to make. If the prospect of competition that is embedded in any negotiation raises a man's testosterone level, that rise in testosterone may help him feel more confident about setting higher targets for the negotiation and making a more aggressive first offer—taking greater risks in order to get as much as he can. Once the negotiation has begun, if a man is negotiating effectively, each perceived "win" in the interaction may serve to keep his testosterone elevated, thus maintaining his optimistic outlook, improving his cognitive functioning and concentration, and helping him continue to pursue a more aggressive target settlement. A woman in the same situation, unaided by this biological "facilitator of risk,"[33] may not only set a less aggressive target in the first place, she may also concede more rapidly if she fears that pushing for what she wants is socially risky. Or she may concede more because the man she's negotiating with, urged on by the testosterone in his system, continues pushing for his goal much longer.

Just as excessive optimism can be problematic for men, however, "testosterone-driven impatience may lead to poor decision-making,"[34] which can leave men with bad agreements, with no aggreements, or with relationship problems created by their overly aggressive behavior.

The Confidence Gap

Women also set lower targets and settle for less in their negotiations because they lack confidence in their ability to negotiate effectively.[35] Assuming that they're no good at negotiating, they conclude that they won't be able to attain higher goals.

Psychologists have demonstrated that the more self-confident people feel about a particular task, the more likely they are to set high goals for that task and persist in trying to achieve those goals. More self-confident people stay in the game, that is, trying to find ways to get what they want; less-confident people give up sooner.[36] Lindsey, 41, a research chemist, although quite successful, conforms to this pattern:

I get so nervous in negotiating that I capitulate very quickly. So, for instance... when I took my previous job, I felt as though for form's sake... you shouldn't take what you're offered, you should always ask for a little more. So... I go in there and say it, and the person to whom I say it sits back and says, 'Well, what do you mean by that?' Or 'Are you saying blah, blah, blah?' And then I find myself going, 'Oh, never mind, I didn't really mean it. I'm happy to have the job,' or whatever. And I just capitulate so quickly after just making a show of trying to get something, because... I'm not very good at professional negotiating.

Lindsey's lack of self-confidence prevents her from "sticking to her guns" and holding out for what she wants.

In addition to limiting the goals women set for themselves, their lack of self-confidence can undermine women's efforts in another way. A 1983 study by the psychologists Debra Instone, Brenda Major, and Barbara Bunker examined the interrelationships among self-confidence, influence attempts, and gender. They divided students into groups of four and assigned one student in each group to supervise the other three while they performed a set task. During this exercise, the researchers observed the extent to which the "supervisors" attempted to influence the productivity of their "workers" and the types of influence strategies they used. Separately, the researchers also measured the supervisors' self-confidence about their managerial ability using a simple five-point scale. They found that the male "supervisors" felt more confidence in their managerial ability than the women (the men's average scores were 31 percent higher than the women's)—and that the male "supervisors" made more attempts than the female supervisors to influence the productivity of their "workers." Even more to the point, the higher the supervisors scored on the self-confidence scale, the more frequently they tried to influence the productivity of their workers. Had the male and female supervisors had similar levels of self-confidence about their managerial ability, this suggests, there would have been no difference in the frequency of their influence attempts.[37]

How does this relate to negotiation? As we've already noted, negotiation is essentially a mutual influence-attempt process—it's all about trying to influence another person or group of people to do something or give you something you want. Since women as a group feel less self-confident about their negotiating abilities, they not only attempt fewer negotiations, they also try to influence the decision of the opposite negotiator fewer times: Their lack of confidence impels them to try only once or twice to get what they want before conceding.

Lana, a trauma surgeon at a New York hospital and a friend of Linda's, applied for parental leave before the birth of her first child. The hospital's policy was to give new mothers six weeks of pregnancy leave and then four additional months during which they were exempt from working night and weekend shifts. But when Lana asked her department head for the leave, he said they were short-staffed and she could only have two months off from night and weekend call. Having asked once and been turned down, Lana wasn't going to try again. She thought she had no choice but to take the two months he'd offered and then go back to her usual grueling schedule. Fortunately, she mentioned what had happened to Linda, and Linda convinced her that she was entitled to the full benefits stipulated by hospital policy. Lana went back to her department head, tried again, and this time persuaded him to give her the full four months off. Like many other women, Lana's lack of self-confidence, particularly around negotiating, had led her to concede too soon.

Interestingly, however, the psychologist Ellen Lenney has found that gender differences in self-confidence depend upon context and situation, with women's perceptions of their ability more context-dependent than men's. This means that women's feelings of self-confidence fluctuate more than men's in response to the specifics of a situation.[38] Following up on this research, the psychologists Sylvia Beyer and Edward Bowden found that women tend to feel more self-confident about certain types of activities than others—and especially lack confidence about activities that are strongly identified with men.[39] Some researchers believe that negotiation, particularly on one's own behalf, is one of those activities.[40] This makes a lot of sense to us, since negotiation falls more in line with social expectations for male behavior (being self-promoting and aggressive) than with those for female behavior (being other-directed and selfless). Not surprisingly, this is what Linda and her colleagues found in their web survey—that people's estimations of their own ability as negotiators differed noticeably by gender, with men rating their ability higher on average than women.[41]

Increasing Control

Is there hope? Are there ways for women to improve their self-confidence around negotiating—and achieve better outcomes? Although very little research has been done on training or tactics that will improve women's negotiating results, one study offers some useful clues. After demonstrating distinct gender differences in negotiated outcomes among a group of MBA students, three professors of management, Cynthia Kay Stevens, Anna Bavetta, and Marilyn Gist, explored whether these differences could be eliminated by different types of training interventions.[42] In the first stage of the study, the researchers gave a group of students four hours of classroom training in useful tactics for salary negotiations. Then they asked each student to negotiate a salary for a hypothetical job. Confederates of the researchers played the role of a personnel director at a firm that wanted to hire the students, and all the confederates used identical "scripts." This was called the "baseline" negotiation, and the researchers found that gender differences in goals (men's were higher) closely paralleled the gender gap in negotiated results (the men negotiated better salaries).

After this negotiation, the student subjects attended two more hours of training, but this time they were separated into two groups. One group attended a session about goal-setting while the other attended a session about "self-management" techniques. The "goals" session showed how the use of challenging goals can improve performance and described ways to set appropriate goals for salary negotiations. The instructors did not tell the students what goals to set, however. They merely taught them how to set aggressive goals and emphasized the importance of doing so. In the other training session, students were taught five "self-management" principles. These included anticipating performance obstacles by identifying situations that might cause them anxiety or stress and planning to overcome those performance obstacles by developing strategies to deal with anxiety-producing situations. They also included practicing their responses with a partner to build their self-confidence. In addition, students were encouraged to set performance goals by evaluating all potential outcomes and ranking their priorities, identifying "giveaways," and settling on targets as well as "reserves" (the minimum they would accept). They were also taught to monitor their progress by tracking the goals they attained and to reward themselves by celebrating the goals they achieved.[43]

The researchers hoped that this type of training might enhance performance by improving each negotiator's sense of control over the negotiation. They thought that higher levels of perceived control might help the students feel more self-confident and that this would translate into "greater effort, persistence, and performance."[44]

After the second round of training, the students participated in another negotiation. The researchers found that the training in goal-setting increased the goals of both men and women and led to improvements in negotiated results for both. However, gender gaps in performance remained because the women and the men increased their goals by about the same amount and consequently raised the salaries they negotiated by about the same amount—and the average difference between them did not change. So the men still did better than the women. This tells us that goal-setting can indeed increase women's negotiated outcomes, but if men receive similar training, gender gaps will persist.

The "self-management" training produced more dramatic results. This training, the researchers found, increased the salaries negotiated by both men and women but increased them far more for women—and completely eliminated the gender gap in performance. To explore whether they were correct that the "self-management" training increased the students' feelings of control during their negotiations, the researchers measured the students' perceived control before and after the training. As the researchers suspected, the women's perceived levels of control increased significantly after the training, but the men's did not (presumably because the men already felt fairly high levels of control before the training). The researchers concluded that changing the women's feelings of control over the negotiation process eliminated the gender gap in performance. They also concluded that this type of self-management training program can be extremely effective in improving the agreements negotiated by women who have the "tactical knowledge" they need to negotiate (they have studied basic negotiating tactics) but lack the self-confidence and skills to use that knowledge—to translate that knowledge into action.[45]

Linda proved the efficacy of this approach. Once she realized that her female Ph.D. students were not asking for or getting what they wanted enough of the time, she organized a series of workshops for female graduate students. In the workshops, she helped the women articulate the barriers and challenges they faced in obtaining what they wanted. She encouraged them to examine which of these barriers and challenges were real and which were imagined. She shared many of the ideas that formed the foundation of this book, talked about ways students could increase their feelings of control over the negotiation process, and encouraged the women to try out these ideas in their daily lives.

The results were striking. Paula, a senior graduate student, reported that she had chosen not to teach for several summers in order to focus on her own research. Then, the summer after she participated in Linda's workshop, an associate dean asked her to teach again. She agreed—with the condition that she teach precalculus, which wouldn't require much preparation because she'd taught it before. A few weeks later, the associate dean told her that he really needed her to teach calculus instead. This required all new preparation and a big time commitment. Paula was reluctant to agree, but the associate dean was in a bind and she finally said okay—provided she could have a teaching assistant for the course.

When the summer session began, only five students had scored high enough on the placement exam to enroll in calculus. At the first meeting for summer instructors, the program coordinator told Paula that her teaching assistant would be reassigned to a precalculus class and she would have to do all the grading and administrative work for her five students herself. Paula was sure that before taking Linda's workshop she would have accepted this. Instead, she told the coordinator that she had an arrangement with the associate dean and she still wanted the teaching assistant. But, since the grading would not be as time-consuming with only five students, Paula offered to split the T.A. with the precalculus instructor.

The coordinator seemed shocked that Paula was insisting on a T.A. for such a small class. He thought it perfectly reasonable to ask her to do all of the work associated with the course. But she hadn't wanted to teach in the first place; she was doing the associate dean a favor; and she had a lot of her own work to do that summer. At another time in her life, Paula would have felt guilty about making trouble and would have conceded to the change without a fight. Instead, with her confidence bolstered by Linda's workshop, she not only insisted, she felt fully justified in insisting. She thought she had offered a reasonable compromise and wasn't required to consider further concessions. Paula got the half-time T.A. and felt good about how she'd handled the situation.

Another student, Marie, told Linda about shopping with her husband for air conditioners at a large national chain. They were purchasing three units, so Marie asked the sales clerk for a quantity discount of 15 percent. The clerk said he couldn't do that. Instead of backing down immediately as she would have before Linda's workshop, Marie counteroffered and asked for 10 percent off. The clerk said okay. When Marie and her husband got home, they found that the boxes had already been opened and the units appeared to have been used. Marie called the store and asked them to pick up the old ones and deliver new ones. She also asked for an additional 10 percent off the units for her trouble. To her husband's astonishment, they agreed. Marie had never raised her voice, threatened to sue, or used harsh language. She determined what she felt was fair (a discount, delivery), and calmly asked for it. Her husband, who until then had rarely seen her stand up for herself, was stunned and delighted.

The rest of the workshop participants reported similar successes. Very quickly, these women stopped accepting the status quo and began challenging it; they aimed higher in their negotiations and resisted conceding too much or too soon. As a result, they were able to open up opportunities for themselves, negotiate better salaries and benefit packages, and overcome barriers that previously would have stopped them. Linda keeps in touch with most of these students and regularly hears how, at every stage of their careers, these women continue to examine the circumstances of their lives, identify desirable improvements, and ask for things they haven't been offered. They don't always get all they want, but they don't give up too easily—and rarely fail to improve their lot. Even more important, perhaps, they feel comfortable and confident exerting far more control over their lives and careers.

Wanting Different Things

Sometimes a woman sets a low target for a negotiation not because she lacks self-confidence or perceives asking for more to be too risky, but because she has other goals for the negotiation—goals that are not less important than a man's goals, just different.[46] These may include getting a flexible work schedule or shorter hours so that she can fulfill some of her personal goals, such as being a good mother. Goals of this sort are so important to many women that they will sacrifice many of their professional goals, such as increased job responsibility, higher pay, and greater opportunities for career advancement, in order to get what they want. Although it's important to recognize that women may bring a broader array of personal goals into their job negotiations, in many cases women probably don't need to sacrifice as much as they think they do.

When Melissa, the social worker, went back to work after the birth of her first child, her principal goal, she said, was to get the hours she wanted so that she could pick her daughter up from day care and actively participate in her schooling and her life. Believing that this was a lot to ask, she accepted the first job that agreed to give her the hours she wanted and she accepted the salary she was offered without negotiating. "I did feel like I was conceding other things," she said, but "if they were willing to give me this [the hours], then it didn't matter that this job was kind of a go-nowhere job for me." Her belief that asking for the hours she wanted was a lot to ask impelled her to compromise every other goal she had for her professional life. The lesson here is not that women shouldn't want what they want. Melissa's goal of spending a lot of time with her daughter was a great goal. But she probably didn't have to give up so much else to get it.

Of the adult females in this country who work, only 71 percent work 35 or more hours a week.[47] Many of the others choose to work less than full-time in order to attend to some of their other goals, but it's important to remember that these preferences, to a large degree if not completely, have been socially constructed—and that they can limit the choices of both men and women (working fewer hours may be less socially acceptable for a man than for a woman, for example). In addition, limited opportunities in the labor market may explain some of this difference, with women less able to find full-time jobs than men.

The bottom line is that whatever their personal and professional aspirations, women can achieve more in a negotiation if they walk in with more ambitious goals. Whatever they want, pitching their goals higher helps them focus more, hold their ground, and come away with more.

Not the Whole Story

Will persuading women to raise their targets be enough to get women paid what they deserve? Will helping women increase their self-confidence around negotiating ensure that they get recognized for the work they do? Unfortunately, not always. Despite all the positive change achieved over the past half-century, some employers still will not concede as much to a woman in a negotiation as they will to a man. In addition, employers often make lower first offers to women than they make to men and take it for granted that women will work for less. In the next chapter, we look at the ways in which external forces prevent women from negotiating more successfully even when they set high targets, feel confident about what they deserve, and valiantly resist conceding.

7

JUST SO MUCH AND NO MORE

NEGOTIATION NEVER TAKES PLACE in a vacuum. Everything from where a negotiation takes place (the business world, the political arena, the commercial world, the home), the issue or issues at stake (a price, a vote, who will do the dishes) and the roles, status, and relationships of the parties negotiating (a boss, a business client, a salesperson, a spouse) can influence both the tone and outcome of a negotiation. By now it will come as no surprise that gender norms also influence how most negotiations unfold. This chapter looks at how certain situations can prevent women from getting more of what they want in a negotiation. It looks at how people frequently enforce stricter limits on what they will grant to women in a negotiation, force women to concede more and accept less—and in many cases limit women's ability to exercise both personal and professional power.

Requiring More, Conceding Less

In some situations people routinely take a tougher stance against women than they take against men—this has been conclusively demonstrated. One study by the economists Ian Ayres and Peter Siegelman showed that salespeople in car dealerships consistently quote higher prices to women than to men, for example. The "buyers" in this study were trained by the researchers with the same "script" and all tried to buy the same type of car. They also shared a variety of characteristics, such as age, level of education, attractiveness, and style of dress. The only significant differences among them were whether they were male or female and black or white. But these turned out to be the differences that counted: Consistently, in more than 300 buying attempts, salespeople quoted higher prices to women than to men, and *much* higher prices to African Americans.[1] This tells us that car salespeople, as a group, have learned (or been trained) to make higher first offers in negotiations with women and African Americans. Since we know that higher first offers go hand in hand with higher targets, we can conclude that car salespeople also set higher targets against women and African Americans. And higher targets, as we've already demonstrated, tend to produce higher negotiated outcomes, meaning that women and African Americans usually pay more than white men for their cars. The bad news is inescapable: In negotiations over buying a car, at least, women and African Americans start out at a disadvantage before they even begin.

Another study, by the economist Sara Solnick, used something called the "Ultimatum Game" to look at general attitudes toward men and women when they are negotiating. In the Ultimatum Game, researchers give two people a certain amount of money, such as ten dollars, to divide. One person, the "proposer" suggests a division of the ten dollars between the two players (for example, six dollars for me and four dollars for you). The other person, the "responder," then decides whether to accept this offer. If the responder accepts, the two players are paid the amounts suggested by the proposer. If the responder rejects the offer, both players get nothing and the game is over—and the players know this in advance. This game helps researchers understand people's perceptions of fairness and how those perceptions influence their behavior. If fairness were not an issue, researchers assume, self-interest would motivate most proposers to suggest $9.99 for themselves and one cent for their responders. But once fairness is calculated in, each proposer must guess the minimum amount the responder will accept as fair. The responder must then decide whether the offer is fair enough to be acceptable, or so unfair that getting nothing would be preferable.

To look at how ideas about gender influence behavior, Solnick informed the two halves of each research pair only of the gender of the other player (they never met).[2] She discovered two interesting things. First, she found that both men and women made less generous offers to female responders than to male responders—12 percent lower on average. This makes it clear that people of both sexes expect women to accept less than men and perhaps even think that this is right (women should accept less). Given the demonstrated power of other people's expectations to influence behavior, this expectation alone translates into powerful pressure on women to do exactly that—accept less. Angela, the marketing director for the community development bank, bluntly summed up: "People are a lot more comfortable with giving you less when you're a woman." Solnick's second finding turned out to be the flip side of her first: We don't just insist that women accept less, she discovered; we also demand that women *give away* more. Both male and female responders required much larger offers from women than they required from men to make an offer acceptable (42.5 percent larger on average).

The expectation that women will demand and accept less and give away more was confirmed from a different angle by our interviews. Only 16 percent of the people we interviewed said that they think women make better negotiators than men. Because beliefs can be such powerful determinants of behavior, when translated into practice this belief will lead many people, if not most, to expect that they'll be able to reach better agreements (agreements that are more advantageous to their own side) when they're negotiating with women than when they're negotiating with men. This expectation, consciously or subconsciously, will lead them to set higher targets against women, make tougher first offers, press harder for concessions, and resist conceding more than they would if they were negotiating with men. In other words, they will make negotiations more difficult for women. As we've already shown, in many cases people aren't even aware that they're doing this. And when their tougher stance prevents women from achieving good results, this perpetuates the notion that women make worse negotiators than men.

Even the most successful professional women can find themselves hampered by the widespread tendency to grant inferior agreements to women than to men. Elsbeth, 56, is the founder and artistic director of a regional arts conservatory that regularly gets its dancers accepted into prestigious international competitions. Thoroughly self-confident and savvy, Elsbeth is well respected in the performing arts world and a major force in the cultural life of her state. Her conservatory has also been a major engine of economic recovery in its small rust-belt city. Nonetheless, she struggles against entrenched attitudes toward women in business every day—so much so that she had developed a favorite expression: "I'm going to have my guys deal with that." Time after time, dealing with a contractor, a banker, or a politician, "some man in a man's job," she has found that "the guy who is on my building committee who is a window washer will get further with this guy than I will." During one major initiative, in which her conservatory bought a historic building, restored it, and expanded it to include dormitories, practice rooms, offices, and a radio station, "there were a bunch of men around and a couple of women involved and the women were definitely the brains of the outfit, but the men were able to go out and do things with people in this town that the women were not."

Elsbeth believes that people's attitudes slow down women's progress in business to such a degree that "the average male has a ten-year advantage—at least in our country—a *minimum* of a ten-year advantage on a female. In other words, I'm 56. Most males now in their late forties are experiencing in their businesses the kind of growth I'm experiencing now."

Power Prohibitions

As Elsbeth's experience shows, even successful women can find themselves blocked from achieving the same levels of business success achieved by their male peers. How and why does this happen? In addition to the many reasons we've already explored, extensive research by organizational sociologists and organizational behaviorists has demonstrated the value in business of "social networks"—connections to others within one's organization and at other organizations. Networks, this research has shown, provide broad access to advice, early news of emerging opportunities, and a privileged view of the way an organization works. Networks also position members to be considered as key prospects for advancement.[3] Although building social networks sounds like something women would be good at, sizable barriers frequently prevent them from taking full advantage of this skill. For one thing, workplace networks tend to be relatively gender-segregated: Men network with other men and women network with other women.[4] Because access to men's networks can be extremely important, especially in organizations where men control promotion and salary decisions (most organizations), this gender segregation can leave women without the same access to connections and information that men in their organizations enjoy.

Social scientists have identified two principal types of networks: "instrumental" networks and "friendship" networks. "Instrumental" networks are based on exchanges of advice and information and on a readiness to help each other out, whereas "friendship" networks have a more social function. Typically, men's "instrumental" networks and their "friendship" networks are predominantly male. Women's "instrumental" networks, in contrast, are usually made up of both men and women but their "friendship" networks tend to be predominantly female.[5] As a result, women's ties to the men in their "instrumental" networks—frequently the more powerful members of the group—can be less strong and therefore less valuable. Compounding the problem, in workplace situations in which women are a minority, women are more likely to be marginal members of any informal friendship networks of which they do become members, a marginalization that appears to result "more from exclusionary pressures than from their preferences."[6] This lack of strong personal ties to the men in their "instrumental" networks can make those ties less useful.

Adding another wrinkle, research has shown that men benefit considerably from maintaining numerous ties that are relatively weak, but women and other minorities in an organization (any group of people who need to overcome negative stereotypes) derive little benefit from weak ties.[7] A weak tie is a relationship with someone you'd consider an acquaintance but not a friend—it's a connection based on goodwill and generally positive impressions but not much intimate knowledge of one another.

Since women are in the minority at many organizations, especially at the higher levels, research suggests that women need stronger ties than men need because "strong ties may help women to counteract the effects of bias, gender-typed expectations, and contested legitimacy."[8]

A man may be comfortable doing a favor or providing a reference for another man he doesn't know especially well, for example, but negative stereotypes about women's competence and the widespread tendency to devalue women's performance may make him less comfortable doing the same thing for a woman he doesn't know well. As a result, for a man to do a favor for a woman, he usually needs to know her well enough to feel completely confident in her abilities—his ties to her need to be strong. In an article in the *Harvard Business Review* titled "When the Mentor Is a Man and the Protégée Is a Woman," the authors, Lawton Whehle Fitt and Derek Newton, reported that "two of the men we talked to said that, to protect themselves, they maintain higher standards for female protégés than for male protégés."[9] Another one of their interview subjects admitted: "In the case of women, many people have to be convinced. When you're trying to present a woman to your superiors, you often feel you have to explain everything."[10] Knowing that there will be more resistance to a woman, many men choose the easier path and recommend a man they know will be acceptable. In addition, if a man has to "explain everything"—meaning, presumably, everything a woman has accomplished and everything she can do—this by itself would seem to require a strong tie. Otherwise, the man may not know "everything" he needs to explain. And, as we've said, women rarely have such strong ties to men in their "instrumental" networks who may be in a position to help promote their careers.

Another way in which women can be cut off from exercising power and influence involves a potentially powerful position in a network called a "structural hole." A person who occupies a structural hole maintains connections to people in his or her organization who are not themselves connected to one another. This position can be a very powerful one for men, giving them access to information not necessarily shared by everybody, allowing them to draw on the skills and points of view of a diverse population, and enabling them to be effective at many different levels of an organization. But this position turns out to be less helpful for women.[11] Far more important and useful for women, it turns out, is having a strong advocate in a powerful position in the network: having someone, in other words, with the power and inclination to direct plum assignments their way, push their advancement, and make sure they get appropriate recognition for their achievements. Not to put too fine a point on it, women thrive when they have someone powerful to do a lot of their "asking" for them.

Why the difference? One persuasive theory postulates that it is appropriate for men to use their power directly but less acceptable for women to do so. This means that it can be a gender-role violation for women to take advantage of their position in a "structural hole." Instead, they must rely on a strategic partner or mentor—who must be male—to do so for them.[12] Unfortunately, the subconscious devaluing of women's ability and performance that afflicts so many people, and the pervasive assumption that women are less capable than men at more senior and management-level jobs, makes it much harder for women to find men willing to play this role for them.[13] Cynthia Fuchs Epstein, in her paper "Constraints on Excellence: Structural and Cultural Barriers to the Recognition and Demonstration of Achievement," offers this explanation: "Stratification and ghettoization are...characteristic of most professional domains. Institutions position women, and powerful individuals within these institutions do not commonly challenge tradition by cross-crossing these lines by personally sponsoring women."[14] Thus, cut off from using their positions of power and influence directly, prohibited by gender prejudice from negotiating aggressively on their own behalf, and without a strong advocate, women often find themselves stymied, unable to progress as rapidly or as far in their careers as their abilities should dictate.

Supporting Others

If the world were populated only by women who feel trapped by gender norms and unable to act powerfully and forcefully, it would be a different place from the world in which we all live. For of course there are plenty of women who behave confidently and assertively—we see them every day. In certain situations this kind of behavior by women can even be expected. Looking at those situations can help us to better understand the barriers that hold women back the rest of the time.

So where is this far and distant land, the place where women can freely assert themselves and negotiate and push and ask? It is the land of advocacy—of asking on behalf of others. Helena, 38, an advertising executive, confessed that she feels perfectly comfortable asking her boss for things on behalf of the younger people in her office even though she has a terrible time doing the same for herself:

You know, asking for them to go on [photo] shoots... and asking for them to be paid more money. And then I got Zoë a raise when she was hired back because I said to my boss that I thought it was wrong that the man he hired who had less experience was making more money than she was.... So when he hired her back, she was making more money than both of the young guys.... I'm better at asking for other people, and I can be really direct... but not so much for myself.

Susannah, the political strategist, said that she still has trouble asking for things for herself, even though she has learned that this is necessary. When Sara pointed out that her difficulty with asking was particularly ironic since her job involves asking for things—votes, favorable legislation—on a daily basis, Susannah laughed. "Oh, but those things aren't for me," she said. "Those are for the children!" Mary Wade speculates that women feel more comfortable asking on behalf of others because this activity feels consistent with existing gender norms for women, which require women to take responsibility for other people's interests and needs: "Assertion connotes promoting the self and demanding recognition, rewards, or resources for the self.... Men have traditionally functioned in roles that are enhanced by assertiveness (e.g., aggressive breadwinner, powerful boss, authoritative father), whereas women have traditionally acted as advocates (e.g., supportive assistant, encouraging wife, prodding mother). These expectations remain surprisingly current."[15]

Wade believes that the persistence of these expectations continues to influence the types of assertive behavior that women can safely employ in our society today. In the earliest study of this issue, which we described in chapter 2, male and female students completed a task and then decided either the amount they should be paid for their work or the amount another person who completed the same task should be paid.[16] Confirming expectations, women paid others significantly more than they paid themselves (48 percent more) and men paid others significantly less than they paid themselves (20 percent less).

In a recent study, Mary Wade looked more closely at this difference between men and women.[17] She informed 178 undergraduate student volunteers that they were participating in a study to evaluate students' business skills. Each student was given a job description about a campus internship and asked to write a letter accepting the internship. The students were told to include in the letter what they felt would be an appropriate salary for the position, with the salary falling somewhere between $900 and $3,000. Half the students were told to accept the position for themselves and the other half were told to accept it on behalf of someone else. Also, some of the students were told that a counselor from the career center would evaluate their letters with their names attached and the rest were told that their letters would not be linked with their names.

Wade suspected that female students who believed an evaluator would connect their letters with their names (and therefore would know they were women) would feel compelled to act according to society's expectations for women. This is exactly what happened. Among the students who were told that evaluators would know their names when they read their letters, women made lower requests for themselves than men made (8 percent lower). But, true to Wade's expectations, those women who wrote the letter on someone else's behalf (and knew it would be read by someone who could tell a woman had written it) actually made *larger* payment requests than the men made (9 percent larger).

These results clearly indicate that women know they can campaign strongly for the welfare of others (and may even be expected to do so). They also illuminate the constraints women feel when asking for something for themselves. The power of these constraints was confirmed by the behavior of the students who believed their names would not be linked to their letters. In this condition, women actually made *larger* requests for themselves than the men made (8 percent larger). When they knew that their letters would not be linked with their names and that the evaluators would not know whether they were male or female, the women were able to express a healthy sense of entitlement and advocate well on their own behalf. This suggests that among younger women at least (this study used only undergraduates and was completed in 2002) entitlement issues may play a smaller part than gender-norm pressures in women's reluctance to make strong requests for themselves. As Wade concluded, women's well-founded concerns about provoking negative reactions in others may play a larger role than "self-esteem deficits" in discouraging them from asking for big things for themselves.[18]

Another study Linda conducted with Hannah Riley and Kathleen McGinn in 2000 and 2001 extends this finding to negotiation behavior.[19] For this study, they recruited approximately 200 students from universities in the Boston area to negotiate face-to-face over a single issue. They assigned half the students to represent a fictional retail store negotiating with a web-design company to create a web page for its business. The rest of the students were told that they represented either the owner of the web-design company itself or the undergraduate business and information-systems student who would actually design the page. The negotiation concerned the hourly wage the retail store would pay for the web design. The goal was to observe the differences between how men and women negotiated for another person (when they were playing the owner of the web-design firm negotiating on behalf of the student) compared to how they negotiated for themselves (when they were playing the role of the student designer).

They found that women's goals for the negotiation were 14 percent higher when they were representing another person than when they were representing themselves. Women also indicated that they would make first offers that were 23 percent higher when they were representing someone else than they would make when representing themselves. The opposite was true for men—men set 10 percent higher goals for themselves than for others.

Our female interview subjects repeatedly confirmed the truth of these findings, telling us without prompting (we asked no direct question about this issue) how much more comfortable they feel asking for things on behalf of other people. Geri, the director of the day care center and preschool, said she feels more successful in her professional life than in her personal life, because in her professional capacity, "it's more for a cause and not for myself. . . . I'm not asking for myself." Gillian, the hospital rehabilitation counselor, said of her struggle to negotiate a good new work contract for herself, "I am a fierce tigress for others and a lamb for myself. To do that for myself is a foreign thing. I can do it for my children, my patients, for others, but not for myself."

Role Liberation

Women also find some freedom from gender-role constraints when the professional roles in which they serve are themselves a source of power. That is, they feel free to act assertively when their professional role, by its very nature, requires such behavior. Elaine, the district court judge, believes that female lawyers and judges, for example, can comfortably exercise their authority in the courtroom because the highly structured environment of the courtroom provides for what she calls "aggression in role." By this she means that when a woman performs one of the necessary roles in a courtroom, such as prosecutor, defense attorney, or judge, rather than being perceived as violating female gender norms, she is seen as simply abiding by the requirements of her role. The courtroom, for women, said Elaine, "is structured and comfortable and there are rules that you can follow." But when a woman lawyer meets to negotiate with opposing attorneys outside the courtroom, or a woman judge must mediate such an encounter, her situation becomes much harder. "You get into the back room with the other lawyer, and you start talking about what your case deserves and what they want, and you're dealing with something without a safety net," she said. Similarly,

> For new judges, both male and female, the mediation is the most difficult thing for you to do. It's one thing to come into court with a robe

and a stature and to say, you know, 'I rule this.' That's not easy to do at the beginning, but you get up and get the hang of it after a while. But to go into the back room...a much more informal setting, to mediate, when you have none of the accoutrements of power, is a much more difficult kind of thing.... Power lines are not clear; the rules are not clear.

Although Elaine acknowledges that this is difficult for everyone at the outset, she believes that it's harder for women than for men. Part of the everyday gender role of being male, she said, involves the expectation that you will act aggressively and exercise personal power. "Young male lawyers can pass, and they know they can," she said, "in the sense that...you can walk into a negotiation, you can assume that your opponent will accord you a certain status. As a woman, I didn't feel that right out of the box at all." Tellingly, despite her professional success, Elaine still feels this lack of stature and authority outside the courtroom, where she is not automatically perceived as entitled to exercise personal power. "For something that's personal...I do feel more naked. I don't have the stature to clothe me.... It's almost as if the professional status is like a costume that you put on."

In another field altogether, Heather, the pastor, told a story about negotiating with her city's high school administration because she felt that her foster daughter, a troubled teenager, had been unfairly suspended. First Heather and her husband spoke informally to the high school administrator, with little success. Then they formally appealed the suspension. This required meeting with the high school principal, the administrator, and the two teachers involved. Wanting to make the strongest possible case for her foster daughter, Heather bought herself a pastoral collar of the type used by Protestant ministers and wore it with a dark suit to the meeting. At one point, the principal said to her, "Well, now, Heather, your concerns..." and Heather immediately interrupted him. "You may address me as Reverend Kirk-Davidoff," she said. Her clear feeling, she explained, was that her point of view and her personal power would be greater if she were perceived to be acting not just as a woman and a parent but within her role as a pastor (hence her use of the collar and her professional title)—a role that by its very nature involves advocating for the welfare of others.

A study by the linguist Elizabeth Kuhn sheds revealing light on the ways in which women use their roles to exercise power almost by proxy. Kuhn's study looked at how college professors establish their authority in class. At the beginning of a semester, she found, male professors tended to make direct statements that unequivocally asserted their personal authority, such as "I have two midterms and a final, and I added this first midterm rather early to get you going on the reading." The male professors conveyed that they were in charge and felt comfortable giving directions to their students—and expected them to respond and obey. Female professors, in contrast, used much more indirect speech patterns such as "There are two papers.... Um, there is going to be a midterm and a final. Okay?"[20] Rather than asserting their authority, the women let their role and the situation—this is a class, and a class implies a certain structure of obligations on its participants—impose requirements on the students.

Changing the Context

It's essential to remember, however, that the restraints placed on women are "socially constructed." They aren't physical principles like the law of gravity or mathematical principles like the laws of addition and subtraction, which can't be altered. They are products of our culture and our ideas about the roles that men and women should play. They can be loosened and changed completely *if we want them to change.* Not only can ideas about what is right and wrong or appropriate or inappropriate be changed, the ways in which people behave can be changed as well. This is because one of the most widespread findings in psychology is called the "fundamental attribution error."[21] The fundamental attribution error describes the almost universal human tendency to believe that people's behavior is produced by innate and stable personality characteristics. Research has conclusively demonstrated, however, that this is not the case. People's behavior and their beliefs often change radically when their circumstances change.

Under terrible conditions, people will do things they never thought they could do (such as eating human flesh to survive). Under conditions in which the rules of their culture have changed, making behavior permissible that was previously deemed criminal or antisocial, once peaceable and ordinary-seeming people will commit terrible atrocities (such as murdering their neighbors during the war in Bosnia or persecuting and mass-slaughtering Jews under the Third Reich). People also do remarkable positive things under certain circumstances. The Austrian industrialist Oskar Schindler failed to achieve much professional success before World War II and accomplished very little afterwards. He was a poor businessman, a womanizer, and, according to his wife, lazy and self-indulgent. In a 1973 interview, she said that he'd "done nothing astounding before the war, and had been unexceptional since." Yet during the war he mustered the courage and resourcefulness to save the lives of 1,100 Jews who would otherwise have been murdered by the Nazis. He did this at considerable personal risk and expense, putting his own life in danger and leaving himself, at the end of the war, penniless. Why? His wife says it was because he was fortunate "during that short fierce era" to be surrounded by people "who summoned forth his deeper talents."[22] Schindler had the capacity for heroic behavior, for behavior far more admirable than the spendthrift and irresponsible behavior that characterized much of his life, but it took the right circumstances, the right context, to bring out those qualities in him.

As Schindler's story shows, people's behavior depends to an enormous extent on their environment—not just the environment in which they were raised but the social context in which they live and work every day. And this context can be changed.

Looking Through Female Eyes

It's not hard to understand how individual women will benefit from cultural changes that make it easier for them to pursue their professional ambitions as far as they can go. We've also talked about the damage we do to ourselves as a society by treating half of our population differently and undervaluing their contributions to our shared future. But there's another reason why it's important to make sure that women have the same access as men to leadership roles in our society: Because when women take on those roles, they often bring a fresh approach to situations that have persisted for years. From their particular vantage as women, they question received wisdom, look at familiar ideas from new angles, and sometimes ask if there's not a better way to do things.

Here are a few examples. Until recently, researchers believed that everyone responded in the same way to stress. The presence of danger, they thought, triggered a physiological reaction that motivated a person to either fight the source of danger or flee. This was dubbed the "fight or flight" response, and for years scientists assumed that it was essential to our survival as a species. No one thought to question this view when only men ran their own labs and dictated research directions and strategies. But once women began directing their own research, two female scientists, Shelley Taylor and Laura Klein, noticed that their female and male colleagues behaved differently in challenging situations: "There was this joke that when the women who worked in the lab were stressed, they came in, cleaned the lab, had coffee and bonded. . . . When the men were stressed, they holed up somewhere on their own."[23] When Taylor and Klein realized that the vast majority (a full 90 percent) of all stress research had looked exclusively at males, they decided to investigate whether or not females actually respond to stress in the same ways that men do.

What they found startled the research community. Although women do experience the "fight or flight" response when they're threatened, differences in women's bodies mute the impact of that response. Here's what happens: In situations of extreme stress, the hormone oxytocin is released into the bloodstreams of both men and women. Oxytocin produces a calming effect and promotes caretaking and social-bonding behaviors— but testosterone reduces the effects of oxytocin. Since men have large quantities of testosterone in their systems (especially when stressed), the release of oxytocin into their systems has little impact on their "fight or flight" response. Women have much lower levels of testosterone than men do and much higher levels of estrogen, which magnifies the effects of oxytocin. As a result, in women the release of oxytocin into their bloodstreams can block the "fight or flight" response and prompt them instead to reach out for social support. This finding led Taylor and Klein to dub the female version of the stress response "tend and befriend."[24]

Researchers have only begun to explore the full implications of this difference between men and women. The "tend and befriend" response may help explain why women outlive men, for example, because the calming effect of oxytocin may "reduce women's vulnerability to a broad array of stress-related disorders" such as heart disease, substance abuse, violence, suicide, and stress-related accidents and injuries.[25] Research has also shown that physical contact such as hugging releases oxytocin—meaning that women's impulse to look for social support when they're under stress may be a very healthy adaptive strategy. This is more than merely interesting. It also suggests ways in which a lot of isolated men who "hole up" when things get tough might try to change how they respond to stress— improving their health and maybe even helping them live longer.

Discoveries about the life-threatening risks of hormone replacement therapy, one of the most widely prescribed treatment programs in America, provide another vivid illustration of what can happen when women gain better access to positions of power. When Dr. Bernadine Healy was appointed head of the National Institutes of Health by President George H. W. Bush in 1991, women were routinely excluded from clinical studies of diseases that afflict both men and women. The thinking among researchers was that women's responses often differed from men's, clouding their results and confusing them. It didn't occur to them that they should be studying the different ways in which women's bodies responded to disease or to disease therapy. They wanted to control their lab results, and including women made that more difficult. In addition, at the time many devastating health problems that afflict women alone had not been systematically studied, and numerous routine treatments for women's health problems had never been submitted to rigorous clinical trials. No one really knew whether many of these treatments were indeed beneficial rather than ineffective or—worse yet—damaging. Dr. Healy, approaching the condition of our national health from a woman's perspective, found herself questioning these practices. And with no logical or persuasive answers forthcoming, she asked for some changes.

Against strong opposition from the medical research establishment, Dr. Healy created the Women's Health Initiative to study "the causes, prevention, and treatment of diseases that affect women."[26] Not only must women now be included in any American research that studies conditions affecting both men and women, but within a decade of establishing the Women's Health Initiative, the N.I.H. announced that a certain type of hormone replacement therapy, which had become a commonplace treatment for menopausal women, increases a woman's risk of breast cancer, heart attacks, strokes, and blood clots.[27]

The results of the hormone replacement study alone inspired the *New York Times* to call Dr. Healy an "on-the-job hero," responsible for saving the lives of "tens of thousands of women." The *Times* also noted that "many perfectly capable and good men (liberal ones, too) came before Dr. Healy at the N.I.H."[28] But because none of them were women, they failed to notice this potentially devastating oversight in the way we conducted medical research. It wasn't that these men wanted women to die unnecessarily or to receive inappropriate treatment. They just brought different priorities and a different perspective to the job.

As these two examples demonstrate, allowing women to advance into positions of greater power and influence has the potential not just to improve women's lives but to increase the fund of human knowledge, change what we know about ourselves as a species—and in some cases save thousands of lives.

8

The Female Advantage

Jeremy, 28, a former naval officer who now works as a business analyst for a software firm, described a situation in which he was traveling abroad and spent an hour negotiating for a rug in a Turkish bazaar even though he had no interest in buying the rug. He was negotiating just for the fun of it. Although this story sounds preposterous to many women (and some men), Jeremy explained that he simply enjoys negotiating—enough to waste an hour negotiating for its own sake. "I like the gaming," he said. "It's a little bit of a game." David, the hedge fund manager, described negotiating this way: "When you reach a barrier, the game is just beginning again. It's not whether you get knocked down. It's whether you get up or not—that's the real game." He also said he loves "the theatrical part of it," playacting to intimidate or unsettle an opposing negotiator by hanging up the phone, putting his papers in his briefcase and leaving the room—even taking a call in the middle of a negotiation. To him, negotiation is "a sport, absolutely." And Eli, 56, a structural engineer, said that he views negotiation as "a big analytic jigsaw puzzle."

Whereas men often describe negotiating as a competitive game or a puzzle, women tend to use different language when they talk about it. Ingrid, 30, a city councilwoman, said, "It's not about winning. It's, 'How do I get to my goals and how do I work with this person in this moment to get to my goals?' It's about figuring out very pointedly where I need to go and how to work with this person to get there.... It's also like meeting that person where they're at."

Lory, the theater production manager, explains that her preferred negotiation style is one "in which you make all parties feel included in the discussion, and they go the most flawlessly when everyone in the discussion has a sense of ownership of the final outcome. And whether or not it suits their needs or follows along the lines that they had originally anticipated or advocated, they still understand how we got there." Mercy, the director of space management for a large university, regularly negotiates property purchases and space allocation disputes and knows why she's good at it:

> I tend to work very closely with whatever group I'm working with, whether it be my peers or my supervisors or folks, and inform them and make sure I've done a good job of basically lobbying, so that they sort of come to the conclusion in their own way rather than my going in and saying, "I want this" or something like that. They see the benefit for all parties and they buy into it rather than me being demanding. It's more of an issue of collaborating, getting them to collaborate with you.... I bring people along in the process, and I think I do that very well.

These different perspectives on negotiation—the male view that it's a game or a contest and the female view that it's a collaborative undertaking—lead men and women to approach the process of negotiation very differently.

Up to this point in the book we've focused on the socialization that often prevents women from asking for more of life's bounty—and on the discouraging responses they often get when they do negotiate. But women also have some advantages that can make them outshine men at negotiating. Although the more aggressive approach favored by many men can win good short-term results, women's focus on cooperation and relationship building can be a huge advantage. This is because a multitude of negotiation studies in the past two decades have shown that a cooperative approach, aimed at finding good outcomes for all parties rather than just trying to "win," actually produces solutions that are objectively superior to those produced by more competitive tactics. The influence of this line of research has been so profound, and the behaviors it recommends dovetail so nicely with women's strengths, that negotiation experts often joke that the goal of many negotiation courses today is to train people to negotiate like women. This chapter looks at how powerful the female approach to negotiating can be.

Cooperative Advantage

Why would taking a cooperative approach to a negotiation produce a better solution than just trying to get as much as you can for yourself or "your side"? The answer lies in understanding something negotiation scholars have dubbed "the mythical fixed-pie bias." Many people walk into a negotiation mistakenly assuming that their interests are in direct conflict with those of the other negotiator or negotiators. This attitude, "the mythical fixed-pie bias," creates the belief that "what is good for the other side must be bad for us."[1] Although this is occasionally true, particularly in negotiations in which there's only one issue to be decided ("distributive" negotiations), the vast majority of negotiations are not single-issue negotiations. Much more common are multi-issue negotiations (called "integrative" negotiations), in which more than one issue needs to be decided or more than one problem needs to be solved, and the negotiators typically have different priorities. Because more issues are "in play" in an integrative negotiation, this type of negotiation allows participants to trade things they value less for other things that matter to them more, a practice called "logrolling." Perhaps most important, integrative negotiations allow for resolutions that can be good for both sides.

To better understand the difference between distributive and integrative negotiations, and between "fixed-pie" and "growing-the-pie" approaches to negotiation, consider the following example. Suppose two chefs are preparing a dinner together and each one needs a lemon for one of the dishes he is preparing. Opening the refrigerator, the two men discover that there is only one lemon left. The two of them might fight over this lone lemon, with each one arguing that he should get the whole lemon (that would be each chef's "position"). This would represent a "fixed-pie" approach to the situation. But what if one chef really wants the lemon rind for a cake and the other wants the juice for a marinade (these would be their "interests")? If the two chefs describe their interests to each other, they should be able to work out a solution that not only benefits both (one man gets the whole rind and the other gets all the juice) but is better than a straightforward distributive solution (one gets the whole lemon and the other gets nothing) and better than another possible solution, such as each cook getting half the lemon.

Surprisingly, very few people who have not been trained in negotiation realize the full benefits of an integrative approach. The negotiation professor Leigh Thompson estimates that at least two-thirds of untrained negotiators suffer from the "mythical fixed-pie bias."[2] Although the origin of the bias is unknown, it is reinforced by negotiation books with titles such as *Secrets of Power Negotiating*, which offer advice such as: "The more you think of negotiating as a game, the more competitive you'll become . . . and the better you'll do."[3] Encouraged by books like this, people frequently end up with inferior agreements because they've been so busy competing with each other that they've overlooked potential agreements that would have been better for *both* parties than the deals they made. The effects of this bias are so extreme that even in situations in which the parties would actually prefer the same outcome, they're often so busy resisting each other's points of view that they fail to realize they have the same preference about half the time.[4]

Since the publication in 1981 of *Getting to Yes*, which popularized the view that most negotiations have integrative or "win/win" potential,[5] negotiation scholars have explored strategies for finding these superior solutions. Most of this research has focused on one key factor: increasing the flow of information between the parties and finding out as much as possible about the other side's needs, interests, and preferences.[6] This can be done directly (by asking questions) or indirectly (by asking whether the other negotiator would be willing to give a little on issue X in exchange for getting a little on issue Y). It can be done by sharing information, listening closely, and talking about interests rather than positions. Although this

might seem like an obvious tactic to use, research suggests that most people don't do this unless they've been trained to do so. In one study, Leigh
Thompson found that only 7 percent of untrained negotiators try to discover information about the other side's preferences and priorities in a
negotiation.[7]

Integrative tactics (asking questions, listening, sharing information,
and trying to find solutions that satisfy the needs of both sides) differ dramatically from the competitive tactics (staking out extreme positions,
bluffing, resisting concessions) that can be effective in classic distributive
(one-issue) negotiations. Perhaps most important, integrative tactics involve behaviors at which women often excel.

Real Differences

We've said that women take a more cooperative approach to negotiation
and that men are usually more competitive in their attitude. But do we
know this for a fact? Although this area of research is relatively new, a few
studies have found that women do indeed behave differently from men
when they negotiate.

In one of the earliest studies to look at this question, the researchers
divided subjects into same-sex pairs to conduct a negotiation that could
be settled in a distributive (i.e., competitive—I win, you lose) fashion but
could also be settled more creatively so that both sides would benefit. They
observed that men used distributive tactics (making threats, insulting the
other side, and staking out inflexible positions) much more than women
did.[8] In two other studies that compared the characteristics of male and female managers, the business writer and consultant Sally Helgesen found
that men were much less likely than women to share information.[9] A
meta-analysis that quantified the results of numerous research studies also
found differences in the ways in which men and women behave in negotiations, with women more likely to behave cooperatively than men.[10]

Another study, by the negotiation scholars Jennifer Halpern and Judi
McLean Parks, also separated subjects (undergraduates in a negotiations
class) into same-sex groups of two. These all-male or all-female pairs were

asked to conduct a negotiation about allocating public money to build a children's playground. One member in each pair played the role of a representative from the Parks Department and the other played a representative of a community volunteer organization.[11]

The differences between the all-male and all-female pairs were dramatic. Males were more likely than females to talk about their positions (how much they wanted to see allocated to the project), with all of the male pairs discussing their positions but only 17 percent of the female pairs doing so. Males also used confrontational bargaining techniques (making threats or posing ultimatums) more, with men using confrontational tactics nine times as much as women did. (Only two of the 12 female pairs became confrontational at all.)

On the other side of the equation, the female pairs talked about personal information far more than the males (92 percent of the females compared to 23 percent of the males introduced information about themselves into the negotiation). The women weren't simply making small talk, however, or asking random questions about each other's private lives. The personal information the women discussed was directly relevant to what each side wanted, and introducing this information into their negotiations helped expand their shared understanding of the goals on both sides. In addition, when the women discussed personal information, they did so within the first five minutes of the negotiation (suggesting a more efficient process) but the men who introduced personal information did so only after 20 minutes of negotiation, and only when they were having difficulty reaching an agreement.

Another interesting finding from this study involved the different ways in which the male and female negotiating teams used the case information provided to them. Whereas 50 percent of the female pairs discussed how the playground would affect a senior citizens' home nearby (falling in line with women's prescribed role as caretakers who look out for the interests of others), none of the male pairs took notice of this factor. On the other hand, 58 percent of the males but only 8 percent of the females discussed legal liability issues. This was particularly noteworthy because legal issues were not part of the case materials—the men introduced them on their own.

The results of the playground study strongly suggest that men typically focus more on the competitive elements of a negotiation (discussing their positions from the outset, resorting to confrontational behavior, talking about each side's legal responsibilities) while women focus more on the relational aspects—the needs of both sides and how the outcome of the negotiation will affect other people, such as the senior citizens. Because increasing the flow of information between the negotiators is essential to achieving a superior solution in an integrative bargain, and the female pairs exchanged much more information than the male pairs, this study suggests that women not only employ a more productive process when they negotiate—they're more likely to produce better agreements for both sides.

Our interviews turned up many examples of women quite purposefully taking a collaborative approach to negotiating because they know that this works better. Cheryl, the toy store owner, said of the negotiation process, "It's really important to just listen to somebody. Listening is at the top of the list. That way you get to know that person better. And then you'll be able to negotiate better or get what you want out of it and get what they want out of it." Lory, the theater production manager, said, "I like getting people to tell me what they think—especially if they didn't want to. And especially if it helps us get to where we need to go, find an answer.... I like to hash it out with people, and I like reaching mutually beneficial goals." These women's comments reveal their understanding that getting a good agreement depends on sharing and requesting information. These women understand that the final agreement in any negotiation shouldn't merely fulfill their own interests, it also needs to meet the interests of the other side—a key element in an integrative approach to bargaining.

Women Are Better

If integrative bargaining methods produce superior results in many types of negotiations, and women are more likely than men to use these methods, this should mean that women actually make better negotiators than men. Actually, this appears to be true—at least in situations in which women's cooperative overtures are reciprocated. In one of Linda's negotiation experiments, she and her colleague Hannah Riley asked pairs of MBAs to conduct a multi-issue negotiation that possessed integrative potential. Some possible negotiated agreements could be terrific for both parties and other possible agreements could be terrible for both parties, with a wide range of alternatives in between. Linda and Hannah Riley had chosen the issues to be negotiated so that finding the better outcomes required the negotiators to share information, and when they compared outcomes they discovered that the all-female pairs had outperformed the all-male pairs. The agreements reached by the all-female pairs were better for both negotiators than those reached by the all-male pairs on average.[12] This strongly suggests that the female pairs shared more information and that the male and female pairs used different techniques and behaviors to achieve their results.

Our interviews revealed that many women recognize the differences between their approach and that of the men around them and believe that their less-competitive approach is superior. Ingrid, the city councilwoman, explained why she thinks she's a better negotiator than many men:

> I don't think it's about me. I can listen, and I have an ability to meet people where they're at, and to negotiate with a diverse set of personalities and I think this can sometimes hold men back. I sort of lack the ego that it's about me and it's about winning. It's about the goal.... It's about figuring out very pointedly where I need to go and how to work with this person to get there. Men I know who are even good negotiators often can't check their ego at the door and that can limit their effectiveness.

Angela, the community development bank marketing director, said:

> I think I have a less aggressive negotiating style, or less abrasive... So, when I was lobbying lots of times I would go on visits with various

people who wanted the same things. . . . I know that in some cases my style was more attractive to who we were trying to persuade than others. . . . I think that I'm more genuine in thinking, "you've got something to contribute, I've got something to contribute, let's get to where we need to get here," rather than, "let me tell you how this is going to go." . . . If it's somebody who wants to know what we can provide, what we can give them, and what we want, and go from there . . . that's more my style, my style is better.

Looked at from this angle, an aggressively distributive approach to negotiating can actually put men at a disadvantage. David, the hedge fund manager, told us:

When I was younger I was a classic male, aggressive, dominant, type-A personality. That worked to my detriment many times, not only because a lot of people don't want to deal with you, but people can take advantage of that—push your buttons a little bit. Over time and with the people I've worked with and for, they said, you know, you really ought to think about doing this a different way. You can't be a bull in a china shop all of the time. You've got to really think about what you want, and the best way to get it. You know, all of those silly clichés play in—you draw more flies with honey than vinegar.

Even when a man takes a competitive approach to negotiation and essentially "wins" by setting aggressive goals and resisting concessions, he may suffer in the long run. Many men recognize this problem. Richard, a microbiologist and the vice president of a pharmaceutical company, said: "Men tend to get aggressive faster and they tend to be more outwardly assertive, more impatient. It is all sort of this cowboy kind of approach. Whereas, women will tend to stay low-key. . . . I think in terms of the long term and being a successful negotiator, the man is at a disadvantage because of that behavior. . . . The approach that females take in general is superior and will get better results over time."

As one set of scholars explains, "Seeking to maximize one's own profit in any one bargaining episode may result in short-term gain, but may eventually prove harmful to a negotiator's bargaining position in future episodes. Thus, cooperation may be a superior bargaining tactic because it offers a long-term perspective."[13] In this, women also have an advantage. Research shows that women are more likely to see a negotiation as one event in a long-term relationship whereas men are more likely to think of it as a "one-shot" deal.[14] Heather, the pastor, gave an example of how an aggressive, short-term perspective can backfire:

> In a lot of negotiations, there is this sense that someone's going to put a claim out there and that they're actually willing to negotiate, but because it's put in such an angry, sort of bullying kind of way, I find it really hard to engage with that. I just want to have nothing to do with that person, if they look like they're trying to intimidate me or shame me.... I'm very conscious about how when you negotiate, you're setting up patterns of communication that the person will use again with you.

Of course, very few men behave this badly. But even for more mild-mannered men who still think every negotiation is a contest, focusing on a short-term perspective may "win the battle, but lose the war."

When Advantage Breaks Down

Although we know that the more cooperative approach women bring to negotiation can produce superior results, a good outcome using this approach is not guaranteed. When both negotiators don't share this view of a negotiation—if a man and a woman take different "scripts" into a negotiation, with the man approaching it as a win/lose situation and the woman seeing it as a search for outcomes to benefit both parties—the woman's strategy, though potentially superior, can leave her vulnerable.

Linda and Hannah Riley's study mentioned above, in which the all-female pairs outperformed the all-male pairs, produced another interesting finding: The mixed female-male pairs produced agreements that were no better than those produced by the all-male pairs. Not only did the females fare much worse when they were negotiating against men than when they were negotiating with women, but the "pies" that the female/male pairs split up were *smaller* than the "pies" divided by the all-female pairs. In other words, by sharing information and working together, the all-female pairs were able essentially to "enlarge the pie."[15] By "logrolling" and together taking an integrative approach to the process, they were able to identify hidden benefits for both sides that went unnoticed by the pairs that took a more competitive approach. This suggests that the best outcomes are produced in situations in which both negotiators take a cooperative rather than an adversarial approach to working out a solution—that it takes two women, in other words, or two people trained to "negotiate like women," to produce a superior outcome.

Unfortunately, this study also reveals that going into a negotiation with a cooperative approach can make it harder to withstand the onslaught of a more competitive approach. Deborah Kolb and Judith Williams, in *The Shadow Negotiation*, describe a conflict between two doctors (a male and a female) in the same practice.[16] Both doctors wanted the same week off, but only the woman worried about the damage to their relationship if they could not agree. She thought hard about how to resolve their conflict and decided to try "logrolling"—she offered to let the other doctor have the week off in return for "first dibs" on the summer schedule. He accepted her concession but refused to make one in return, saying that the second issue had nothing to do with the first. She was expecting a give-and-take interaction in which they each gave up something to get something in return (which in her case, but not in his, included good working relations in the practice). He saw the interaction as "winner-take-all" and interpreted her flexibility not as a desire for a favorable outcome for both but as an indication that she was "weaker" and would give in to his will.

We heard similar stories from women who said that they sometimes need to negotiate differently with men than with women. Louise, the power company executive, said:

> If you're negotiating with a woman who is approaching it from a collaborative point of view, and you are, I think there tends to be more open disclosure about what you're really interested in getting, maybe

more trust earlier in the process, and so it tends to be sort of this process of give-and-take until you both get what you need. In negotiating with men, I think there is less willingness to disclose, and a lot less confidence that you're in a situation where you can trust what you're being told.

Louise described an incident in which the man with whom she was negotiating was "very aggressive, very insistent, trying to force a conclusion as opposed to being willing to talk through the process and figure out what the gain was for both. And it was very uncomfortable. And I think to some degree I compromised my decision process as a result of feeling pressed to behave differently because of his style."

Under these circumstances, the techniques of "negotiation jujitsu" described in chapter 5 can sometimes enable a woman to move all sides toward cooperation. By "stepping to their side"—acknowledging the opposing negotiators' interests and communicating that she understands their points of view, asking questions that will draw out information about their needs, and revealing some information and trying to get them to reciprocate—she can often reframe the interaction.

But sometimes these techniques don't work. Louise said that if none of her more cooperative tactics are working, she will behave "more like a man" to get what she wants. "I may try the collaborative approach," she said, but if that doesn't work, "then I may have to try something different—bluff, or, you know, grandstand, close my file and walk away."

Learning how and when to employ these tactics—and building the self-confidence to do so comfortably—can take time and experience, but women's relationship skills and social good sense can often provide them with a significant advantage in this type of situation as well.

Beyond Negotiation

When Sara interviewed Geri, the day care and preschool director, Geri talked a lot about her inferior negotiating skills, describing what she perceived to be her weaknesses and flaws ("my style is hesitant and unsure or more insecure"). She also said that she dislikes negotiation because she's "not good at it." A few weeks later, Sara interviewed Cecelia, a 46-year-old preschool teacher who had worked for Geri for nine years. One of our standard interview questions was: "Is there anyone whose negotiating tactics you admire?" When Sara asked Cecilia this question, she instantly named Geri, her boss. "What about Geri's negotiating tactics do you admire?" Sara asked. "Geri is a very easy person to talk to," Cecilia said. "She's a good listener.... She's never raised her voice to me. And I've gotten really angry and she's always really calm. I feel comfortable talking to her. I can go to Geri and talk to her about anything." Cecilia was describing key integrative skills—good listening, interest in the other person's needs, and openness to his or her point of view.

A few days after Cecilia's interview, Sara saw Geri (Sara's son attended Geri's school) and mentioned that one of her teachers had named her as a negotiations role model. Geri initially laughed with disbelief. But a few days later she called Sara to describe a situation in which she recognized that her style had been an advantage. She'd met with a representative of the church where the school rents space. The school was in the process of being accredited by the National Academy of Early Childhood Programs and needed some plumbing and electrical work done in order to meet the Academy's safety standards. It was also time to renegotiate the school's rental fee for the space. Geri was a little worried about the meeting because historically the church had been reluctant to make capital improvements to the school's space. She also had to negotiate with a new church warden whom she'd never met. So rather than going in and laying out her demands, Geri decided to approach the meeting simply as an opportunity to get to know the new warden and discuss the issues on both sides. She listened respectfully to the church's complaints about the school (mostly regarding parents parking in church parking spaces), and instead of insisting on the changes she wanted, she asked how they could address the needs of both sides. At the end of the meeting, the new warden agreed to make the needed improvements and only raised the school's rent a small amount. Geri felt sure that her nonconfrontational style had been a major factor in producing such a good outcome.

Geri's story is revealing in several ways. First, it illuminates the difficulty many women have in accurately judging their own skills—and the ten-dency of many women to judge themselves according to a male standard. Deborah Kolb argues that women often don't see their negotiating skills as valuable because their negotiating style differs from the dominant style of conducting negotiations, which is a more competitive, win-or-lose male style. [17] The male approach to negotiation (as in so many areas of life) was long seen as the right way and the female way was regarded as the deviant, inferior way.[18] A lot of research in the past has suggested that the solution is to "fix the woman"—to teach women to do as men do. In more recent years, though, scholars have begun to look at women's negotiation skills in another light—to "see difference and value it," as Kolb writes, and to ac-knowledge that sometimes "a woman's point of view ... brings theretofore unnoticed benefits to the negotiation process and the agreements it pro-duces."[19]

Geri's story also illustrates the ways in which the female advantage in negotiating can extend to other parts of life.[20] As both Cecilia's description of her boss and Geri's own interview made clear, Geri's open, relationship-building approach colors her entire management style, and the positive results are easy to identify. In a field (early education) notorious both for low wages and rapid turnover, Geri's staff is distinguished by remarkable longevity (out of a teaching staff of nine, one teacher has worked there for 15 years, one 13, one 11, and one 9). Although you may think that Geri's "feminine" management style is better suited to running a preschool than to running General Motors, new scholarship suggests that women's styles may produce superior results even in the hard-core business world.

Sources ranging from management gurus such as Peter Drucker to business analysts at consulting firms to self-styled "innovation theorists" have all predicted that new approaches will be required for creating value in the businesses of the future—approaches that correspond in many ways to women's management and leadership styles. In a 1993 *Harvard Business Review* interview, Drucker expressed the opinion that the jobs of man-agers have completely changed: "You no longer evaluate an executive in terms of how many people report to him or her. That standard doesn't mean as much as the complexity of the job, the information it uses and generates, and the different kinds of relationships needed to do the work."[21] In another *Harvard Business Review* article, in 1997, the MIT management professor Peter Senge wrote, "Almost everyone agrees that the command-and-control corporate model will not carry us into the twenty-first century. In a world of increasing interdependence and rapid change, it is no longer possible to figure it out from the top."[22]

Jeffrey Pfeffer of Stanford University goes even further. In *The Human Equation: Building Profits by Putting People First*, he argues that "success comes from successfully implementing strategy, not just from having one," and "this implementation capability derives, in large measure, from the organization's people, how they are treated, their skills and competencies, and their efforts on behalf of the organization."[23] The overarching theme of Pfeffer's argument is that in the new global economy, businesses will only thrive by "putting people first." This creates a pressing need for organizations to focus on the ways in which they manage their people: creating high worker morale and building a shared sense of commitment to the organization's success. Doing this requires the use of management practices that promote mutual trust and reduce status distinctions among workers. It also requires practices that instill a sense of "ownership" among employees, such as sharing information concerning the financial health and performance of the organization and emphasizing that everyone in the organization is working toward common goals.

Research by the psychologists Richard Wagner and Robert Sternberg reinforces the value of this approach to management. Noting the lack of any demonstrated link between IQ and job performance, they conclude that mere intelligence and the types of achievement taught and measured in schools have little bearing on whether or not someone makes a good manager. More important, Wagner and Sternberg contend, is something they call "tacit knowledge"—the practical intelligence that enables people to work well with others and motivate them to do what they want.[24] In an article in the *New Yorker*, Wagner said that "in the real world, everything you do involves working with other people. . . . What I.Q. doesn't pick up is effectiveness at common-sense sorts of things, especially working with people."[25]

Research suggests that women may possess more of this type of "common sense." Studies show that men typically adopt more autocratic (directive, command-and-control) leadership styles while women employ more democratic leadership styles that allow subordinates to participate in decision making.[26] Women's more inclusive, consensus-building leadership styles fit nicely with the ability to manage different kinds of relationships emphasized by Drucker, the more collaborative management style Senge believes will be necessary in the future, Pfeffer's emphasis on "putting people first," and Wagner and Sternberg's belief in the importance of "tacit knowledge." Research has also found that women leaders are more interpersonally oriented than men—more concerned with the welfare of the people they work with and with maintaining good professional relationships.[27] These differences even color how women leaders think about their place in their organizations: Where a male leader is more likely to see himself at the top of his organization, a woman leader is more likely to see herself in the center of hers.[28]

Marcela, the nuclear engineer, described her way of asking the people she supervises to do what she needs: "I talk about working *with* people, that people work with me, not for me.... I tend to couch things in those terms—asking for help, asking for input.... 'I'm in the same boat with everybody else; we need to get this done.'"

Cynthia, the chief executive of a large electronics manufacturer, described an early job at which she inherited an administrative office full of women who were used to an autocratic management approach. (Their previous boss had been male.) Finding this an inefficient, even counterproductive, system, Cynthia took a much more collaborative, democratic, and facilitative approach—a much more "feminine" approach—to managing the office. She pushed her employees to work out problems for themselves and take responsibility for finding solutions. The office rapidly became much more productive, and these gains helped her land an even better job. She has since moved up from position to position and is now the top corporate officer of a Fortune 1000 company.

As more and more organizations change from the pyramid structures of old to flat, more flexible organizations in which power is more diffuse, control is looser, and there is more interdependence,[29] both business scholars and business leaders are starting to recognize the correspondence between the skills of women like Marcela and Cynthia and the new needs of organizations.[30] Pulitzer Prize and National Book Award winner James MacGregor Burns, in his influential book *Leadership*, noted that effective leaders energize and inspire their followers and understand their needs and desires. "The male bias is reflected in the false conception of leadership as mere command or control," he wrote. "As leadership comes properly to be seen as a process of leaders engaging and mobilizing the human needs and aspirations of followers, women will be more readily recognized as leaders and men will change their own leadership styles."[31] Similarly, Judith Rosener observed that "there is a convergence between the need to reinvent today's organizations and the interactive leadership styles of women."[32]

Many women in high management positions are also recognizing the need to reinvent today's organizations—and they feel up to the challenge. "Women's goals used to be to get into management, to get onto the boards of Fortune 500 companies, to become CEO," says Margaret Hefferman. "There is a new goal. The aim now is more radical and more ambitious: It is to change the game entirely."[33]

All of this suggests that women's greater participation in the business world will not just provide more opportunities for women and greater gender equality—it may actually produce a strengthening of business culture. By focusing their efforts on cooperating rather than competing, women may be able to teach men to negotiate and manage—and lead—more effectively. By sharing information rather than hoarding it, women may demonstrate the power of a more collaborative approach and model ways in which both men and women can make the best decisions for themselves and their organizations. By involving others in decision making rather than decreeing solutions, women may set a new standard for motivating workers to take pride in their work. And, as Judith Rosener puts it, by approaching management as a process of linking people rather than ranking them, women may lead the way in designing new organizational structures that achieve far higher levels of efficiency and profitability.[34]

Rather than being a threat to either the power of men or the power of our business culture, as men have sometimes feared, and rather than weakening business culture by introducing an inappropriate emotional dimension or focusing on the wrong things (such as relationships rather than outcomes), "Women can transform the workplace by expressing, not giving up, their personal values," contend business writers John Naisbitt and Patricia Aburdene in *Reinventing the Corporation*.[35] The psychologist Jean Baker Miller envisions it this way: "I am not suggesting that women should soften or ameliorate power—but instead that, by their participation, women can strengthen its appropriate operation. Women can bring more power to power by using it when needed and not using it as a poor substitute for other things—like cooperation."[36]

This is not merely an idealistic goal. It's a practical one as well. Being hampered by the "mythical fixed-pie bias" is like "burning money"—the lesser agreements reached instead are often inefficient and, in dollars and cents, costly. By leading the way in showing us how to reach better overall agreements more of the time, manage more effectively, and develop new forms of leadership for the new times in which we live, women will be contributing to more stable and sophisticated business relationships— relationships based on mutual advantage rather than on cruder, more competitively defined measures of success. And strong business relationships are the hallmark of a healthy economy. By demonstrating the benefits of approaching power differently, women may not only be improving their own position within the larger business world, but—as befits an approach that proceeds from a communal impulse—they may be helping us all.

EPILOGUE

Negotiating at Home

FOR MUCH OF THIS BOOK, we've talked about negotiating in terms of the workplace—how women can get to do the work they want to do, see that their work is fairly evaluated, make sure they're paid what they're worth, and proceed as high into the upper levels of their professions as their talent and ambition will take them. We've focused on workplace negotiations not because they're inherently more important than negotiations in other realms, but because most of the existing research about negotiation looks at workplace situations. We just don't know very much about how the factors that constrain women from negotiating for themselves play out in the private sphere. We know that the gender gap in asking widens in ambiguous situations without clear guidelines,[1] and ideas about proper male and female roles have changed enough in recent years to suggest that many private situations now lack clear guidelines for behavior and feel more ambiguous to women.

We do have plenty of evidence, however, that learning to negotiate more in their private lives, particularly with their spouses or partners, may improve women's lives and their health. Numerous studies, for example, have shown that women do far more housework than men, take more responsibility for caring for their children, and have far less leisure time than their spouses.[2] This is true whether they work full-time, part-time, or work entirely in the home. Virginia Valian reports: "Almost all employed women in heterosexual relationships live in households where the division of labor is grossly and visibly inequitable.... The imbalance exists among all groups of women who live with men, including professional women. Married women who work for pay average about thirty-three hours of housework per week—about two-thirds of the total household work. Married men who are employed do fourteen to eighteen hours of housework a week."[3]

The impact of this unequal division of household labor is substantial and measurable. Research has shown that women with families who work full-time experience far higher levels of stress than their male counterparts, and that their excessive stress is due not to the demands of their employment but to the weight of their responsibilities at home. In one extraordinarily revealing study, researchers periodically measured the blood pressure and norepinephrine levels of managers during the day. (They chose norepinephrine because this hormone responds rapidly to changes in stress.) They found that the male managers' blood pressure and stress-hormone levels dropped dramatically at five P.M. but the women managers' levels actually jacked up as they turned their attention from their "first-shift" jobs to their "second-shift" responsibilities as wives and mothers. Another researcher, who looked at the levels of stress hormones in employed mothers and childless women, found that the women with children at home excreted higher levels of the stress hormone cortisol and reported more stress around home responsibilities. The amount of stress they experienced around their work responsibilities did not differ from the stress experienced by childless women.[4]

These higher levels of both norepinephrine and cortisol represent a genuine threat to women's health. As Linda Austin reports in *What's Holding You Back*, "Chronic elevation of blood pressure caused by norepinephrine secretion...is a significant risk factor for heart disease, the number one killer of women."[5] Dr. Bruce S. McEwen, director of the neuroendocrinology laboratory at Rockefeller University, confirms that "prolonged or severe stress has been shown to weaken the immune system, strain the heart, damage memory cells in the brain and deposit fat at the waist rather than the hips or buttocks (a risk factor for heart disease, cancer, and other illnesses)."[6] In addition to these threats, stress can contribute to aging, depression, rheumatoid arthritis, diabetes, and other illnesses.[7]

Women pay for shouldering more than their share of household work with diminished professional success as well. Numerous studies have noted the fact that, as Linda Austin writes, "high achievement and heavy domestic responsibilities do not mix."[8] This is not because getting married and having children automatically saps a woman's ambition and makes her want to aim less high professionally, but because the burden of her responsibilities at home make it impossible for her to devote the attention, energy, and time to her career that single or childless women can commit. In many cases, this is a choice that women happily make. Nonetheless, research has consistently shown that working mothers experience more stress and depression than working fathers do. And, as Linda Austin writes, "the cause of the stress is frequently misattributed. It is often implied that employment is causing women stress and depression and that the remedy is staying home." In fact the opposite is the case: "A study of 3,800 men and women concluded that paid employment is associated with reduced depression among both husbands and wives, while time spent in housework is associated with increased depression for both genders, regardless of other roles."[9]

This tells us that working outside the home can be good for a woman's mental health, but if she also has children she will find herself desperately in need of the skills necessary to make that balancing act work. One of the most important skills she will need is the ability to negotiate with her spouse or partner. Of course, if her circumstances permit it, a woman can choose to work part-time, choose a less aggressive career track, or decide to put some of her ambitions on hold until her children are older. If she is sufficiently affluent, a woman can hire people to do some of the household labor she doesn't have time to do (housecleaners, nannies, gardeners—even cooks and personal assistants). Any of these are fine choices for a woman to make if she can. And none of them change the fact that caring for children and running a household take a lot of work, and it makes sense for both adult partners in a relationship to do a fair proportion of that work. Negotiation can be a useful strategy for establishing a more equitable distribution of this workload.

Thinking About It Differently

Shortly before her first child was born, Emma, the social science researcher, said to her husband, "How are you going to care for your child while you are at work?" Her husband was taken aback—he had not considered that this was a problem he needed to solve. He'd assumed that Emma would make whatever adjustments needed to be made to see that their child was properly cared for. Emma told Sara that she frequently repeats this story to groups of women, and they always respond with a kind of shocked delight, applauding her for her daring. Their response reveals the assumptions made by most women: Since they have always done the lion's share of the childcare and housework, it seems normal to them that they should continue to do so—and make whatever sacrifices, professional or otherwise, that this may require. They don't question this requirement, even though women's lives have changed markedly since that norm was established.

Women's lives have changed, but our thinking has not. Virginia Valian puts it succinctly: "The usual solutions proffered to solve 'women's' problem are higher-quality, more affordable, more widely available child care; flexible work hours; and family-leave policies. All those improvements are needed, but they fail to question the way the problem is framed. They do not ask why combining work and family is a female problem rather than a human problem, and thus do not address it as a human problem."[10] Valian also points out that until "both parties are willing to resolve conflicts so that sometimes the male's and sometimes the female's work suffers, there will be no change. Change will occur only when each partner believes that the other should have an equal chance for professional and domestic fulfillment and works to make fairness a daily reality."[11] Seeing the home as an arena in which negotiation plays an important role can enable both men and women to start thinking more creatively and more fairly about

ways to share their household responsibilities. Linda Austin puts it another way: "The resolution of these issues in the domestic realm is outside
the reach of political ideology.... Private power relations can only be negotiated by an individual woman relating to an individual man."[12]

Matters of Life and Death

The stress of working full-time and shouldering the majority of the caretaking responsibilities at home, as we've shown, can represent a real threat
to women's health. But there are even more serious health reasons why
women must learn to negotiate in the personal realm. Every minute, between five and six women worldwide are infected with the HIV/AIDS
virus.[13] As of the end of 1999, 14.8 million women in the world were living
with HIV/AIDS;[14] in the year 2000, 10,459 new AIDS cases among women
were reported in the United States alone.[15] Condom use is widely known
to prevent the transmission of HIV, but men don't especially like wearing
condoms and don't often volunteer to do so. This puts women into the almost unavoidably awkward position of *needing to ask*. But asking for what
they want and need, so difficult for women in many circumstances, can
feel close to impossible in this intimate situation. And needless to say, not
asking can have drastic life consequences.

   Research has begun to focus on why condoms are not used more frequently, despite the obvious risks of not using them. A 1993 study of the
HIV/AIDS epidemic in Haiti points to two principal issues: women's economic dependency and their concern with fostering and protecting their
relationships.[16] After conducting gender-segregated focus groups with men
and women, the researchers concluded that because men bring in most or
all of the family's income, women receive little respect and have "little influence on household decisions."[17] In Haiti, many men exercise a lot of sexual freedom outside the home. This makes it doubly important for women
to wield some influence over the "household decision" of whether or not
their partners wear condoms during sexual activity. But women who receive little respect because of their economic dependency often can't do
this. Making their problem more difficult, "the high value women attach to

harmony in long-term unions leads them to condone or overlook a man's sexual activity outside the home in the interest of protecting the partnership."[18] This characteristically female commitment to protecting relationships—one of women's best and most enduring qualities—in this context could literally be killing them.

The situation of women in Haiti is pretty extreme, and other Western societies may not be quite so imbalanced in terms of sexual power-sharing. But researchers in the United States have found that women often don't ask their partners to use condoms for similar reasons—because they're concerned that doing so will damage their relationships.[19] If their unwillingness to ask their partners to use condoms doesn't always cost American women their lives, it often leaves them with unwanted pregnancies or venereal diseases—such as herpes simplex—that may be with them for the rest of their lives. It also puts their future sexual partners and the rest of us (who until now have avoided an epidemic similar to Haiti's) at risk.

This one public health crisis, as much as any other example, highlights the importance of women not simply learning that they *can* ask for what they want and need, but that they *must* learn to ask—in all parts of their lives. Because men are the ones who wear condoms, women must clearly learn how to negotiate better in the private realms of their lives. But as the situation in Haiti so dramatically reveals, they need to learn how to negotiate outside the bedroom as well—because when women improve their economic status, they increase their clout in private as well as in professional negotiations. Once that happens (when women achieve economic parity with men and can wield equal power in the bedroom and the boardroom), men may be unable to find women who will *allow* them to have sex without using condoms. They may even find themselves living in a society so profoundly changed that protecting the health of their intimate partners earns them respect and admiration.

We like this vision of the future, and we hope that helping women learn to negotiate both at home and at work—and teaching society to accept women's need and right to negotiate—will make our world a better, healthier, and more just place for our children to inherit and enjoy.

ACKNOWLEDGMENTS

We have many people and organizations to thank for their help with this project. The National Science Foundation, the Heinz Family Foundation, and the Heinz School at Carnegie Mellon provided generous support for Linda's research. Max Bazerman and Mark Kamlet encouraged Linda to write a book about her ideas. Nikki Sabin of the Harvard Business School Press recommended that she write it with Sara, kicking off what we expect will be years of fruitful work together. Linda's Ph.D. students Deborah Small and Heidi Stayn contributed hundreds of hours of hard work and along with Michele Gelfand and Hannah Riley collaborated with Linda on much of the important research in the book; Jon Baron hosted our survey on his website; and Jennifer Lerner taught Linda a great deal about psychology and directed her to relevant research. Linda's research assistants Jo Ann Shoup and Luisa Blanchfield and the students in Linda's negotiation classes helped her refine, develop, and find confirmation for her ideas. Linda's colleagues at Carnegie Mellon made the writing process easier and more enjoyable by making the Heinz School a fun and stimulating place to work.

We would also like to thank the hundreds of scholars whose important work in gender studies helped pave the way for this work. The scholarship of the following researchers, in particular, contributed immeasurably to the substance of this book and the development of our ideas: Lisa Barron, Linda Carli, Ann Crittenden, Faye Crosby, Kay Deaux, Alice Eagly, Peter Glick, Madeline Heilman, John Jost, Rosabeth Moss Kanter, Deborah Kolb, Eleanor Maccoby, Brenda Major, Cecilia Ridgeway, Judith Rosener, Laurie Rudman, Deborah Tannen, Virginia Valian, and Mary Wade.

Ann Laschever, Richard and Roberta Gross, Mike and Ann Moore, Charlie Moore, and Mande and Dave Mischler extended their hospitality to Sara's entire family while she was traveling around the country interviewing people. They also put her in touch with a raft of good potential interview subjects. Rachel Asher, Hilary Blair, Ellen Brodsky, Judith Fisher, Lucia Gemmell, JoAnn Griffin, Michele LaForge, Dolores and Barney Laschever, Julia Lieblich, Karen Lynch, Jenny Mikesell, Lynn Osborn, Ann Riley, Marilyn Griggs Riley, Diane Schilder, Mary Snyder, Pamela Sutherland, and Vic Svilik also directed Sara to people with good stories to tell and a wide range of experiences with negotiating.

We extend special thanks to the many people who took time out of their busy lives to let us interview them. We heard far more wonderful and illuminating stories than we could include here, and everyone we talked to enhanced our appreciation of the forces that constrain women from asking. In many cases, we have changed their names and a few details about their lives to protect their privacy, but the essence of their stories remains intact.

Cynthia and Jan Babcock, Lisa Barron, Jonathan Caulkins, Jennifer Lerner, Julia Lieblich, Hannah Riley, Joyce Roe, Denise Rousseau, Gerhard Sonnert, Kathleen McGinn, and Sara's husband, Tim, as well as members of Ann English's book club in Pittsburgh read early versions of the manuscript and shared their excellent suggestions.

Dick Thaler introduced us to Peter Dougherty, our wonderful editor, who has been an ardent champion of this project from the beginning. The book has benefited immeasurably from his acute suggestions, broad knowledge, and constant enthusiasm.

Brenda Peyser was a steady source of encouragement for Linda; Anne Blumberg and Jonathan Dorfman cheered Sara on at every step along the way; and our husbands, Mark Wessel and Tim Riley, provided nonstop support, enthusiasm, tolerance, and help with the kids.

This book could not have been written without the dedicated efforts of Carly Canning, Noeleen Geaney, and the staffs of the Cyert Center for Early Education at Carnegie Mellon and the Bigelow Cooperative Daycare Center in Cambridge, Massachusetts, who took such good care of our children while we were working on it. Last but not least, we want to thank our children for their patience as we labored on long after we promised we'd be done—and for entertaining us, making us laugh, and distracting us, even when we wished they wouldn't.

NOTES

The research we have used in this book looks at average differences between men and women, using samples of people in the United States. Although we included people from a variety of racial backgrounds in our research and interview samples, the average person in the United States is white, and we haven't (and by and large others have not) collected large enough samples within racial groups to say anything about how gender differences may vary across racial groups. As a result, there may be important differences that we aren't picking up. This research needs to be done (and in some cases is in the process of being done) and we hope that the issues raised in this book will inspire more of this type of work.

Preface

1. Fisher 1999; Pasternak and Viscio 1998; Helgesen 1990.
2. Rousseau 2001.
3. U.S. Department of Labor, Bureau of Labor Statistics 2000.
4. U.S. Department of Labor, Bureau of Labor Statistics 2002a.
5. U.S. Department of Labor, Bureau of Labor Statistics 2002b.
6. Fullerton and Toossi 2001.
7. U.S. Small Business Administration 2001.
8. U.S. divorce statistics, available from www.divorcemag.com/statistics/statsUS.
9. Ibid.
10. Weitzman 1985.

11. Ventura and Bachrach 2000.

12. Detailed income tabulations from the Current Population Survey, http:// www. census.gov/hhes/income/dinctabs.html; U.S. Department of Labor 2000.

13. Committee on the Status of Women in the Economics Profession 2002; Blank 1994.

14. Shemo 2002.

INTRODUCTION

1. Babcock 2002.

2. Small, Babcock, and Gelfand 2003.

3. Only 2.5 percent of the female subjects but 23 percent of the male subjects asked for more.

4. Babcock, Gelfand, Small, and Stayn 2002. The survey was hosted by Jonathan Baron's website at the University of Pennsylvania.

5. Another interpretation is possible, however. Men may not really be doing more negotiating than women; men and women may behave in the same ways but label or describe their behavior differently. That is, what a man calls a negotiation, a woman calls something else. This interpretation seems less plausible because it suggests that men and women define a common word in our language differently. But even if it is true, it still has implications for behavior. If women aren't calling their interactions negotiations and men are, women may not be viewing those encounters as strategically and instrumentally as men do and may therefore gain less from them in significant ways.

6. Although we strove to make our sample as representative as possible of the full diversity of women in Western culture, we used the interviews only to illustrate the ideas in the book and did not try to ensure that our sample exactly matched current demographic patterns in the population. We also interviewed far more women than men.

7. Babcock, Gelfand, Small, and Stayn 2002.

8. Gerhart 1990.

9. Pinkley and Northcraft 2000. Example is from page 6.

10. Ibid.

11. Janoff-Bulman and Wade 1996.

12. Malhotra 2002.

13. Martell, Lane, and Emrich 1996.

14. Valian 1998. Quotation is from page 3.

15. Ibid. Idea introduced on pages 4–5.

16. Pinkley and Northcraft 2000. Quotation is from page 6.

17. Babcock, Gelfand, Small, and Stayn 2002.

18. Ibid.

19. For good texts that summarize negotiation research, see Thompson 1998; Raiffa 1982; Lewicki, Saunders, and Minton 1997; Neale and Bazerman 1991.

20. Janoff-Bulman and Wade 1996; Gerhart and Rynes 1991; Kaman and Hartel 1994.

21. Gladwell 2000. Quotation is from page 258.

22. Ibid. Quotation is from page 259.

23. Ibid. Quotation is from page 11.

24. Information on Deloitte and Touche's program is drawn from McCracken 2000.

25. Ibid.

26. Kanter 1990. Quotation is from page 11.

27. Ibid. Quotation is from page 13.

Chapter 1: Opportunity Doesn't Always Knock

1. Babcock, Gelfand, Small, and Stayn 2002.

2. Rotter 1966.

3. Crandall and Crandall 1983.

4. Strickland and Haley 1980; Parkes 1985; Kunhikrishnan and Manikandan 1995; Wade, T. J. 1996.

5. Smith, Dugan, and Trompenaars 1997.

6. Austin 2000. Quotation is from page 39.

7. These statistics are from the Catalyst website, 2001 Catalyst census of women board of directors of the Fortune 1000 (www.catalystwomen.org). Catalyst is a non-profit research and advocacy organization.

8. Rosenthal and Rodrigues 2000.

9. Inter-parliamentary Union 2000.

10. Austin 2000. Quotation is from page 39.

11. Fiske and Taylor 1984.

12. For research on the development of gender schemas, see Maccoby 1966; Liben and Signorella 1987; Mussen 1983.

13. Valian 1998. Quotation is from page 48.

14. Fiske and Taylor 1984.

15. Beal 1994.

16. Rubin, Provenzano, and Luria 1974.

17. Goodnow 1988.

18. Chodorow 1978.

19. Orenstein 1994. Quotation is from page xiv.

20. Barron 2003.

21. Tannen 1994.

22. Carpenter and Huston 1980.

23. Carpenter and Huston 1980; Fagot 1978; Huston and Carpenter 1985.

24. Carpenter, Huston, and Holt 1986.

25. Babcock, Gelfand, Small, and Stayn 2002.

26. Cohoon 2001.

CHAPTER 2: A PRICE HIGHER THAN RUBIES

1. Sauser and York 1978.

2. Crosby 1982.

3. Graham and Welbourne 1999.

4. Major and Konar 1984.

5. Martin 1989.

6. Major and Konar 1984.

7. Jackson, Gardner, and Sullivan 1992.

8. Porter and Lawler 1968; Locke 1976.

9. Proverbs 31:10.

10. Crittenden 2001. Quotation is from page 2.

11. Ibid. Quotation is from page 5.

12. Ibid. Quotation is from page 17.

13. Ibid. Quotation is from page 17.

14. Eckert 1993. Quotation is from page 34.

15. Goodnow 1988.

16. Ibid.

17. Valian 1998. Quotation is from page 32.

18. Ibid. Quotation is from page 33.

19. Weitzman 1985.

20. Crosby 1982; Goodman 1974.

21. Bylsma and Major 1994; Crosby 1982.

22. U.S. Department of Labor, Bureau of Labor Statistics 2001.

23. Roberts and Nolen-Hoeksema 1989; Roberts and Nolen-Hoeksema 1994; Schwalbe and Staples 1991; Lenney 1977.

24. Roberts and Nolen-Hoeksema 1989.

25. Callahan-Levy and Messe 1979.

26. Major, McFarlin, and Gagnon 1984.

27. Ibid.

28. Barron 2003.

29. Babcock, Gelfand, Small, and Stayn 2002.

30. Taylor and Brown 1988; Taylor and Brown 1994.

31. Brown, Andrews, Bifulco, and Veiel 1990.

32. Stermer 2003.

33. Lemonick 2003.

34. Ibid.

35. Beyer and Bowden 1997. Quotation is from page 169.

36. Crittenden 2001. Quotation is from page 6.

37. www.psych.ucsc.edu/Faculty/Crosby.shtml; see also Crosby 1984.

38. Crosby, Pufall, Snyder, O'Connell, and Whalen 1989.

39. Rosenthal and Rodrigues 2000.

40. Almer 2000.

41. Pfeffer 1998.

42. Epstein 1991. Quotation is from page 251.

43. Ibid. Quotation is from page 257.

44. Major, McFarlin, and Gagnon 1984.

45. Bylsma and Major 1992.

46. Riley, Babcock, and McGinn 2003.

CHAPTER 3: NICE GIRLS DON'T ASK

1. For reviews, see Eagly 1987; Heilman 1995.

2. Deaux and Major 1987; Eagly 1995.

3. Heilman 1995.

4. Bakan 1966; Eagly 1987.

5. Desmarais and Curtis 1997.

6. Major, McFarlin, and Gagnon 1984.

7. Archer 1996.

8. Eagly 1987; Deaux and Major 1987.

9. Statistics on occupations are from U.S. Department of Labor, Bureau of Labor Statistics 2001. Statistics on corporate officers are from the Catalyst website, 2001 Catalyst census of women board of directors of the Fortune 1000 (www.catalystwomen.org).

10. Cejka and Eagly 1999.

11. Tomaskovic-Devey 1995.

12. Eagly 1987.

13. Babcock, Gelfand, Small, and Stayn 2002.

14. Maccoby 1988; Maccoby 1990; Maccoby and Jacklin 1987; Serbin, Sprafkin, Elman, and Doyle 1984; Chodorow 1978.

15. Maccoby 1988. Quotation is from page 759.

16. Kubik 2000.

17. *Getting the message* 1997.

18. Brazleton and Sparrow 2001; Cassell and Jenkins 1998.

19. *Getting the message* 1997.

20. Lytton and Romney 1991; Stern and Karraker 1989.

21. Callahan-Levy and Messe 1979.

22. Kling, Shelby-Hyde, Showers, and Buswell 1999; Feingold 1994.

23. Kling, Shelby-Hyde, Showers, and Buswell 1999. Quotation is from page 472.

24. Stein, Newcomb, and Bentler 1992.

25. Eagly 1987; Deaux and Major 1987; Eagly 1997.

26. Rosenthal and Jacobson 1968.

27. Ibid. Quotation is from page 66.

28. Harris and Rosenthal 1985.

29. For a review, see Gilbert 1995.

30. Eagly 1987; Deaux and Major 1987.

31. Gilbert 1995; Cantor and Mischel 1979; O'Sullivan and Durso 1984.

32. Gilbert 1995.

33. Wade, M. E. 2001.

34. Kray, Thompson, and Galinsky 2001.

35. Jost 1997.

36. Ibid. Quotation is from page 388.

37. Ibid. Quotation is from page 387.

38. Ross and Sicoly 1979.

39. Sonnert and Holton 1995.

40. Widnall 1988. Quotation is from page 1743. Cited in Sonnert and Holton 1995, page 10.

41. Hornig 1987; Widnall 1988.

42. Orenstein 1994. Quotation is from page xxxi.

43. Crosby and Ropp 2002. Quotation is from page 394.

44. Nussbaum 2001.

45. Heilman 1995. Quotation is from page 8.

46. Steele and Aronson 1995; Steele 1997; Aronson, Lustina, Good, Keough, Steele, and Brown 1999.

47. Spencer, Steele, and Quinn 1999.

48. Steele and Aronson 1995.

49. Kray, Thompson, and Galinsky 2001; Aronson, Good, and Harder 1998.

50. Spencer, Steele, and Quinn 1999.

51. Ibid.

52. Inzlicht and Ben-Zeev 2000.

53. Sue Molina, personal communication, 14 March 2003.

54. Quotations obtained from the Accenture website, www.accenture.com.

55. Bigg 1991.

56. Quotation from the Catalyst website, www.catalystwomen.org.

57. www.workingmother.com/thinkoutside.shtml

Chapter 4: Scaring the Boys

1. Banerjee 2001.

2. *BBC News Online: Business* 2001.

3. Banerjee 2001.

4. Ibid.

5. Ibid.

6. O'Connor 2000.

7. Ridgeway and Dickeman 1989; Ridgeway, Diekeman, and Johnson 1995; Burgoon, Birk, and Hall 1991.

8. Copeland, Driskell, and Salas 1995.

9. Carli 1990.

10. Carli 2001; Carli 1998.

11. Case 1990. Quotation is from page 108.

12. Heilman 1995.

13. Wade, M. E. 2001.

14. Ibid. Quotation is from page 65.

15. Costrich, Feinstein, Kidder, Marecek, and Pascale 1975; Rudman 1998.

16. Carli 1990; Wade, M. E. 2001.

17. Heatherington, Crown, Wagner, and Rigby 1992; Miller, Cooke, Tsang, and Morgan 1992.

18. Miller, Cooke, Tsang, and Morgan 1992.

19. Carli 2001; Glick, Zion, and Nelson 1988.

20. Jones and Pittman 1982.
21. Rudman 1998. Quotation is from page 629.
22. Carli 1990; Case 1990; Rudman 1998; Burgoon, Dillard, and Doran 1983.
23. Case 1990. Quotation is from page 108.
24. Statham 1987.
25. Eagly, Makhijani, and Klonsky 1992.
26. Butler and Geis 1990.
27. Schein 1973; Schein 1975.
28. Powell and Butterfield 1989.
29. Norris and Wylie 1995; Tomkiewicz and Adeyemi-Bello 1995; Deal and Stevenson 1998.
30. Deal and Stevenson 1998.
31. Schein and Mueller 1992; Schein, Mueller, Lituchy, and Liu 1996.
32. Khurana 2002. Quoted in Useem 2002, page 90.
33. Heilman 1995. Quotation is from page 8.
34. Kanter 1977.
35. Heilman 1980.
36. Bertrand and Hallock 2000.
37. Heffernan 2002.
38. Ibid. Quotation is from page 60.
39. Cejka and Eagly 1999.
40. Lashinsky 2002. Quotation is from page 104.
41. Ibid. Quotation is from page 106.
42. Ibid. Quotation is from page 98.
43. Neumark 1996.
44. Goldin and Rouse 2000.
45. Valian 1998. Quotation is from page 214.
46. Llewellyn-Williams 2002.
47. Blau and Kahn 2000.
48. Heffernan 2002. Quotation is from page 62.
49. Faludi 1991. The story of Diane Joyce is recounted on pages 388–393.
50. Ibid. Quotation is from page 390.
51. Ibid. Quotation is from page 391.
52. Ibid. Quotation is from page 391.
53. Rosener 1998.
54. The Yankelovich Monitor poll, cited in Faludi 1991, page 65.
55. Wade, M. E. 2001; Eagly 1987.
56. Wise 2002; Gregorian 2002; Judd 2001.

57. Faludi 1991. Quotation is from page 70.

58. Satel 2001.

59. Shalit 1999.

60. Graglia 1998.

61. Sommers 2000.

62. For a summary of the literature, see Wade, M. E. 2001.

63. Major, McFarlin, and Gagnon 1984.

64. Daubman, Heatherington, and Ahn 1992.

65. Kahn, O'Leary, Krulewitz, and Lamm 1980. Quotation is from page 176.

66. Wade, M. E. 2002.

67. Gneezy, Niederle, and Rustichini 2001.

68. Hewlett 2002. Quotation is from page 41.

69. Dowd 2002.

70. Chupack 2000–2001.

71. Carli, LaFleur, and Lober 1995.

72. Ridgeway 1982. Quotation is from page 81.

73. Ridgeway 2001. Quotation is from pages 649–650.

74. Rudman and Glick 2001; Rudman and Glick 1999.

75. Rudman and Glick 2001. Quotation is from page 743.

76. Carli, LaFleur, and Lober 1995.

77. Ridgeway 2001. Quotation is from pages 649–650.

78. Rudman and Glick 2001. Quotation is from page 758.

79. Yoder 2001. Quotation is from page 819.

80. Carli 2001.

81. Carli 1990.

82. Eagly and Johannesen-Schmidt 2001.

83. Rynecki 2002.

84. Yoder 2001; Tolbert, Simons, Andrews, and Rhee 1995.

85. Fiske and Taylor 1984; Heilman 2001.

86. Heilman, Haynes, and Goodman 2001.

87. Boyle 2002. Quotations are from page 208.

88. Valian 1998. Quotation is from page 291.

89. *Price Waterhouse v. Hopkins* (490 U.S. 228 [1989]). Quotation is from pages 1790–1791.

90. Valian 1998. Quotation is from page 16.

CHAPTER 5: FEAR OF ASKING

1. Babcock, Gelfand, Small, and Stayn 2002.
2. Michele Gelfand, personal communication, 22 February 2002.
3. Babcock, Gelfand, Small, and Stayn 2002.
4. Purohit and Sondak (2001). Gender results were not in the paper but came to us in a personal communication from Harris Sondak, 30 August 2001.
5. Bill Betts, General Motors, personal communication.
6. For an extensive literature review, see Cross and Madson 1997.
7. McGuire and McGuire 1982.
8. McCrae and Costa 1988.
9. Bybee, Glick, and Zigler 1990.
10. Clancy and Dollinger 1993.
11. Taylor 2002.
12. Cross and Madson 1997.
13. Dunn, Bretherton, and Munn 1987; Fivush 1992.
14. Sociologists call these "self-concept" or "identity" differences.
15. Fiske and Taylor 1984.
16. Cross and Madson 1997. For alternative views on independent and interdependent self-schemas, see Baumeister and Sommer 1997; Gabriel and Gardner 1999.
17. Cross and Madson 1997. Quotation is from page 7. These two different schemas, independent as opposed to interdependent, were originally proposed to summarize Eastern and Western cross-cultural differences. See Markus and Kitayama 1991.
18. King and Hinson 1994; Gelfand, Smith-Major, Raver, and Nishii 2000; Greenhalgh and Gilkey 1993.
19. Barron 2003.
20. Kolb and Coolidge 1991. Quotations are on pages 262 and 267.
21. Maccoby 1988; Maccoby 1990; Maccoby and Jacklin 1987.
22. Kraft and Vraa 1975; Maccoby 1990.
23. Serbin, Sprafkin, Elman, and Doyle 1984; Maltz and Borker 1983.
24. Lever 1976.
25. Humphreys and Smith 1987.
26. Miller, Danaher, and Forbes 1986; Maltz and Borker 1983; Maccoby 1988.
27. Sheldon 1990.
28. Lever 1976.
29. Maccoby 1990.

30. Tannen 1994. Quotation is from page 58.
31. Ibid.
32. Tannen 1990.
33. Kolb and Coolidge 1991.
34. Maccoby 1990.
35. Josephs, Markus, and Tafarodi 1992.
36. Miller 1986. Quotation is from page 83.
37. Hodgins, Liebeskind, and Schwartz 1996.
38. Josephs, Markus, and Tafarodi 1992.
39. Kolb and Williams 2000. Quotation is from page 184.
40. Fisher and Ury 1981. Quotation is from page 40. Story is taken from a paper that Mary Parker Follett presented to a Bureau of Personnel Administration conference group in January 1925. The paper was later published in a book of her collected papers, Fox and Urwick (eds.) 1973.
41. Ibid.; Ury 1991.
42. Fisher and Ury 1981. See also Thompson 1998.
43. Hatfield, Caccioppo, and Rapson 1992.
44. Carnevale and Isen 1986; Barry and Oliver 1996; Allred, Mallozzi, Matsui, and Raia 1997.
45. Fisher and Ury 1981. Quotation is from page 108.
46. Allred 1999.
47. Ury 1991.
48. Ibid.

CHAPTER 6: LOW GOALS AND SAFE TARGETS

1. Bergmann 1986.
2. Stevens, Bavetta, and Gist 1993; Barron 2003; King and Hinson 1994; Riley, Babcock, and McGinn 2003; Stuhlmacher and Walters 1999; Riley 2001.
3. Riley, Babcock, and McGinn 2003.
4. Gerhart and Rynes 1991.
5. Stevens, Bavetta, and Gist 1993; Riley, Babcock, and McGinn 2003.
6. Locke and Latham 1990.
7. Riley, Babcock, and McGinn 2003.
8. Author's calculation based on data in Riley, Babcock, and McGinn 2003.
9. White and Neale 1994; Galinsky, Mussweiler, and Medvec 2002.
10. Galinsky, Mussweiler, and Medvec 2002.

11. Ibid.

12. Barron 2003.

13. Riley, Babcock, and McGinn 2003.

14. Stevens, Bavetta, and Gist 1993.

15. Kaman and Hartel 1994.

16. Riley, Babcock, and McGinn 2003.

17. Slovic 2000; Lerner, Gonzalez, Small, and Fischhoff 2003.

18. Slovic 2000. Quotation is from page 402.

19. Riley, Babcock, and McGinn 2003.

20. Ibid.

21. Ibid.

22. Rowland, Franken, and Harrison 1986; Braathen and Svebak 1992; Svebak and Kerr 1989; Ellis 1986; Jelalian, Spirito, Raile, Vinnick, Rohrbeck, and Aarrigan 1997.

23. Zuckerman 1974; Zuckerman 1978; Zuckerman, Buchsbaum, and Murphy 1980.

24. Arch 1993. Quotation is from page 3.

25. For a good review, see Mazur and Booth 1998.

26. Sullivan 2000.

27. Booth, Shelley, Mazur, Tharp, and Kittok 1989; Mazur, Susman, and Edelbrock 1997.

28. Daltzman and Zuckerman 1980.

29. Kemper 1990; Klaiber, Broverman, Vogel, Abraham, and Cone 1971.

30. Booth, Shelley, Mazur, Tharp, and Kittok 1989.

31. Dabbs, de la Rue, and Williams 1990.

32. Mazur and Booth 1998.

33. Sullivan 2000. Quotation is from page 51.

34. Ibid. Quotation is from page 69.

35. Babcock, Gelfand, Small, and Stayn 2002.

36. Bandura and Wood 1989; Bandura 1977.

37. Instone, Major, and Bunker 1983.

38. Lenney 1977.

39. Beyer and Bowden 1997.

40. Kolb and Putnam 1997.

41. Babcock, Gelfand, Small, and Stayn 2002.

42. Stevens, Bavetta, and Gist 1993.

43. Gist, Stevens, and Bavetta 1991; Stevens, Bavetta, and Gist 1993.

44. Stevens, Bavetta, and Gist 1993. Quotation is from page 726.

45. Ibid.
46. Kolb and Coolidge 1991; Kolb and Putnam 1997; Jackson, Gardner, and Sullivan 1992.
47. These statistics are available at www.census.gov, table P064 from the 2000 census.

CHAPTER 7: JUST SO MUCH AND NO MORE

1. Ayres and Siegelman 1995. With both a man and a woman trying to buy a car at each of 153 dealerships, the "dealer mark-up" in the first prices quoted to white women was an average of 11 percent higher than the mark-up in the prices quoted to white men. The mark-up in the prices quoted to black women was 31 percent higher.
2. Solnick 2001.
3. Burt 1992.
4. Brass 1985.
5. Ibarra 1997; Ibarra 1992.
6. Mehra, Kilduff, and Brass 1998: Quotation is from page 441.
7. Granovetter 1982.
8. Ibarra 1997. Quotation is from page 99.
9. Fitt and Newton 1981. Quotation is from page 58.
10. Ibid. Quotation is from page 56.
11. Burt 1992.
12. Ibid.
13. Fitt and Newton 1981.
14. Epstein 1991. Quotation is from page 251.
15. Wade, M. E. 2001. Quotation is from page 66.
16. Callahan-Levy and Messe 1979.
17. Wade, M. E. 2002.
18. Ibid.
19. Riley, Babcock, and McGinn 2003.
20. Kuhn 1992. Described in Tannen 1994, pages 175–176.
21. Gilbert 1995.
22. Quotations are from the Tulane University Teaching Guide, Schindler after the Second World War, available at http://www.tulane.edu/~so-inst/slguid5.html.
23. Michaud 2001.
24. Taylor, Klein, Lewis, Gruenewald, Gurung, and Updegraff 2000.
25. Ibid. Quotation is from page 424.

26. Dranginis 2002.
27. Announced in the 9 July 2002 National Institutes of Health (NIH) news release "NHLBI Stops Trial of Estrogen Plus Progestin Due to Increased Breast Cancer Risk, Lack of Overall Benefit." Available at http://www.nih.gov.
28. Dranginis 2002.

CHAPTER 8: THE FEMALE ADVANTAGE

1. Bazerman and Neale 1992. Quotation is from page 16.
2. Thompson 1998. Statistic is from page 49.
3. Dawson 2000. Quotation is from page 248.
4. Thompson 1991.
5. Fisher and Ury 1981.
6. Thompson 1991; Lax and Sebenius 1986; Pruitt and Rubin 1986; Fisher and Ury 1981; Raiffa 1982.
7. Thompson 1991.
8. Kimmel, Pruitt, Magenau, Konar-Goldband, and Carnevale 1980.
9. Helgesen 1990.
10. Walters, Stuhlmacher, and Meyer 1998.
11. Halpern and Parks 1996.
12. Riley and Babcock 2002.
13. Stuhlmacher and Walters 1999. Quotation is from page 656.
14. Greenhalgh and Gilkey 1993.
15. Riley and Babcock 2002.
16. Kolb and Williams 2000. Story is on pages 31–34.
17. Kolb 2000.
18. Gray 1994.
19. Kolb 2000. Quotation is from page 3.
20. Sally Helgesen's book *The Female Advantage* explores the benefits of women's approaches to leadership.
21. Harris 1993. Quotation is from page 115.
22. Senge 1997. Quotation is from page 9.
23. Pfeffer 1998. Quotation is from page 17.
24. For a review of this research, see Sternberg 1999; Wagner and Sternberg 1991.
25. Quoted in Gladwell 2002. Quotation is on page 29.
26. Eagly and Johannesen-Schmidt 2001; Rosener 1990.
27. For a review of the research on leadership, see Eagly and Johannesen-Schmidt 2001.

28. Helgesen 1990.

29. Fisher 1999; Rosener 1995.

30. Fisher 1999; Rosener 1995; Helgesen 1990.

31. Burns 1978. Quotation is from page 50.

32. Rosener 1995. Quotation is from page 6.

33. Heffernan 2002. Quotation is from page 64.

34. Rosener 1995.

35. Naisbitt and Aburdene 1986. Quotation is from page 242.

36. Miller 1986. Quotation is from page 118.

EPILOGUE

1. Riley, Babcock, and McGinn 2003.

2. Biernat and Wortman 1991; Lennon and Rosenfield 1994; Robinson 1988.

3. Valian 1998. Quotation is from page 39.

4. Pollard, Ungpakorn, and Parkes 1996. Described in Austin 2000, pages 185–186.

5. Austin 2000. Quotation is from page 186.

6. Goode 2001.

7. Epel, McEwen, Seeman, Matthews, Castellazzo, Grownell, Bejj, and Ickovia 2000; McEwen 2000.

8. Austin 2000. Quotation is from page 187.

9. Ibid. Quotation is from page 186. The study she refers to is Glass and Fujimoto 1994.

10. Valian 1998. Quotation is from page 45.

11. Ibid. Quotation is from page 46.

12. Austin 2000. Quotation is from pages 192–193.

13. Briggs 2000.

14. Ibid.

15. Centers for Disease Control and Prevention, Divisions of HIV/AIDS Prevention 2002.

16. Ulin, Cayemittes, and Metellus 1993.

17. Ibid. Quotation is from page 2 of executive summary.

18. Ibid. Quotation is from page 2 of executive summary.

19. Gomez and Marin 1996; Williams, Gardos, Ortiz-Torres, Tross, and Ehrhardt 2001.

REFERENCES

Allred, K. 1999. Anger and retaliation: Toward an understanding of impassioned conflict in organizations. *Research on Negotiation in Organizations* 7:27–58.

Allred, K. G., J. S. Mallozzi, F. Matsui, and C. P. Raia. 1997. The influence of anger and compassion on negotiation performance. *Organizational Behavior and Human Decision Processes* 70(3): 175–187.

Almer, E. 2000. Management: What women need to know about starting up. *New York Times,* 4 October, page C9.

Arch, E. C. 1993. Risk-taking: A motivational basis for sex differences. *Psychological Reports* 73:3–11.

Archer, J. 1996. Sex differences in social behavior: Are the social role and evolutionary explanations compatible? *American Psychologist* 51:909–917.

Aronson, J., C. Good, and J. A. Harder. 1998. Stereotype threat and women's calculus performance. University of Texas, Austin. Unpublished manuscript.

Aronson, J., M. J. Lustina, C. Good, K. Keough, C. M. Steele, and J. Brown. 1999. When white men can't do math: Necessary and sufficient factors in stereotype threat. *Journal of Experimental Social Psychology* 35:29–46.

Austin, L. 2000. *What's holding you back? 8 critical choices for women's success.* New York: Basic Books.

Ayres, I., and P. Siegelman. 1995. Race and gender discrimination in bargaining for a new car. *American Economic Review* 85(3):304–321.

Babcock, L. 2002. Do graduate students negotiate their job offers? Carnegie Mellon University. Unpublished report.

Babcock, L., M. Gelfand, D. Small, and H. Stayn. 2002. Propensity to initiate negotiations: A new look at gender variation in negotiation behavior. Carnegie Mellon University. Unpublished manuscript.

Bakan, D. 1966. *The duality of human existence: An essay on psychology and religion.* Chicago: Rand McNally.

Bandura, A. 1977. Self-efficacy: Toward a unifying theory of behavioral change. *Psychological Review* 84:191–215.

Bandura, A., and R. Wood. 1989. Effect of perceived controllability and performance standards on self-regulation of complex decision-making. *Journal of Personality and Social Psychology* 56(5):805–814.

Banerjee, N. 2001. Some "bullies" seek ways to soften up: Toughness has risks for women executives. *New York Times*, 10 August, pages C1–C2.

Barron, L. A. 2003. Ask and you shall receive: Gender differences in negotiators' beliefs about requests for a higher salary. *Human Relations*, forthcoming.

Barry, B., and R. L. Oliver. 1996. Affect in dyadic negotiation: A model and propositions. *Organizational Behavior and Human Decision Processes* 67(2): 127–144.

Baumeister, R. F., and K. L. Sommer. 1997. What do men want? Gender differences and two spheres of belongingness: Comment on Cross and Madison (1997). *Psychological Bulletin* 122(1):38–44.

Bazerman, M., and M. Neale. 1992. *Negotiating rationally.* New York: Free Press.

BBC News Online: Business. 2001. Bitchy bosses go to boot camp, 8 August.

Beal, C. R. 1994. *Boys and girls: The development of gender roles.* New York: McGraw-Hill.

Bergmann, B. 1986. *The economic emergence of women.* New York: Basic Books.

Bertrand, M., and K. F. Hallock. 2000. The gender gap in top corporate jobs. National Bureau of Economic Research Working Paper #7931.

Beyer, S., and E. M. Bowden. 1997. Gender differences in self-perceptions: Convergent evidence from three measures of accuracy and bias. *Personality and Social Psychology Bulletin* 23(2):157–172.

Biernat, M., and C. B. Wortman. 1991. Sharing of home responsibilities between professionally employed women and their husbands. *Journal of Personality and Social Psychology* 60:844–860.

Bigg, D. 1991. In the Supreme Court of the United States, Price Waterhouse v. Ann B. Hopkins amicus curiae brief for the American Psychological Association. *American Psychologist* 46(10):1061–1070.

Blank, R. M. 1994. Report of the Committee on the Status of Women in the Economics Profession. *American Economic Review* 84:491–495.

Blau, F. D., and L. Kahn. 2000. Gender differences in pay. National Bureau of Economic Research Working Paper #7732.

Booth, A., G. Shelley, A. Mazur, G. Tharp, and R. Kittok. 1989. Testosterone, and winning and losing in human competition. *Hormones and Behavior* 23:556–571.

Boyle, M. 2002. Just right. Goldilocks had it easy: Choosing a bowl of porridge is a lot easier than deciding between jobs. *Fortune*, 10 June, pages 207–208.

Braathen, E. T., and S. Svebak. 1992. Motivational differences among talented teenage athletes: The significance of gender, type of sport, and level of excellence. *Scandinavian Journal of Medicine and Science in Sports* 2:153–159.

Brass, D. J. 1985. Men's and women's networks: A study of interaction patterns and influence in an organization. *Academy of Management Journal* 28(2):327–343.

Brazleton, T. B., and J. D. Sparrow. 2001. *Touchpoints three to six: Your child's emotional and behavioral development*. Cambridge, Mass.: Perseus.

Briggs, C. 2000. *Women with HIV: A global fact sheet*. National Pediatric and Family HIV Resource Center, March. Available at www.pedhivaids.org/fact/women_fact_g.html.

Brown, G. W., B. Andrews, A. Bifulco, and H. Veiel. 1990. Self-esteem and depressions: I. Measurement issues and prediction of onset. *Social Psychiatry and Psychiatric Epidemiology* 25:200–209.

Burgoon, M., T. S. Birk, and J. R. Hall. 1991. Compliance and satisfaction with physician-patient communication: An expectancy theory interpretation of gender differences. *Human Communication Research* 18:177–208.

Burgoon, M., J. P. Dillard, and N. E. Doran. 1983. Friendly or unfriendly persuasion: The effects of violations of expectations by males and females. *Human Communication Research* 10(2):283–294.

Burns, J. M. 1978. *Leadership*. New York: Harper Torchbooks.

Burt, R. 1992. *Structural holes: The social structure of competition*. Cambridge, Mass.: Harvard University Press.

Butler, D., and F. L. Geis. 1990. Nonverbal affect responses to male and female leaders: Implications for leadership evaluation. *Journal of Personality and Social Psychology* 58:48–59.

Bybee, J., M. Glick, and E. Zigler. 1990. Differences across gender, grade level, and academic track in the content of the ideal self-image. *Sex Roles* 22:349–358.

Bylsma, W. H., and B. Major. 1992. Two routes to eliminating gender differences in personal entitlement. *Psychology of Women Quarterly* 16:193–200.

———. 1994. Social comparisons and contentment. *Psychology of Women Quarterly* 18:241–249.

Callahan-Levy, C. M., and L. A. Messe. 1979. Sex differences in the allocation of pay. *Journal of Personality and Social Psychology* 37(3):433–446.

Cantor, N., and W. Mischel. 1979. Prototypes in person perception. In *Advances in experimental social psychology*, ed. L. Berkowitz, volume 12, pages 3–52. New York: Academic Press.

Carli, L. L. 1990. Gender, language, and influence. *Journal of Personality and Social Psychology* 59:941–951.

———. 1998. Gender effects in social influence. Wellesley College. Unpublished manuscript.

———. 2001. Gender and social influence. *Journal of Social Issues* 57:725–741.

Carli, L. L., S. J. LaFleur, and C. C. Lober. 1995. Nonverbal behavior, gender, and influence. *Journal of Personality and Social Psychology* 68:1030–1041.

Carnevale, P., and A. Isen. 1986. The influence of positive affect and visual access on the discovery of integrative solutions in bilateral negotiations. *Organizational Behavior and Human Decision Processes* 37:1–13.

Carpenter, C. J., and A. C. Huston. 1980. Activity structure and sex-typed behavior in preschool children. *Child Development* 51:862–872.

Carpenter, E. J., A. C. Huston, and W. Holt. 1986. Modification of preschool sex-typed behavior by participation in adult-structured activities. *Sex Roles* 14 (11/12):603–615.

Case, S. S. 1990. Communication styles in higher education: Differences between academic men and women. In *Women in higher education: Changes and challenges*, ed. L. B. Welch, pages 94–118. New York: Praeger.

Cassell, J., and H. Jenkins. 1998. *From Barbie to Mortal Kombat: Gender and computer games*. Cambridge, Mass.: MIT Press.

Cejka, M. A., and A. H. Eagly. 1999. Gender-stereotypic images of the occupations correspond to the segregation of employment. *Personality and Social Psychology Bulletin* 25(4):413–423.

Centers for Disease Control and Prevention. Divisions of HIV/AIDS Prevention. 2002. *HIV/AIDS surveillance in women: L264 slides series*, 1 March. Available at www.cdc.gov/hiv/graphics/women.htm.

Chodorow, N. 1978. *The reproduction of mothering: Psychoanalysis and the sociology of gender*. Berkeley: University of California Press.

Chupack, C. 2000–2001. *Sex and the City*, season 3, episode 42. Broadcast on Home Box Office (HBO).

Clancy, S. M., and S. J. Dollinger. 1993. Photographic depictions of the self: Gender and age differences in social connectedness. *Sex Roles* 29(7/8):477–495.

Cohoon, J. M. 2001. Toward improving female retention in the computer science major. *Communications of the ACM* 44(5):108–114.

Committee on the Status of Women in the Economics Profession. 2002. Annual report. *Newsletter*, winter, pages 3–4.

Copeland, C. L., J. E. Driskell, and E. Salas. 1995. Gender and reactions to dominance. *Journal of Social Behavior and Personality* 10:53–68.

Costrich, N., J. Feinstein, L. Kidder, J. Marecek, and L. Pascale. 1975. When stereotypes hurt: Three studies of penalties for sex-role reversals. *Journal of Experimental Social Psychology* 11:520–530.

Crandall, V. C., and B. W. Crandall. 1983. Maternal and childhood behaviors as antecedents of internal-external control perceptions in young adulthood. In *Research with the locus of control construct*, ed. H. LeCourt, volume 2, pages 53–103. New York: Academic Press.

Crittenden, A. 2001. *The price of motherhood: Why the most important job in the world is still the least valued.* New York: Metropolitan Books.

Crosby, F. 1982. *Relative deprivation and working women.* New York: Oxford University Press.

———. 1984. The denial of personal discrimination. *American Behavioral Scientist* 27:371–386.

Crosby, F., A. Pufall, R. C. Snyder, M. O'Connell, and P. Whalen. 1989. The denial of personal disadvantage among you, me, and all the other ostriches. In *Gender and thought: Psychological perspectives*, ed. M. Crawford and M. Gentry. New York: Springer-Verlag.

Crosby, F., and S. A. Ropp. 2002. Awakening to discrimination. In *The justice motive in everyday life*, ed. M. Ross and D. T. Miller, pages 382–396. Cambridge, Eng.: Cambridge University Press.

Cross, S. E., and L. Madson. 1997. Models of the self: Self-construals and gender. *Psychological Bulletin* 122(1):5–37.

Dabbs, J. M., D. de la Rue, and P. M. Williams. 1990. Salivary testosterone and occupational choice: Actors, ministers, and other men. *Journal of Personality and Social Psychology* 59(6):1261–1265.

Daltzman, R., and M. Zuckerman. 1980. Disinhibitory sensation seeking, personality, and gonadal hormones. *Personality and Individual Differences* 1:103–110.

Daubman, K. A., L. Heatherington, and A. Ahn. 1992. Gender and the self-presentation of academic achievement. *Sex Roles* 27:187–204.

Dawson, R. 2000. *Secrets of power negotiating*, 2d edition. Franklin Lakes, N.J.: Career Press.

Deal, J. J., and M. A. Stevenson. 1998. Perceptions of female and male managers in the 1990s: Plus ça change . . . *Sex Roles* 38:287–300.

Deaux, K., and B. Major. 1987. Putting gender into context: An interactive model of gender-related behavior. *Psychological Review* 94(3):369–389.

Desmarais, S., and J. Curtis. 1997. Gender and perceived pay entitlement: Testing for effects of experience with income. *Journal of Personality and Social Psychology* 72(1):141–150.

Dowd, M. 2002. The baby bust. *New York Times*, 10 April.

Dranginis, A. M. 2002. Why the hormone study finally happened. *New York Times*, 15 July.

Dunn, J., I. Bretherton, and P. Munn. 1987. Conversations about feeling states between mothers and their young children. *Developmental Psychology* 23:132–139.

Eagly, A. H. 1987. *Sex differences in social behavior: A social role interpretation.* Hillsdale, N.J.: Erlbaum.

———. 1995. The science and politics of comparing women and men. *American Psychologist* 50(3):145–158.

———. 1997. Sex differences in social behavior: Comparing social role theory and evolutionary psychology. *American Psychologist* 52(12):1380–1383.

Eagly, A. H., and M. C. Johannesen-Schmidt. 2001. The leadership styles of women and men. *Journal of Social Issues* 57(4):781–797.

Eagly, A. H., M. G. Makhijani, and B. G. Klonsky. 1992. Gender and the evaluation leaders: A meta-analysis. *Psychological Bulletin* 111(1):3–22.

Eckert, P. 1993. Cooperative competition in adolescent "girl talk." In *Gender and conversational interaction*, ed. D. Tannen, pages 32–61. New York: Oxford University Press.

Ellis, L. 1986. Evidence of neuroandrogenic etiology of sex roles from a combined analysis of human, nonhuman primates, and nonprimate mammalian studies. *Personality and Individual Differences* 7:519–552.

Epel, E., B. McEwen, T. Seeman, K. Matthews, G. Castellazzo, K. Grownell, J. Bejj, and J. Ickovia. 2000. Stress and body shape: Stress-induced cortisol secretion is consistently greater among women with central fat. *Psychosom Med* 62(5):623–632.

Epstein, C. F. 1991. Constraints on excellence: Structural and cultural barriers to the recognition and demonstration of achievement. In *The outer circle: Women in the scientific community*, ed. H. Zuckerman, J. R. Cole, and J. T. Bruer, pages 239–258. New York: W. W. Norton.

Fagot, B. I. 1978. The influence of sex of child on parental reactions to toddler children. *Child Development* 49:30–36.

Faludi, S. 1991. *Backlash: The undeclared war against American women*. New York: Doubleday.

Feingold, A. 1994. Gender differences in personality: A meta-analysis. *Psychological Bulletin* 116(3):429–456.

Fisher, H. 1999. *The first sex: The natural talents of women and how they are changing the world*. New York: Random House.

Fisher, R., and W. Ury. 1981. *Getting to yes: Negotiating agreement without giving in*. New York: Houghton Mifflin.

Fiske, S., and S. E. Taylor. 1984. *Social cognition*. New York: Random House.

Fitt, L. W., and D. A. Newton. 1981. When the mentor is a man and the protégée is a woman. *Harvard Business Review* March–April:56–60.

Fivush, R. 1992. Gender differences in parent-child conversations about past emotions. *Sex Roles* 27:683–698.

Fox, E. M., and L. Urwick, eds. 1973. *Dynamic administration: The collected papers of Mary Parker Follett*. London: Pitman.

Fullerton, H., and M. Toossi. 2001. Labor force projections to 2010: Steady growth and changing composition. *Monthly Labor Review* November:21–38.

Gabriel, S., and W. L. Gardner. 1999. Are there "his" and "hers" types of interdependence? The implications of gender differences in collective versus relational interdependence for affect, behavior, and cognition. *Journal of Personality and Social Psychology* 77(3):642–655.

Galinsky, A., T. Mussweiler, and V. H. Medvec. 2002. Disconnecting outcomes and evaluations: The role of negotiator reference points. *Journal of Personality and Social Psychology* 83(5):1131–1140.

Gelfand, M. J., V. Smith-Major, J. Raver, and L. Nishii. 2000. Gender, self, and negotiation: Implications of relational self-construals for negotiations. University of Maryland. Unpublished manuscript.

Gerhart, B. 1990. Gender differences in current and starting salaries: The role of performance, college major, and job title. *Industrial and Labor Relations Review* 43(4):418–433.

Gerhart, B., and S. Rynes. 1991. Determinants and consequences of salary negotiations by male and female MBA graduates. *Journal of Applied Psychology* 76:256–262.

Getting the message. 1997. Publication of the nonprofit organization Children Now (available at www.childrennow.org).

Gilbert, D., 1995. Attribution and interpersonal perception. In *Advanced social psychology*, ed. A. Tesser, pages 99–148. New York: McGraw-Hill.

Gist, M., C. K. Stevens, and A. Bavetta. 1991. Effects of self-efficacy and post-training intervention on the acquisition and maintenance of complex interpersonal skills. *Personnel Psychology* 44:837–861.

Gladwell, M. 2000. *The tipping point: How little things can make a big difference.* New York: Little, Brown.

———. 2002. The talent myth. *New Yorker*, 22 July.

Glass, J., and T. Fujimoto. 1994. Housework, paid work, and depression among husbands and wives. *Journal of Health and Social Behavior* 35(2):179–191.

Glick, P., C. Zion, and C. Nelson. 1988. What mediates sex discrimination in hiring decisions? *Journal of Personality and Social Psychology* 55:178–186.

Gneezy, U., M. Niederle, and A. Rustichini. 2001. Performance in competitive environments. Harvard University. Unpublished manuscript.

Goldin, C., and C. Rouse. 2000. Orchestrating impartiality: The impact of "blind" auditions on female musicians. *American Economic Review* 90(4):715–742.

Gomez, C., and B. V. Marin. 1996. Gender, culture, and power: Barriers to HIV-prevention strategies for women. *Journal of Sex Research* 33(4):355–362.

Goode, E. 2001. The heavy cost of chronic stress: Some can be benign, but too much is lethal. *New York Times*, 17 December, page D1.

Goodman, P. 1974. An examination of references used in the evaluation of pay. *Organizational Behavior and Human Performance* 12:170–195.

Goodnow, J. J. 1988. Children's household work: Its nature and functions. *Psychological Bulletin* 103(1):5–26.

Graglia, C. F. 1998. *Domestic tranquility: A brief against feminism.* Dallas: Spence Publishing Company.

Graham, M. E., and T. M. Welbourne. 1999. Gainsharing and women's and men's relative pay satisfaction. *Journal of Organizational Behavior* 20:1027–1042.

Granovetter, M. 1982. The strength of weak ties. *American Journal of Sociology* 6:1360–1380.

Gray, B. 1994. The gender-based foundations of negotiation theory. *Research on Negotiations in Organizations* 4:3–36.

Greenhalgh, L., and R. W. Gilkey. 1993. The effect of relationship orientation on negotiators' cognitions and tactics. *Group Decision and Negotiation* 2:167–186.

Gregorian, V. 2002. Bobsledder shows no remorse dropping partner; Jean Racine says winning the gold is all that matters. *St. Louis Post-Dispatch*, 17 February, page D18.

Halpern, J. J., and J. M. Parks. 1996. Vive la difference: Differences between males and females in process and outcomes in a low-conflict negotiation. *International Journal of Conflict Management* 7(1):45–70.

Harris, M. J., and R. Rosenthal. 1985. Mediation of interpersonal expectancy effects: 31 meta-analyses. *Psychological Bulletin* 97:363–386.

Harris, T. G. 1993. The post-capitalist executive: An interview with Peter F. Drucker. *Harvard Business Review*, May/June, pages 115–122.

Hatfield, E., J. T. Caccioppo, and R. L. Rapson. 1992. Primitive emotional contagion. In *Review of personality and social psychology*, ed. M. S. Clark, volume 14, pages 151–177. Newbury Park, Calif.: Sage.

Heatherington, L., J. Crown, H. Wagner, and S. Rigby. 1992. Toward an understanding of social consequences of "feminine immodesty" about personal achievements. *Sex Roles* 20(7/8): 371–380.

Heffernan, M. 2002. The female CEO: ca. 2002. *Fast Company*, August, pages 58–66.

Heilman, M. E. 1980. The impact of situational factors on personnel decisions concerning women: Varying the sex composition of the applicant pool. *Organizational Behavior and Human Performance* 26:286–295.

———. 1995. Sex stereotypes and their effects in the workplace: What we know and what we don't know. *Journal of Social Behavior and Personality* 10(6):3–26.

———. 2001. Description and prescription: How gender stereotypes prevent women's ascent up the organizational ladder. *Journal of Social Issues* 57(4): 657–674.

Heilman, M. E., M. Haynes, and A. D. Goodman. 2001. Denying women credit for their successes: Gender stereotyping as a function of group vs. individual level performance information. New York University. Unpublished manuscript.

Helgesen, S. 1990. *The female advantage: Women's ways of leadership.* New York: Doubleday/Currency.

Hewlett, S. A. 2002. *Creating a life: Professional women and the quest for children.* New York: Talk Miramax Books.

Hodgins, H. S., E. Liebeskind, and W. Schwartz. 1996. Getting out of hot water: Face-work in social predicaments. *Journal of Personality and Social Psychology* 71:300–314.

Hornig, L. S. 1987. Women graduate students. In *Women: Their underrepresentation and career differentials in science and engineering*, ed. L. S. Dix, pages 103–122. Washington, D. C.: National Academy Press.

Humphreys, A. P., and P. K. Smith. 1987. Rough and tumble, friendships, and dominance in schoolchildren: Evidence for continuity and change with age. *Child Development* 58:201–212.

Huston, A. C., and C. J. Carpenter. 1985. Gender differences in preschool classrooms: The effects of sex-types activity choices. In *Gender-related differences in the classroom*, ed. L. C. Wilkinson and C. B. Marett. New York: Academic Press.

Ibarra, H. 1992. Homophily and differential returns: Sex differences in network structure and access in an advertising firm. *Administrative Science Quarterly* 37:422–447.

———. 1997. Paving an alternative route: Gender differences in managerial networks. *Social Psychology Quarterly* 60(1):91–102.

Instone, D., B. Major, and B. B. Bunker. 1983. Gender, self-confidence, and social influence strategies: An organizational simulation. *Journal of Personality and Social Psychology* 44(2):322–333.

Inter-parliamentary Union. 2000. *Women in politics, 1945–2000.* Report #37. Geneva: United Nations.

Inzlicht, M., and T. Ben-Zeev. 2000. A threatening intellectual environment: Why females are susceptible to experiencing problem-solving deficits in the presence of males. *Psychological Science* 11(5):365–371.

Jackson, L. A., P. D. Gardner, and L. A. Sullivan. 1992. Explaining gender differences in self-pay expectations: Social comparison standards and perceptions of fair pay. *Journal of Applied Psychology* 77(5):651–663.

Janoff-Bulman, R., and M. B. Wade. 1996. The dilemma of self-advocacy for women: Another case of blaming the victim? *Journal of Social and Clinical Psychology* 15(2):143–152.

Jelalian, E., A. Spirito, D. Raile, L. Vinnick, C. Rohrbeck, and M. Aarrigan. 1997. Risk-taking, reported injury, and perception of future injury among adolescents. *Journal of Pediatric Psychology* 22:513–531.

Jones, E. E., and T. S. Pittman. 1982. Toward a general theory of strategic self-presentation. In *Psychological perspectives on the self*, ed. J. Suls, volume 1, pages 231–262. Hillsdale, N.J.: Erlbaum.

Josephs, R. A., H. R. Markus, and R. W. Tafarodi. 1992. Gender and self-esteem. *Journal of Personality and Social Psychology* 63:391–402.

Jost, J. 1997. An experimental replication of the depressed-entitlement effect among women. *Psychology of Women Quarterly* 21:387–393.

Judd, R. 2001. Golden dreams shattered as bobsled duo hits the brakes. *Seattle Times*, 16 December, page C2.

Kahn, A., V. E. O'Leary, J. E. Krulewitz, and H. Lamm. 1980. Equity and equality: Male and female means to a just end. *Basic and Applied Social Psychology* 1(2):173–197.

Kaman, V. S., and C. E. Hartel. 1994. Gender differences in anticipated pay negotiation strategies and outcomes. *Journal of Business and Psychology* 9(2):183–197.

Kanter, R. M. 1977. *Men and women of the corporation.* New York: Basic Books.

———. 1990. Foreword: Special issue on women and economic empowerment. *New England Journal of Public Policy* 6 (spring/summer): 11–14.

Kemper, T. D. 1990. *Social structure and testosterone.* New Brunswick, N.J.: Rutgers University Press.

Khurana, R. 2002. *Searching for a corporate savior: The irrational quest for charismatic CEOs.* Princeton, N. J: Princeton University Press.

Kimmel, M., D. G. Pruitt, J. M. Magenau, E. Konar-Goldband, and P. Carnevale. 1980. Effects of trust, aspiration, and gender on negotiation tactics. *Journal of Personality and Social Psychology* 38(1):9–22.

King, W. C., and T. D. Hinson. 1994. The influence of sex and equity sensitivity on relationship preferences, assessment of opponent, and outcomes in a negotiation experiment. *Journal of Management* 20(3):605–624.

Klaiber, L., D. Broverman, W. Vogel, G. Abraham, and F. Cone. 1971. Effects of infused testosterone on mental performances and serum LH. *Journal of Clinical Endocrinology* 32:341–349.

Kling, K. C., J. Shelby-Hyde, C. J. Showers, and B. N. Buswell. 1999. Gender differences in self-esteem: A meta-analysis. *Psychological Bulletin* 125(4): 470–500.

Kolb, D. M. 2000. Renewing our interest in gender negotiations: What's new or what would really be new? Paper presented at the Academy of Management meeting, August.

Kolb, D. M., and G. G. Coolidge. 1991. Her place at the table: A consideration of gender issues in negotiation. In *Negotiation theory and practice,* ed. J. W. Breslin and J. Z. Rubin, pages 261–277, Cambridge, Mass.: Program on Negotiation and Harvard Law School.

Kolb, D. M., and L. L. Putnam. 1997. Through the looking glass: Negotiation theory refracted through the lens of gender. In *Workplace dispute resolution: Directions for the 21st century,* ed. S. Gleason. East Lansing: Michigan State University Press.

Kolb, D. M., and J. Williams. 2000. *The shadow negotiation: How women can master the hidden agendas that determine bargaining success.* New York: Simon and Schuster.

Kraft, L. W., and C. W. Vraa. 1975. Sex composition of groups and pattern of self-disclosure by high school females. *Psychological Reports* 37:733–734.

Kray, L., L. Thompson, and A. Galinsky. 2001. Battle of the sexes: Stereotype confirmation and reactance in negotiations. *Journal of Personality and Social Psychology* 80(6):942–958.

Kubik, M. 2000. Women rarely quoted as business experts. *Business Journal Online,* mid-February.

Kuhn, E. D. 1992. Playing down authority while getting things done: Women professors get help from the institution. In *Locating power: Proceedings of the second Berkeley women and language conference,* ed. K. Hall, M. Bucholtz, and B. Moonwomon, volume 2, pages 318–325. Berkeley: Berkeley women and language group, University of California, Berkeley.

Kunhikrishnan, K., and K. Manikandan. 1995. Sex difference in Locus of Control: An analysis based on Calicut L.O.C. Scale. *Psychological Studies* 37:121–125.

Lashinsky, A. 2002. Now for the hard part. *Fortune,* 18 November, pages 95–106.

Lax, D., and J. Sebenius. 1986. *The manager as negotiator.* New York: Free Press.

Lemonick, M. D. 2003. The power of mood. *Time,* 20 January, page 65.

Lenney, E. 1977. Women's self-confidence in achievement settings. *Psychological Bulletin* 84:1–13.

Lennon, M. C., and S. Rosenfield. 1994. Relative fairness and the division of housework: The importance of options. *American Journal of Sociology* 100:506–531.

Lerner, J., R. Gonzalez, D. Small, and B. Fischhoff. 2003. Effects of fear and anger on perceived risks of terrorism: A national field experiment. *Psychological Science* 14:144–150.

Lever, J. 1976. Sex differences in the games children play. *Social Problems* 23:478–487.

Lewicki, R., D. Saunders, and J. Minton. 1997. *Essentials of negotiation.* Boston, Mass.: Irwin / McGraw-Hill.

Liben, L. S., and M. L. Signorella, eds. 1987. *Children's gender schemata.* San Francisco: Jossey-Bass.

Llewellyn-Williams, M. 2002. *The C200 Business Leadership Index 2002: Annual report on women's clout in business.* San Francisco: BrandMechanics.

Locke, E. A. 1976. The nature and causes of job satisfaction. In *The handbook of industrial and organizational psychology,* ed. M. D. Dunnette, pages 1297–1349. Chicago: Rand McNally.

Locke, E. A., and G. Latham. 1990. *A theory of goal setting and task performance.* Englewood Cliffs, N.J.: Prentice-Hall.

Lytton, H., and D. M. Romney. 1991. Parents' differential socialization of boys and girls: A meta-analysis. *Psychological Bulletin* 109(2):267–296.

Maccoby, E. E. 1966. *The development of sex differences.* Stanford, Calif.: Stanford University Press.

Maccoby, E. E. 1988. Gender as a social category. *Developmental Psychology* 24(6): 755–765.

———. 1990. Gender and relationships: A developmental account. *American Psychologist* 45(4):513–520.

Maccoby, E. E., and C. N. Jacklin. 1987. Gender segregation in childhood. In

Advances in childhood development, ed. E. H. Reese, volume 20, pages 239–287. New York: Academic Press.

Major, B., and E. Konar. 1984. An investigation of sex differences in pay expectations and their possible causes. *Academy of Management Journal* 27:777–792.

Major, B., D. B. McFarlin, and D. Gagnon. 1984. Overworked and underpaid: On the nature of gender differences in personal entitlement. *Journal of Personality and Social Psychology* 47(6):1399–1412.

Malhotra, D. 2002. Let's take this outside: Some striking results of students negotiating in the real world. Paper presentation at the International Association for Conflict Management annual meeting, June.

Maltz, D., and R. Borker. 1983. A cultural approach to male-female miscommunication. In *Language and social identity,* ed. J. A. Gumperz, pages 195–216. New York: Cambridge University Press.

Markus, H. R., and S. Kitayama. 1991. Culture and the self: Implications for cognition, emotion, and motivation. *Psychological Review* 98:224–253.

Martell, R. F., D. M. Lane, and C. Emrich. 1996. Male-female differences: A computer simulation. *American Psychologist* 51:157–158.

Martin, B. A. 1989. Gender differences in salary expectations when current salary information is provided. *Psychology of Women Quarterly* 13:87–96.

Mazur, A., and A. Booth. 1998. Testosterone and dominance in men. *Behavioral and Brain Sciences* 21:353–397.

Mazur A., E. J. Susman, and S. Edelbrock. 1997. Sex differences in testosterone response to a video game context. *Evolution and Human Behavior* 18(5):317–326.

McCracken, D. 2000. Winning the talent war for women: Sometimes it takes a revolution. *Harvard Business Review,* November/December, pages 59–167.

McCrae, R. R., and P. T. Costa Jr. 1988. Age, personality, and the spontaneous self-concept. *Journal of Gerontology: Social Sciences* 43:S177–S185.

McEwen, B. 2000. The neurobiology of stress: From serendipity to clinical relevance. *Brain Research* 886(1–2):172–189.

McGuire, W. J., and C. V. McGuire. 1982. Significant others in self-space: Sex differences and developmental trends in the social self. In *Psychological Perspectives on the Self,* ed. J. Suls, volume 1, pages 71–96. Hillsdale, N.J.: Erlbaum.

Mehra, A., M. Kilduff, and D. J. Brass. 1998. At the margins: A distinctiveness approach to the social identity and social networks of underrepresented groups. *Academy of Management Journal* 41(4):441–452.

Michaud, E. 2001. Your secret weapon against stress. *Prevention,* August, pages 130–137.

Miller, J. B. 1986. *Toward a new psychology of women.* Boston: Beacon Press.

Miller, L. C., L. L. Cooke, J. Tsang, and F. Morgan. 1992. Should I brag? Nature and impact of positive and boastful disclosures for women and men. *Human Communication Research* 18(3):364–399.

Miller, P. M., D. L. Danaher, and D. Forbes. 1986. Sex-related strategies for coping with interpersonal conflict in children aged five and seven. *Developmental Psychology* 22(4):543–548.

Mussen, P. H., ed. 1983. *Handbook of child psychology,* 4th edition. New York: Wiley.

Naisbitt, J., and P. Aburdene. 1986. *Reinventing the corporation.* New York: Warner Books.

Neale, M. A., and M. H. Bazerman. 1991. *Cognition and rationality in negotiation.* New York: Free Press.

Neumark, D. M. 1996. Sex discrimination in restaurant hiring: An audit study. *Quarterly Journal of Economics* 11(3):915–941.

Norris, J. M., and A. M. Wylie. 1995. Gender stereotyping of the managerial role among students in Canada and the United States. *Group and Organization Management* 20:167–182.

Nussbaum, E. 2001. Peers: Great expectations. *New York Times Magazine,* 9 September, pages 118–122.

O'Connor, C. 2000. Finishing school. *Business 2.0,* April.

O'Sullivan, C. S., and F. T. Durso. 1984. Effects of schema-incongruent information on memory for stereotypical attributes. *Journal of Personality and Social Psychology* 47:55–70.

Orenstein, P. 1994. *Schoolgirls: Young women, self-esteem, and the confidence gap.* New York: Doubleday.

Parkes, K. R. 1985. Dimensionality of Rotter's Locus of Control Scale: An application of the "Very Simple Structure" techniques. *Personality and Individual Differences* 6:115–119.

Pasternak, B., and A. Viscio. 1998. *The centerless corporation: A new model for transforming your organization for growth and prosperity.* New York: Simon and Schuster.

Pfeffer, J. 1998. *The human equation: Building profits by putting people first.* Boston, Mass.: Harvard Business School Press.

Pinkley, R. L., and G. B. Northcraft. 2000. *Get paid what you're worth.* New York: St. Martin's Press.

Pollard, T. M., H. Ungpakorn, and K. R. Parkes. 1996. Epinephrine and cortisol responses to work: A test of the models of Frankenhaeuser and Karasek. *Annals of Behavioral Medicine* 18(4):229–237.

Porter, L. W., and E. E. Lawler. 1968. *Managerial attitudes and performance.* Homewood, Ill.: Dorsey.

Powell, G. N., and D. A. Butterfield. 1989. The "good manager": Did androgyny fare better in the 1980s? *Group and Organization Studies* 14:216–233.

Pruitt, D., and J. Rubin. 1986. *Social conflict: Escalation, stalemate, and settlement.* New York: Random House.

Purohit, D., and H. Sondak. 2001. Fear and loathing at the car dealership: The perceived fairness of pricing policies. Duke University and University of Utah. Unpublished manuscript.

Raiffa, H. 1982. *The art and science of negotiation.* Cambridge, Mass.: Harvard University Press.

Ridgeway, C. L. 1982. Status in groups: The importance of motivation. *American Sociological Review* 47:76–88.

———. 2001. Gender, status, and leadership. *Journal of Social Issues* 57(4):637–655.

Ridgeway, C. L., and D. Diekeman. 1989. Dominance and collective hierarchy formation in male and female task groups. *American Sociological Review* 54:79–83.

Ridgeway, C. L., D. Diekeman, and C. Johnson. 1995. Legitimacy, compliance, and gender in peer groups. *Social Psychology Quarterly* 58:298–311.

Riley, H. C. 2001. "When does gender matter in negotiation? The case of distributive bargaining." Ph. D. diss., Harvard Business School.

Riley, H. C., and L. Babcock 2002. Gender differences in distributive and integrative negotiations. Carnegie Mellon University. Unpublished manuscript.

Riley, H. C., L. Babcock, and K. McGinn. 2003. Gender as a situational phenomenon in negotiation. Carnegie Mellon University. Unpublished manuscript.

Roberts, T., and S. Nolen-Hoeksema. 1989. Sex differences in reactions to evaluative feedback. *Sex Roles* 21:725–747.

———. 1994. Gender comparisons in responsiveness to others' evaluations in achievement settings. *Psychology of Women Quarterly* 18:221–240.

Robinson, J. P. 1988. Who's doing the housework? *American Demographics* 10:24–28.

Rosener, J. B. 1990. Ways women lead. *Harvard Business Review,* November/ December, pages 119–125.

———. 1995. *America's competitive secret: Women managers.* New York: Oxford University Press.

———. 1998. Remarks at the conference "The corporate state: A women's CEO and senior management summit," 18 September, New York City.

Rosenthal, B., and M. Rodrigues. 2000. *Women-owner firms attract investors for business growth.* Washington, D.C.: National Foundation for Women Business Owners.

Rosenthal, R., and L. Jacobson. 1968. *Pygmalion in the classroom*. New York: Holt, Rinehart, and Winston.

Ross, M., and F. Sicoly. 1979. Egocentric biases in availability and attribution. *Journal of Personality and Social Psychology* 37:322–336.

Rotter, J. B. 1966. Generalized expectancies for internal versus external control of reinforcement. *Psychological Monographs* 80(1).

Rousseau, D. 2001. The idiosyncratic deal: Flexibility versus fairness? *Organizational Dynamics* 29(4):260–273.

Rowland, G. L., R. E. Franken, and K. Harrison. 1986. Sensation-seeking and participating in sporting activities. *Journal of Sport Psychology* 8:212–220.

Rubin, J. Z., F. J. Provenzano, and Z. Luria. 1974. The eye of the beholder: Parents' views on sex of newborns. *American Journal of Orthopsychiatry* 44(4):512–519.

Rudman, L. A. 1998. Self-promotion as a risk factor for women: The costs and benefits of counterstereotypical impression management. *Journal of Personality and Social Psychology* 74(3):629–646.

Rudman, L. A., and P. Glick. 1999. Feminized management and backlash toward agentic women: The hidden costs to women of a kinder, gentler image of middle managers. *Journal of Personality and Social Psychology* 77(5):1004–1010.

———. 2001. Prescriptive gender stereotypes and backlash toward agentic women. *Journal of Social Issues* 57(4):743–762.

Rynecki, D. 2002. The Bernstein way. *Fortune*, 10 June, page 86.

Satel, S. 2001. Feminism is bad for women's health care. *Wall Street Journal*, March 8.

Sauser, W., and M. York. 1978. Sex differences in job satisfaction: A reexamination. *Personnel Psychology* 31:537–547.

Schein, V. E. 1973. The relationship between sex role stereotypes and requisite management characteristics. *Journal of Applied Psychology* 57:95–100.

———. 1975. Relationships between sex role stereotypes and requisite management characteristics among female managers. *Journal of Applied Psychology* 60:340–344.

Schein, V. E., and R. Mueller. 1992. Sex-role stereotyping and requisite management characteristics: A cross-cultural look. *Journal of Organizational Behavior* 13:439–447.

Schein, V. E., R. Mueller, T. Lituchy, and J. Liu. 1996. Think manager—think male: A global phenomenon? *Journal of Organizational Behavior* 17:33–41.

Schwalbe, M. L., and C. L. Staples. 1991. Gender differences in sources of self-esteem. *Social Psychology Quarterly* 54:158–168.

Senge, P. M. 1997. Communities of leaders and learners. *Harvard Business Review*, September/October, pages 9–10.

Serbin, L. A., C. Sprafkin, M. Elman, and A. Doyle. 1984. The early development of sex-differentiated patterns of social influences. *Canadian Journal of Social Science* 14:350–363.

Shalit, W. 1999. *A return to modesty: Discovering the lost virtue.* New York: Simon and Schuster.

Sheldon, A. 1990. Pickle fights: Gendered talk in preschool disputes. In *Gender and conversational interaction*, ed. D. Tannen, pages 83–109. New York: Oxford University Press.

Shemo, D. J. 2002. Women who lead colleges see slower growth in ranks. *New York Times*, 9 December, page A19.

Slovic, P. 2000. *The perception of risk.* London: Earthscan Publications.

Small, D., L. Babcock, and M. Gelfand. 2003. Why don't women ask? Carnegie Mellon University. Unpublished manuscript.

Smith, P. B., S. Dugan, and F. Trompenaars. 1997. Locus of control and affectivity by gender and occupational status: A 14-nation study. *Sex Roles* 36:51–57.

Solnick, S. J. 2001. Gender differences in the ultimatum game. *Economic Inquiry* 39:189–200.

Sommers, C. H. 2000. *The war against boys: How misguided feminism is harming our young men.* New York: Simon and Schuster.

Sonnert, G., and G. Holton. 1995. *Who succeeds in science? The gender dimension.* New Brunswick, N.J.: Rutgers University Press.

Spencer, S. J., C. M. Steele, and D. Quinn. 1999. Stereotype threat and women's math performance. *Journal of Experimental Social Psychology* 35:4–28.

Statham, A. 1987. The gender model revisited: Differences in the management styles of men and women. *Sex Roles* 16(7/8):408–429.

Steele, C. M. 1997. A threat in the air: How stereotypes shape intellectual identity and performance. *American Psychologist* 52:613–629.

Steele, C. M., and J. Aronson. 1995. Stereotype threat and the intellectual test performance of African Americans. *Journal of Personality and Social Psychology* 69(5):797–811.

Stein, J. C., M. D. Newcomb, and P. M. Bentler. 1992. The effect of agency and communality on self-esteem: Gender differences in longitudinal data. *Sex Roles* 26:465–483.

Stermer, D. 2003. Through the ages. *Time*, 20 January, pages 82–83.

Stern, M., and K. H. Karraker. 1989. Sex stereotyping of infants: A review of gender labeling studies. *Sex Roles* 20(9/10):501–522.

Sternberg, R. J. 1999. The theory of successful intelligence. *Review of General Psychology* 3(4):292–316.

Stevens, C. K., A. G. Bavetta, and M. E. Gist. 1993. Gender differences in the acquisition of salary negotiation skills: The role of goals, self-efficacy, and perceived
control. *Journal of Applied Psychology* 78(5):723–735.

Strickland, B. R., and W. E. Haley. 1980. Sex differences on the Rotter I-E scale.
Journal of Personality and Social Psychology 39(5):930–939.

Stuhlmacher, A. F., and A. E. Walters. 1999. Gender differences in negotiation outcome: A meta-analysis. *Personnel Psychology* 52(3):653–677.

Sullivan, A. 2000. The he hormone. *New York Times Magazine*, 2 April, pages 46–74.

Svebak, S., and J. H. Kerr. 1989. The role of impulsivity in preference for sports.
Personality and Individual Differences 10(1):51–58.

Tannen, D. 1990. *You just don't understand: Women and men in conversation.* New
York: William Morrow.

———. 1994. *Talking from 9 to 5: Women and men in the workplace: Language, sex,
and power.* New York: Avon Books.

Taylor, S. 2002. Relationship and negotiation. Schenley High School. Unpublished
manuscript.

Taylor, S. E., and J. D. Brown. 1988. Illusion and well-being: A social psychological
perspective on mental health. *Psychological Bulletin* 103:193–210.

———. 1994. Positive illusions and well-being revisited: Separating fact from fiction. *Psychological Bulletin* 116:21–27.

Taylor, S. E., L. Klein, B. Lewis, T. Gruenewald, R. Gurung, and J. Updegraff. 2000.
Biobehavioral responses to stress in females: Tend-and-befriend, not fight-or-
flight. *Psychological Review* 107(3):411–429.

Thompson, L. 1991. Information exchange in negotiation. *Journal of Experimental
Social Psychology* 27(2):161–179.

———. 1998. *The mind and heart of the negotiator.* Upper Saddle River, N.J.:
Prentice-Hall.

Tolbert, P. S., T. Simons, A. Andrews, and J. Rhee. 1995. The effects of gender composition in academic departments on faculty turnover. *Industrial and Labor
Relations Review* 48:562–579.

Tomaskovic-Devey, D. 1995. Sex composition and gendered earnings inequality: A
comparison of job and occupational models. In *Gender inequality at work*, ed.
J. A. Jacobs, pages 23–56. Thousand Oaks, Calif.: Sage.

Tomkiewicz, J., and T. Adeyemi-Bello. 1995. A cross-section analysis of attitudes of
Nigerians and Americans toward women as managers. *Journal of Social
Behavior and Personality* 10:189–198.

Ulin, P. R., M. Cayemittes, and E. Metellus. 1993. *Haitian women's role in sexual decision-making: The gap between AIDS knowledge and behavior change,* February. Available at www.fhi.org.

Ury, W. 1991. *Getting past no: Negotiating your way from confrontation to cooperation.* New York: Bantam Books.

U.S. Department of Labor. 2000. *Facts on working women: Earnings differences between women and men.*

U.S. Department of Labor. Bureau of Labor Statistics. 2000. *Report USDL 00–245,* 29 August.

————. 2001. *Table 39: Median weekly earning of full-time wage and salary workers by detailed occupation and sex.*

————. 2002a. *Report USDL 02–415,* 30 July.

————. 2002b. *Union Members Summary, Press Release,* 17 January.

U.S. Small Business Administration. 2001. *Women in business, 2001 report.*

Useem, J. 2002. Tyrants, statesmen, and destroyers: A brief history of the CEO. *Fortune,* 18 November, pages 82–90.

Valian, V. 1998. *Why so slow? The advancement of women.* Cambridge, Mass.: MIT Press.

Ventura, S., and C. Bachrach. 2000. *National Vital Statistics Reports* 48(16). National Center for Health Statistics, Centers for Disease Control and Prevention, 18 October.

Wade, M. E. 2001. Women and salary negotiation: The costs of self-advocacy. *Psychology of Women Quarterly* 25:65–76.

————. 2002. Audience and advocacy: When gender norms become salient during salary requests. Manhattan College. Unpublished manuscript.

Wade, T. J. 1996. An examination of locus of control/fatalism for blacks, whites, boys, and girls over a two-year period of adolescence. *Social Behavior and Personality* 24:239–248.

Wagner, R. K., and R. J. Sternberg. 1991. Tacit knowledge inventory for managers. Yale University. Unpublished research instrument.

Walters, A. E., A. F. Stuhlmacher, and L. L. Meyer. 1998. Gender and negotiator competitiveness: A meta-analysis. *Organizational Behavior and Human Decision Processes* 76(1):1–29.

Weitzman, L. J. 1985. *The divorce revolution: The unexpected social and economic consequences for women and children in America.* New York: Free Press.

White, S. B., and M. A. Neale. 1994. The role of negotiator aspirations and settlement expectancies in bargaining outcomes. *Organizational Behavioral and Human Decision Processes* 57:303–317.

Widnall, S. E. 1988. Voices from the pipeline (AAAS presidential lecture). *Science* 241:1740–1745.

Williams, S. P., P. S. Gardos, B. Ortiz-Torres, S. Tross, and A. Ehrhardt. 2001. Urban women's negotiation strategies for safer sex with their male partners. *Women and Health* 33(3/4):133–148.

Wise, M. 2002. Changing sports, keeping a teammate. *New York Times*, 21 February, section D1, page 5.

Yoder, J. 2001. Making leadership work more effectively for women. *Journal of Social Issues* 57(4):815–828.

Zuckerman, M. 1974. The sensation-seeking motive. In *Progress in experimental personality research*, ed. B. A. Maher, volume 7. New York: Academic Press.

———. 1978. Sensation-seeking. In *Dimensions of personality*, ed. H. London and J. Exner Jr. New York: Wiley.

Zuckerman, M., M. S. Buchsbaum, and D. L. Murphy. 1980. Sensation-seeking and its biological correlates. *Psychological Bulletin* 88(1):187–214.

INDEX

Aburdene, Patricia, 197
Accenture, 90
"accumulation of disadvantage," 8–9
advice for managers: on the benefits of
    female management styles, 193–197;
    on fairly evaluating women's job
    performance, 89, 119–122; on
    improving the working climate for
    women, 16–18, 89–92; on reducing
    turnover among female staff, 16–18,
    40–41, 63–64; on the success of
    Deloitte and Touche and other
    organizations in retaining women
    and reducing turnover costs, 16–18,
    89–92; on treating employees
    equitably, 39–41; on utilizing
    resources most effectively, 61–64
advice for parents: on assigning chores to
    children that don't reinforce gender
    roles, 33, 39; on avoiding directing
    girls toward more structured play
    activities, 38–39; on being role
    models, 39; on not reinforcing
    traditional gender roles, 89. *See also*
    socialization of children
advice for society: on changing images of
    and commentary about women in
    the media, 42; on communicating
unintended messages to girls at
    school, 42; on examining widely
    held beliefs and stereotypes,
    120–121, 175–176; on mentoring
    women, 39–40
advice for women: on avoiding low
    expectations, 65–67; on being
    assertive without fear of sanctions,
    114–118; on building networks,
    119; on choosing organizations that
    are hospitable to women, 119–120;
    on goal setting, 157–158, 161–162;
    on increasing their feelings of
    control during negotiations,
    157–160; on learning to negotiate at
    home, 200–203; on recognizing
    more opportunities in their
    circumstances, 41–44; on reducing
    anxiety around negotiating,
    135–142, 157–160; on reframing
    negotiations from competitive to
    cooperative interactions, 135–137,
    139–142, 183–184; on seeking
    comparison information about
    their market value and pay scales
    for similar work, 55, 65–67,
    150–152; on using agents, 139; on
    using emotion in negotiations, 138

LINDA BABCOCK is James M. Walton Professor of Economics at the H. John Heinz III School of Public Policy and Management of Carnegie Mellon University in Pittsburgh, Pennsylvania.

SARA LASCHEVER'S work has been published by the *New York Times,* the *New York Review of Books,* and *Vogue,* among other publications. She lives in Concord, Massachusetts.